Palgrave Hate Studies

Series Editors
Neil Chakraborti
School of Criminology
University of Leicester
Leicester, UK

Barbara Perry
Faculty of Social Science and Humanities
University of Ontario
Oshawa, ON, Canada

This series builds on recent developments in the broad and interdisciplinary field of hate studies. Palgrave Hate Studies aims to bring together in one series the very best scholars who are conducting hate studies research around the world. Reflecting the range and depth of research and scholarship in this burgeoning area, the series welcomes contributions from established hate studies researchers who have helped to shape the field, as well as new scholars who are building on this tradition and breaking new ground within and outside the existing canon of hate studies research.

Editorial Advisory Board:
Tore Bjorgo (Norwegian Institute of International Affairs)
Jon Garland (University of Surrey)
Nathan Hall (University of Portsmouth)
Gail Mason (University of Sydney)
Jack McDevitt (Northeastern University)
Scott Poynting (The University of Auckland)
Mark Walters (University of Sussex) and
Thomas Brudholm (University of Copenhagen)

Mark Austin Walters
Criminalising Hate
Law as Social Justice Liberalism

Mark Austin Walters
School of Law, Politics and Sociology
University of Sussex
Brighton, UK

ISSN 2947-6364 ISSN 2947-6372 (electronic)
Palgrave Hate Studies
ISBN 978-3-031-08124-8   ISBN 978-3-031-08125-5 (eBook)
https://doi.org/10.1007/978-3-031-08125-5

© The Editor(s) (if applicable) and The Author(s), under exclusive licence to Springer Nature Switzerland AG 2022

This work is subject to copyright. All rights are solely and exclusively licensed by the Publisher, whether the whole or part of the material is concerned, specifically the rights of translation, reprinting, reuse of illustrations, recitation, broadcasting, reproduction on microfilms or in any other physical way, and transmission or information storage and retrieval, electronic adaptation, computer software, or by similar or dissimilar methodology now known or hereafter developed.

The use of general descriptive names, registered names, trademarks, service marks, etc. in this publication does not imply, even in the absence of a specific statement, that such names are exempt from the relevant protective laws and regulations and therefore free for general use.

The publisher, the authors, and the editors are safe to assume that the advice and information in this book are believed to be true and accurate at the date of publication. Neither the publisher nor the authors or the editors give a warranty, expressed or implied, with respect to the material contained herein or for any errors or omissions that may have been made. The publisher remains neutral with regard to jurisdictional claims in published maps and institutional affiliations.

This Palgrave Macmillan imprint is published by the registered company Springer Nature Switzerland AG.
The registered company address is: Gewerbestrasse 11, 6330 Cham, Switzerland

Acknowledgements

This book draws on research I have undertaken over the past ten years, both in an independent capacity and as part of a team of researchers on numerous research projects, including the UK-based Sussex Hate Crime Project and EU-based Life Cycle of a Hate Crime project. Both projects involved multiple scholars who have helped to generate new knowledge on the nature and impacts of hate crime, and how criminal justice responses are being used to tackle the problem.

I would like to thank Kay Goodall for all of her research support, without whom this book would not have been completed this year. I would also like to thank my close friend and confidante Jennifer Schweppe, who entertains my random thoughts and questions day and night, who continues to inspire me to be a better scholar, and who persistently challenges me during our spirited mobile phone discussions on the purpose and practice of hate crime law. I thank her for her encouragement with this book, and I look forward to reading her own work on this topic.

During the writing of this book I have received incredibly insightful and helpful feedback on various chapters and aspects of my research from colleagues, including Chara Bakalis, Stavros Demetriou, Zoe James, Tarik Kochi, Tanya Palmer, Shirin Sinnar and Richard Vogler. Thank you to everyone who contributed their thoughts on its contents. All remaining errors remain my own.

I am grateful also to the commissioning editor and series editors of Palgrave's Hate Studies book series who have been very patient and supportive during the completion of this book.

Finally, I would like to thank my caring and loving husband Daniel Lambourne whose strength and level-headedness keep me on track on what is often a rocky and emotional road in researching the harms of hate crime.

Contents

1 Introduction 1

2 Social Justice Liberalism 19

3 Social Justice Liberalism and the Criminalisation of Hate 51

4 Redrawing the Boundaries of Hate Crime: What Characteristics Should Be "Protected" in the Criminal Law? 95

5 Legislating for Hate Crime Globally: Putting "Social Justice" Into Practice, Part 1 127

6 Legislating for Hate Crime Globally: Putting "Social Justice" Into Practice, Part 2 161

7 Punish or Repair? Where Is the "Social Justice" in Hate Crime Laws? 205

8 Conclusion: Expanding the Criminal Justice Lens 235

Appendix A: Examples of Hate Crime Laws from Around the World 245

Author Index 267

Place Index 269

Subject Index 271

List of Figures

Fig. 3.1	Empathy for victims of hate motivated vs. random acts of vandalism. (Adapted from Paterson and others 2018a (see Footnote 78) 25)	72
Fig. 3.2	Flow chart illustrating the process of hate crime harms. (Adapted from Paterson and others 2018a (see Footnote 78) 30)	76
Fig. 3.3	The distinct harms of hate crimes	85
Fig. 5.1	Types of hate crime legislation used globally	157
Fig. 6.1	Constructing hate crime provisions	163

List of Tables

Table 3.1 Words/slurs appearing in the Metropolitan Police Service's police crime reporting information system before and after the EU referendum   84

Table 3.2 Legislative developments in criminalising (race) hate crime in England and Wales   89

1

Introduction

The twentieth century was marked by some of the worst hate motivated atrocities known to humankind.[1] The democracies of the Global North responded by forming a number of supranational entities with the aim of bringing peace to parts of the world previously torn apart by conflicts marked by national, ethnic and religious hostilities.[2] In turn, a raft of national and international instruments were ratified by newly signed up member states that sought to prevent the recurrence of these most odious of identity-based atrocities. Among them was the Universal Declaration of Human Rights (UDHR) adopted in 1948, which set out under Article 1 that "All human beings are born free and equal in dignity and rights". These rights were to apply universally and "without distinction of any kind, such as race, colour, sex, language, religion, political or other opinion, national or social origin, property, birth or other status".[3]

The UDHR was a ground-breaking marker of the triumph of liberalism over totalitarian and fascist forms of governance. Yet the international codification of liberalism's commitments to "freedom" and

---

[1] Including the Holocaust which occurred between 1941 and 1945 and resulted in the killing of 6 million Jews.
[2] Most prominently the United Nations Charter.
[3] Article 2.

© The Author(s), under exclusive license to Springer Nature Switzerland AG 2022
M. A. Walters, *Criminalising Hate*, Palgrave Hate Studies,
https://doi.org/10.1007/978-3-031-08125-5_1

"equality" by no means reflected liberal democratic nations' resolution of their own histories of group-based oppression. The spread of race riots during the 1950s in the United Kingdom (UK), a result of systemic prejudices towards people of colour and the perceived threats they represented due to mass migration, grew steadily as the country began to rebuild its infrastructure in the aftermath of WWII.[4] In the United States (US), the Jim Crow laws that enforced racial segregation in the Southern United States were still in place at the start of the 1950s, while lynching and other forms of racial violence remained endemic across the country.[5] It was not until the 1960s that the social conservatism of the US and parts of Europe began to give way to a more permissive age, at least legally. It was during this decade that a cultural revolution ushered in a more socially liberal way of responding to issues relating to women's rights, racial justice and lesbian and gay equality.[6] The civil rights movement that emerged during this period also began to shine a light on the disproportionate and targeted nature of violence directed towards certain social groups. However, it was not until the early 1980s that an anti-hate movement was birthed, bringing with it sustained attention to, and calls for legislative protection against, violence targeted at marginalised groups in society—what was later to become known as "hate crime".[7]

The first modern form of hate crime legislation was enacted as part of the US federal Civil Rights Act 1968, protecting individuals participating in certain state or local activities from victimisation committed because of their race, colour, religion or national origin.[8] Ten years later California became the first state to legislate for hate crime in 1978,[9] followed by a plethora of similar laws enacted across the country during the

---

[4] For a chronology of events see Ben Bowling, *Violent Racism: Victimization, Policing, and Social Context* (OUP 1998); Rob Witte, *Racist Violence and the State*, (Routledge 1996).

[5] Jason Morgan Ward, 'Racial Violence in the United States since the Civil War', in Louise Edwards, Nigel Penn and Jay Winter (eds), *The Cambridge World History of Violence: Vol. 4* (CUP 2020), 88–109.

[6] See for example the International Covenant on the Elimination of All Forms of Discrimination (ICERD) adopted and opened for signature by the United Nations General Assembly in 1965.

[7] Terry A Maroney, 'The Struggle Against Hate Crime: Movement at a Crossroads' (1998) 73 New York U Law Rev 564; Valerie Jenness and Ryken Grattet, *Making Hate a Crime: From Social Movement to Law Enforcement* (Russell Sage 2001).

[8] Civil Rights Act 1968, § 245 (b)(2).

[9] Titled California Section 190.2, codified in California Penal Code § 422.55 & §422.6.

1980s and 1990s. The main purpose of enacting these laws was to significantly enhance the penalties of those convicted of hate-based criminal conduct.[10] It did not take long for this punitive turn to criminalising hate to make its way across the Atlantic, with the first hate crime offences entering the statute books in the United Kingdom (UK) in 1998.[11] Countries across continental Europe were not far behind, and in 2008 the European Union enacted legislation requiring all member states to aggravate the punishments of hate-based criminal offenders.[12]

Several other intergovernmental organisations have been instrumental in internationalising the concept and its legislative proscription across parts of Europe and beyond.[13] The Office for Democratic Institutions and Human Rights (ODIHR) part of the Organisation for Security and Co-operation in Europe has been particularly active in this area, promoting a practical guide for its members to legislate against hate crime.[14] Most recently, the United Nations has outlined a commitment to "[d]evelop effective strategies, including by enhancing the capacity of criminal justice professionals, to prevent, investigate and prosecute hate

---

[10] The terms hate crime and hate-based criminal conduct is used interchangeably. Hate crime is defined as hate-based conduct (as distinguished from speech alone), which includes acts, omissions, or states of affair, that is considered by lawmakers to be worthy of criminal proscription, based primarily on an assessment of the harms it is likely to cause. The word "hate" (or "hate-element") is inclusive of both states of mind and actions that demonstrate hatred, bias, prejudice, identity-based hostility and/or contempt towards a victim with a protected characteristic, and which underpins, or partly forms, the proscribed conduct. The reasons for this phraseology are more fully outlined in Chaps. 3, 5 and 6. NB., although this book focuses in most part on "hate crime" the theoretical framework outlined here applies to the criminalisation of all forms of hate (i.e. hate speech), and should also have relevance to criminalisation theory more generally.

[11] Sections 28–32 of the Crime and Disorder Act 1998 (UK) bringing in a raft of "racially aggravated" offences. Note, the offence of incitement to racial hatred (hate speech) was first created under the Race Relations Act 1965, s 6. Internationally, the UN Convention on Elimination of All Forms of Racial Discrimination (CERD), which entered into force in 1969, included a requirement to criminalise incitement of racial hatred (Article 4).

[12] See for example European Union Framework Decision on Racist and Xenophobic Crime (2008/913/JHA).

[13] See generally, Jennifer Schweppe and Mark A Walters, *The Globalization of Hate: Internationalizing Hate Crime?* (OUP 2016).

[14] For example OSCE Office for Democratic Institutions and Human Rights, *Hate Crime Laws—A Practical Guide* (OSCE ODIHR 2009); See also the work of the European Union Agency for Fundamental Rights

crimes" as part of the draft Kyoto Declaration signed in March 2021.[15] Such has been the popularity to criminalise hate globally, that as of 2022 legislative provisions to enhance penalties for hate crime can be found in jurisdictions in all inhabited continents across the world.[16]

The proliferation of hate crime laws has not been without controversy. Policy makers and scholars have tended to justify their use through the exposition of liberal criminal law doctrine together with retributive and consequentialist punishment theories.[17] Arguments have tended to pivot around the concept of "harm-culpability", whereby the level of criminal responsibility for any given offence is dictated by the degree of harm it causes combined with how blameworthy someone is for its commission.[18] Starting with harm, Iganski helped to popularise the notion that "hate crimes hurt more" due to their more violent and targeted nature.[19] The idea that hate crimes are more harmful than parallel offences has gained significant traction amongst domestic and international legislatures persuaded by an expanding evidence base that has shown how hate-based criminal conduct is *more likely* to involve physical violence and cause more significant emotional and behavioural harms to both individual victims and others who share their identity characteristics—resulting in what Iganski refers to as "waves of harm".[20]

The retributive principle of proportionality dictates that criminal sanctions should be commensurate with the seriousness of an offence. This typically starts with an assessment of how much (additional) harm has been caused to a victim and more broadly to society. Such a task is not without its difficulties. Indeed, despite what is now a significant body of empirical evidence, it remains unclear the precise *extent* to which the

---

[15] Kyoto Declaration on Advancing Crime Prevention, *Criminal Justice and the Rule of Law: Towards the Achievement of the 2030 Agenda for Sustainable Development*, Fourteenth United Nations Congress on Crime Prevention and Criminal Justice Kyoto, Japan, 7–12 March 2021, A/CONF.234/L.6.

[16] Barring Antarctica, see Appendix A.

[17] Both retributive and consequentialist, see for example Frederick M Lawrence, *Punishing Hate: Bias Crimes under American Law* (Harvard UP 1999); OSCE ODIHR 2009 (see Footnote 14).

[18] Lawrence 1999 (see Footnote 17); Paul Iganski, 'Hate crimes hurt more' (2001) 45(4) Am Behav Sci 626.

[19] Iganski 2001 (see Footnote 18). See also, Brian Levin, 'Hate Crime: Worse by Definition' (1999) 15(1) J Contemp Just 6; Lawrence (1999) (see Footnote 17).

[20] Iganski 2001 (ibid.).

hate-element of a crime "aggravates" its underlying harms. Some critics have asserted that as no *exact* amount of harm can be calculated for the hate-element of *all* hate crimes the application of penalty enhancements cannot be justified.[21] For instance, the physical harm caused by a hate-based assault may be no greater than the harm to a victim of a non-hate motivated assault. If a particularly resilient victim of the hate-based assault does not experience the typical emotional traumas caused by such an act, it has been asserted that it would be disproportionate to punish the hate motivated offender more severely compared with the non-hate motivated offender.[22] In fact, research by Iganski and Lagou found that while on average hate crime victims tend to be more emotionally and psychologically affected by their victimisation, some types of hate crime victims experience less trauma. They conclude thus that a blanket uplift in penalty in every hate crime case "cannot be justified if the justification for sentence uplift is to give offenders their just deserts for the harms they inflict".[23]

The lack of evidence to show conclusively that all hate crimes cause elevated emotional harms has not prevented legislatures from enacting significant penalty uplifts for such crimes. In jurisdictions where new penalty ranges have been prescribed in law some legislatures have doubled maximum penalties,[24] while others have even quadrupled them.[25] Research by this author has also found that in one jurisdiction where legislation gives discretion to judges to determine the amount of penalty uplift very different approaches were taken by sentencers. Some sentencers added 30 per cent to a sentence to reflect the increased seriousness of

---

[21] See, Mohamad Al-Hakim and Susan Dimock, 'Hate as an Aggravating Factor in Sentencing' (2012) 15(4) New Crim LR 572.

[22] Ibid.

[23] Paul Iganski and Spiridoula Lagou, 'Hate crimes hurt some more than others: Implications for the just sentencing of offenders' (2015) 30(10) J Interpers Violence 1696, 1696; see also Michael Cavadino, 'Should Hate Crime Be Sentenced More Severely?' (2014) 13(1) Contemporary Issues in Law 1.

[24] For example § 12-19-38. Hate Crimes Sentencing Act (Rhode Island, US) where a court can impose up to double the sentence of the basic offence.

[25] For example Crime and Disorder Act 1998 (UK) s. 29, which increases the sentence maximum for a racially aggravated assault from six months for the basic offence to two years for the aggravated version.

the hate-element, while others stated they consistently added 100 per cent.[26] Clearly then there is no consistent approach to punishing offenders, either within jurisdictions or across them.

It is not only the question of harm that has resulted in such a diverse range of perspectives within academic discourse and criminal justice practice. The second element of the "harm-culpability" calculation is to assess how blameworthy the offender is for expressing hatred through action.[27] Typical of many hate crime statutes, but by no means not all, is the introduction of "motive" into the fault element of offences. The insertion of motive in the mens rea element of an offence is arguably new to criminal law doctrine,[28] it typically being used instead post-conviction as a form or aggravating or mitigating factor that can be used to enhance or reduce an offender's culpability for the offence committed.[29] As many hate crime provisions apply only at the sentencing stage of the criminal process there should be little issue of whether hate motivation can increase the seriousness of an offence. However, statutes that introduce this element at the front end of the criminal process through the creation of new substantive offences must be able to show that it can justifiably enhance culpability in terms of criminal responsibility. The argument here is that a hate crime offender has not only formed the necessary mens rea for the basic offence (such as intention or recklessness) but in addition has demonstrated a further mens rea element of hate motivation.[30] It is this additional mens rea which is considered to be more morally repugnant than other mental states, thereby increasing the offender's level of blameworthiness.[31] For example, if a person commits a crime because of their racial hatred this is said to establish a higher level of moral culpability than

---

[26] For example an additional value to a fine, or more months onto a prison sentence. Mark Walters, Susann Wiedlitzka and Abenaa Owusu-Bempah, *Hate Crime and the Legal Process: Options for Law Reform* (University of Sussex 2017) ch. 9.

[27] Lawrence (1999) (see Footnote 17).

[28] Though many have provided examples of how motive has been used to construct certain specific intent crimes, see Mark A Walters, 'Hate crimes in Australia: introducing punishment enhancers' (2005) 29(4) Crim Law J 201.

[29] For example Premeditated revenge or acting out of compassion.

[30] Though see Al-Hakim and Dimock 2012 (see Footnote 21) who challenge whether motive can fall within the meaning of mens rea within conventional criminal law doctrine.

[31] Lawrence 1999 (see Footnote 17).

someone who acts out of revenge or lust. This is because unlike the latter motives, the offender's purpose is to attack the dignity and social standing of the victim. At the same time, the offender's expression of hatred or prejudice through criminal action directly undermines broader liberal democratic values of respect and equality.[32] This collectively gives rise to a greater level of moral blameworthiness that increases the seriousness of an offence, meaning that an offender is deserving of a higher level of punishment.[33]

Not all criminal law theorists have accepted that hate motivation increases moral blameworthiness, with some even asserting that such a position is illiberal. Heidi Hurd's doctrinal analysis of criminal law positioned hate crime statutes as unfairly punishing a defendant's inner thoughts.[34] Hurd claimed that unlike other types of mens rea, hate motivation is an emotion or belief which forms part of an individual's disposition, whether genetically or socially curated. As such, it makes up part of an individual's character. Liberal criminal law must only regulate *conduct* that is harmful to others, leaving individual thoughts and character beyond its remit. Hurd asserts that even if we wished to punish emotions, it cannot be determined with any objective certainty that prejudiced beliefs are any worse than other motives such as greed, jealousy, revenge or cowardliness.[35] Therefore, hate crime laws breach liberal doctrine by attempting to affect people's moral character.[36] Within a liberal society the state must not interfere with people's choices to believe what they

---

[32] John Stanton-Ife, *Criminalising Conduct with Special Reference to Potential Offences of Stirring Up Hatred against Disabled or Transgender Persons* (Law Commission 2013); Gail Mason and Andrew Dyer, '"A negation of Australia's fundamental values": Sentencing prejudice-motivated crime' (2013) 36 Melbourne UL Rev 871.

[33] As we will see in this book there may well be a diverging range of mens rea elements for hate crime, including those who intentionally express hatred, those who do so recklessly, and those who do so unwittingly. Iganski and Lagou 2015 (see Footnote 23) assert that there must be flexibility in the system of sentencing to reflect the different degrees of blameworthiness that such mental states give rise to.

[34] Heidi M Hurd, 'Why liberals should hate "hate crime legislation"' (2001) 20 Law & Phil 215. See also, Heidi M Hurd and Michael S. Moore, 'Punishing Hatred and Prejudice' (2004) 56(5) Stanford L Rev 1081.

[35] Heidi M Hurd 2001 (see Footnote 34), 226; see also Claudia Card, "Is Penalty Enhancement a Sound Idea?' (2001) 20(2) Law Philos 195.

[36] Or what Kahan describes as an implicit "bad-value added tax" on violence. Dan M Kahan, 'Two liberal fallacies in the hate crimes debate' (2001) 20 Law & Phil 175, 177.

want. Indeed, it is incumbent upon liberal states to protect the marketplace of ideas, no matter how repugnant people might find some of these.

Other commentators have refuted these claims noting that punishing character is consistent with western conceptions of criminal law,[37] while for some it is argued that hate crime laws do not sanction character or thought specifically but are instead aimed at punishing offenders for choosing to act on their prejudices.[38] What really is being punished is a form of conduct that carries with it a potent message that the individual being targeted is unwelcome and unwanted in society. In this regard, the totality of "hate crime"—as a specific type of offence—should be understood as being greater than the sum of its parts. By this it is asserted that the joining of a crime with hate motivation changes the *quality* of the conduct under scrutiny.[39] For example, a racist assault is not just the infliction of unlawful personal violence coupled with a bad motive, but instead is the infliction of violence that has the purpose, or at least the effect, of subjugating the victim's very essence as a human being, while additionally sending a terroristic message to others who share their identity.[40]

Given that hate crimes have an *in terrorem* effect, it makes sense that the symbolism of the law should be used to counter incidents. Consequentialists have therefore argued that hate crime statutes assist in deterring individuals from reoffending or deter would-be offenders from acting on their identity-based biases.[41] While there is little empirical evidence to back up such consequentialist claims of prevention, there has nonetheless been extensive support for the law's expressive role in challenging hate in society. A number of scholars have recognised the potency

---

[37] Mohamad Al-Hakim, 'Making Room for Hate Crime Legislation in Liberal Societies' (2010) 4(3) Crim L & Phil 341.

[38] John Stanton-Ife 2013 (see Footnote 32); David Brax, 'Motives, Reasons, and Responsibility in Hate/Bias Crime Legislation' (2016) 35(3) Criminal Justice Ethics 230.

[39] Mark A Walters, 'Conceptualizing "hostility" for hate crime law: Minding "the minutiae" when interpreting section 28(1)(a) of the Crime and Disorder Act 1998' (2014b) 34(1) OJLS 47.

[40] Barbara Perry and Alvi Shahid, '"We are all vulnerable": The in terrorem effects of hate crimes' (2012) 18(1) Int Rev Vict 57.

[41] Especially used by judges when determining sentence in hate crime cases, see Walters et al. 2017 (see Footnote 26), Section 9; Tilman Klumpp, and Hugo M Mialon, 'On Hatred' (2013) 15(1) Am Law Econ Rev 39.

of hate crime legislation as a form of public censure. Iterations of its application and enforcement serve to publicly denounce hate-based conduct, which not only directly challenges hate-based offences as immoral, but indirectly promotes social mores that embrace respect for "difference".[42] In this sense Mason has reflected that hate crime laws "implicitly claim that prejudice itself, not just in criminal manifestation, is wrong".[43] Such a position elicits a role for legal moralism in the criminalisation of hate in which hate crime law is conceptualised as a public declaration in favour of identity-based equality—what Mason refers to as the "re-moralization" of society.[44]

Beyond these more conventional criminal justice debates, commentators have argued that hate crime laws have a broader role in the restructuring of society by reversing the historical disadvantage and structural violence experienced by certain identity groups.[45] For instance, Harel and Parchomovsky critiqued the harm-culpability justification of hate crime legislation arguing that the wrongfulness of an act and the offender's culpability for it does not extend to considerations of how vulnerable a victim group is to victimisation.[46] Instead they posited that a "fair protection paradigm" can be used to justify enhanced punishments by requiring the state to take account of disparities among individuals who are more vulnerable to victimisation. The fair protection paradigm is grounded in the value of providing equality of protection against crime to victims. But, as the authors also point out, it can also be interpreted as giving priority to protect the most vulnerable victim groups. In identifying groups for special legislative protection, and punishing offenders who target them more, the state is in effect attempting to reverse the disadvantage that certain

---

[42] Paul Iganski, *Hate Crime and the City* (Policy Press 2008); Mark A Walters, 'Readdressing hate crime: Synthesizing law, punishment and restorative justice' in Thomas Brudholm and Birgitte S Johansen (eds), *Hate, Politics, Law* (OUP 2018) 150–171.
[43] Gail Mason, 'The symbolic purpose of hate crime law: Ideal victims and emotion' (2014a) 18 Theo Crim 75, 75.
[44] Mason 2014a (ibid.).
[45] Iganski 2008 (see Footnote 42): Ch 4; Alon Harel and Gideon Parchomovsky, 'On hate and equality' (1999) 109(3) Yale LJ 507; Chara Bakalis, 'The victims of hate crime and the principles of the criminal law' (2017) 37 LS 718.
[46] Harel and Parchomovsky 1999 (see Footnote 45). I counter this assertion through the analysis of the discriminatory model of legislation in Chap. 6.

minority groups have faced due to structural inequality.[47] Such a position asserts that it is only by giving formal recognition to the experiences of violence by the most marginalised in society that we can move to a place where those most disadvantaged can fully participate in society as equals. This in turn creates a system whereby historically persecuted groups become more confident in demonstrating their group-based rights by, for example, reporting incidents to the law enforcement agencies.[48]

Harel and Parchomovsky's theory offers a perspective that moves beyond the traditional lens of harm-culpability by incorporating the principle of equality and the notion of disadvantage into the penalty enhancement equation. However, the theory provides limited explication for the criminalisation of hate itself, beyond their thesis that hate motivation justifies greater punishment of offenders. They do not use the concept of equality or their notion of fair protection to offer a vision of why or whether the criminal law, as against sentencing provisions, should be used to combat hate crime. Instead, they assert that punishment enhancements "equalize the distribution of protection by deterring offenders from committing crimes against certain victims",[49] concurring with other consequentialist approaches to criminalising hate and in so doing subjecting their thesis to the same critique of whether punishing more effectively deters crime.

While the arguments that have been put forward in favour of criminalising hate in an attempt to recognise structural forms of identity-based oppression are persuasive, there has been renewed scepticism as to its efficacy in reducing social inequality. Within the United Kingdom, the Minister for Women and Equalities, Liz Truss, made the following speech in December 2020 on the Government's approach to addressing social inequality:

> this focus on groups at the expense of individuals has led to harmful unintended consequences…Too often, the equality debate has been dominated by a small number of unrepresentative voices, and by those who believe

---

[47] See also Lawrence 1999 (see Footnote 17).
[48] Paul Iganski, "Why make 'hate' a crime?" (1999) 19(3) Crit Soc Policy 386.
[49] Harel and Parchomovsky 1999 (see Footnote 45) 529.

people are defined by their protected characteristic, and not by their individual character. This school of thought says that if you are not from an 'oppressed group' then you are not entitled to an opinion, and that this debate is not for you. I wholeheartedly reject this approach.[50]

The UK government's move away from identifying and responding to experiences of victimisation linked to specific identity characteristics echoed a political stance taken prominently by several US-based critics in the latter part of the twentieth century. Jacobs and Potter's influential work on hate crimes law in the US argued that a hate crime epidemic had been socially constructed via a surge in identity politics that was in danger of creating the "balkanisation of ... society".[51] Rather than enhancing freedom, the additional penalties imposed by hate crime statutes were said to have a polarising effect on society, thereby reducing its social cohesiveness. The concern was that these new laws would create divisions between communities by highlighting the visibility of social chasms; the focus of which served to antagonise pre-existing tensions between identity groups. Jacobs and Potter argued that the groups with the most political clout had managed to convince legislatures to provide special protection to them, when criminal laws were already in place to punish harmful conduct.

Mason reflected later in the 2010s that identity politics had ultimately led to different identity groups having to convince the public that they did not deserve to be the targets of bias offending, which had in turn resulted in a hierarchy of victimhood. Those deserving or undeserving of special protection depended on how much power and influence each group had had in generating sufficient public sympathy and compassion. This, it has been argued, means that only those who can garner sufficient sympathy are included under hate crime laws, while some erstwhile deserving groups are left outside its protective walls.[52]

---

[50] Liz Truss, 'Fight For Fairness' (17 December 2020).
[51] James B Jacobs and Kimberly Potter, *Hate Crimes: Criminal Law and Identity Politics* (OUP 1998), 8.
[52] Mason 2014a (see Footnote 43); see also Jennifer Schweppe, 'Defining characteristics and politicising victims: A legal perspective' (2012) 10 J Hate Stud 173. I explore the role of identity politics and criteria for inclusion in hate crime legislation in Chap. 4.

Finally, some scholars have resisted hate crime laws, not only for failing to adequately protect all vulnerable groups from targeted victimisation, but because as a form of liberal criminal law they are purported to be yet another tool of oppression devised and administered by social elites to maintain, rather than challenge, existing power structures.[53] Swiffen highlights a new resistance to hate crime laws, especially amongst LGBTQ+ groups that have stressed how punitive laws potentially expose minority groups to the institutional prejudices of criminal justice systems.[54] This critical approach to hate studies positions punishment enhancements as representing a neoliberal response to crime that aims at individualising culpability; thereby masking structural causes and responsibility for hate-based criminality. In other words, hate crime laws not only fail to protect vulnerable groups but may in fact be used as a weapon to help dominant identity groups maintain social, political and economic control.[55]

The polemics of hate crime discourse are without doubt essential to the knowledge accretion of what remains a relatively new area of study. Nonetheless, several limitations can be observed within the extant literature. The first is that critical thinking remains firmly wedded to the idea that the criminalisation of hate automatically equates to enhanced punishment. Little has been said about the role of criminal law in furnishing the boundaries of acceptable behaviour through non-punitive measures.[56] Moreover, both sides of the debate on justifying punishment enhancements have tended to analyse the legitimacy of punishment enhancement through a narrow lens of liberal criminal law theory. Commentators typically support or reject the use of legislation based on conventional

---

[53] Doug Meyer, 'Resisting Hate Crime Discourse: Queer and Intersectional Challenges to Neoliberal Hate Crime Laws' (2014) 22(1) Crit Criminol 113, 120; Dean Spade, *Normal Life: Administrative Violence, Critical Trans Politics and the Limits of the Law* (South End Press 2011).

[54] Amy Swiffen 'New Resistance to hate Crime Legislation and the Concept of Law' (2018) 14(1) *Law, Culture and the Humanities* 121.

[55] Jon Burnett, 'Britain: racial violence and the politics of hate' (2013) 54(4) Race & Class 5.

[56] See, Mark A Walters, *Hate Crime and Restorative Justice: Exploring Causes, Repairing Harms* (OUP 2014a); Mark A Walters, 'Challenging orthodoxy: towards a restorative approach to combating the globalization of hate' in Jennifer Schweppe and Mark A Walters, *The Globalization of Hate: Internationalizing Hate Crime?* (OUP 2016) 294–313; Mark A Walters, 'Readdressing hate crime: Synthesizing law, punishment and restorative justice' in Brudholm and Johansen 2018 (see Footnote 42) 150–171.

1 Introduction

wisdom, by observing what types of crimes are *already* codified in law and then evaluating whether "hate motivation" can be conceptualised within conventional definitions of "harm" and "culpability" that are attached to these offences. Even those who have stepped outside of these conventional analyses have sought justifications for punishment enhancements for hate crime rather than reconceptualising more broadly *why* and *how* we ought to criminalise hate.[57]

In fact, the vast majority of those who have argued in favour of hate crime laws have done so by defining it as a pre-existing criminal offence which is motivated by some form of hate or prejudice.[58] Yet there has been little to no scrutiny within legal scholarship that seeks to examine whether existing criminal laws already cover *all* types of hate-based conduct that a liberal democratic society ought to consider worthy of criminal proscription. Legal scholarship has failed to recognise that there are likely to be hate-based acts, activities and states of affair that occur across society on a daily basis that are either not yet criminalised (but ought to be),[59] or which are (partly) criminalised but in a way that does not adequately reflect their unique dynamics or harms.[60] As I will explore throughout this book, if the criminal law is to truly address hate-based criminal conduct it must expand its lens to include the myriad individual, community and cultural harms that different types of hatred are likely to cause. I argue that if the current framework of criminal law does not reflect the multi-layered harms of hate and prejudice, it cannot meaningfully respond to the phenomenon of "hate crime".

Part of this quandary is that few scholars have fully conceptualised the type of liberalism that hate crime laws ought to be constructed upon. This book therefore challenges conventional wisdom by constructing a

---

[57] See for example Harel and Parchomovsky 1999 (see Footnote 45).
[58] See for example Jennifer Schweppe, 'What is a hate crime?' (2021) 7(1) Cogent Social Sciences, https://doi.org/10.1080/23311886.2021.1902643; Lawrence 1999 (see Footnote 17).
[59] That is conduct which is currently considered legal within a conventional framework of criminal law but which might be considered worthy of proscription under a modified lens of what conduct amounts to harm. See analysis in Chap. 3 and then examples of such conduct in Chap. 5.
[60] Linked to the concept of fair labelling. For example, certain cyber offences which are ill-defined or equipped to cover the types of hate-based offences currently occurring online. See for example Chara Bakalis, 'Rethinking cyberhate laws' (2017) 27(1) Information and Communications Technology Law 86.

new theoretical framework for the criminalisation of hate based on what I term "social justice liberalism". Chapter 2 begins by explaining what is meant by this term. It is argued that the neoliberal turn of the later part of the twentieth and early part of the twenty-first centuries has neither decreased social inequality nor prevented the proliferation of prejudice and hate-based conduct that its protagonists purport. The chapter argues that rather than rejecting "liberalism" as a political philosophy that helps to shape our social reality, we must move to a different practice of liberalism that seeks to ensure social justice and equality is advanced through legal frameworks that seek to protect pluralism through individual rights, while anchoring public policy and state regulation (including criminal law) more firmly to a communitarianism that seeks to identify, uncover and challenge social injustice.[61]

Key to the development of this theoretical groundwork is the work of Iris Young, whose "faces of oppression" is used to inform the framework for both the justification and limits of hate crime legislation.[62] Central to the book's thesis is the argument that if a liberal democracy is to genuinely attempt to dismantle the social inequalities that continue to pervade twenty-first century society, it must look beyond the narrow lens of classical (and neo) liberal harm principles to find ways in which it can effectively challenge forms of criminality that furnish the social structures that are causal to group-based oppression.[63]

In Chap. 3 I use this new normative framework to develop a more expansive theory of criminalisation that seeks to infuse the aims of liberalism *and* social justice into our understanding of harm. The chapter asserts that the harms of hate-based criminal conduct should be conceptualised as *distinct* from so-called parallel offences because expressions of hate (through conduct) have unique individual, community and societal impacts. In order to more fully articulate the distinctive harms of "hate crime" I map my own (and others') empirical findings on the impacts of

---

[61] John Rawls, *A Theory of Justice* (Belknap 1971).
[62] Iris Marion Young, *Justice and the Politics of Difference* (Princeton UP 2011).
[63] Such a criminal law cannot achieve such a task alone. It is beyond the scope of this book to offer a treatise on social justice and the radical reforms that are required in economic policy. It does, however, offer a vision of how law can better seek to identify and control hate-based criminal conduct.

hate-based conduct onto four of Young's faces of oppression, including: violence, marginalisation, powerlessness and imperial colonialism (what I will refer to as cultural harm).

The chapter asserts that fundamental to the exposition of hate's distinct harms in each of the faces of oppression is *group identity*. It is argued that without group identity, the distinct nature and harms of "hate crime" become nebulous and fluid, ultimately undermining its potency as a concept. Most importantly, within the framework of social justice liberalism, the failure to outline and evidence the distinct harms caused by specific types of hate is likely to directly undermine other key liberal legal principles, including fair punishment, fair labelling and proportionate sentencing. The chapter concludes that it is only by understanding hate crime as involving these multi-layered individual, community and cultural harms that the state can position itself to affect a genuine strategy for prevention.

Chapter 4 continues the reconstructing of "hate crime" by exploring who ought to be protected under such laws. Here I highlight how scholarship has failed to provide any clear criteria for inclusion of protected characteristics within either law or policy. The chapter emphasises how current conceptualisations, while undoubtedly valuable in enhancing knowledge about the nature and dynamics of different forms of hate and hostility, have failed to adequately synthesise criminological and victimological knowledge about the phenomenon with theories of criminalisation. The aim of the chapter is to synthesise these understandings via the framework of social justice liberalism, allowing for a more concise and coherent framework that can be used to determine how hate crime legislation should operate and for whom it should protect. This is assisted through the establishment of criteria that draws upon the book's theoretical framework. I argue that the criteria for inclusion (with a specific focus on creating new substantive offences) requires evidence of the distinct harms, as outlined in Chap. 3. Without such evidence, policy makers will struggle to justify the re-codification of criminal law within any framework of liberalism.

It is at this stage of the book that I argue "in defence of identity politics". Contrary to Jacobs and Potter, and a broader accord forming within the hate studies literature, I outline why contemporary identity politics enables the advancement of social justice for minority groups through participatory democracy. This is not to suggest that identity politics is unproblematic in addressing hate crime. Jacobs and Potter argued over 20 years ago that its use as a political tool risks over inflating the problem and risked balkanising society, resulting in siloed groups competing with each other for special protection. Others have reiterated these tensions,[64] all critiquing the role of identity politics as failing to produce fully inclusive hate crime policies that encompass those groups without political clout. The book concurs that the role of identity politics within a neoliberal framework of governance can be problematic when embraced within a political climate that promotes competition (rather than solidarity) between groups. However, identity politics need not be understood as a divisive tool of separation and competition but of cooperation, solidarity and celebration of "difference" in all of its guises. The importance of identity politics is linked to the liberal concept of freedom of association and the importance of political engagement that goes beyond voting. Identity politics should also be acknowledged as an important form of identity expression and celebration which serves to normalise and usualise identity difference within erstwhile hegemonic social structures.

Understanding *why* we ought to criminalise hate and *who* should be included are only two parts of what can be an incredibly complex legal puzzle. Often overlooked in discussions on the workability of hate crime laws is *how* the law is constructed. The way in which laws are drafted can have a significant impact on the operationalisation of hate crime as a concept and the extent to which the law is in turn enforced. Chapter 5 therefore begins the examination of how social justice liberalism can be "put into practice" through the application of hate crime legislation. This involves a detailed empirical investigation of the divergent "types" of law that have been enacted globally. In total, just over 190 legal jurisdictions were identified as having enacted hate crime law around the world.[65] Using the theoretical framework for the book, each statute (or relevant

---

[64] Jennifer Schweppe, 'Defining characteristics and politicising victims: A legal perspective' (2012) 10 J Hate Stud 173; Neil Chakraborti and Jon Garland, 'Reconceptualizing hate crime victimization through the lens of vulnerability and "difference"' (2012) 16 Theo Crim 499; Mason 2014a (see Footnote 43).

[65] Further information on the methodology is set out in Chap. 5.

section of a jurisdiction's penal code) was coded and separated out into one of three main types of legislation (sentence uplifts; substantive offences; hybrid), as well as one of four subtypes (penalty enhancements; sentence aggravation; aggravated offences; conduct-based offences).[66] Based on this data, as well as previous comparative research conducted by the author on how some jurisdictions are putting such laws into practice, I outline the strengths and weaknesses of each approach.

Chapter 6 builds upon the analyses of Chap. 5 by exploring the complexities involved in constructing the legal "model" (e.g. animus vs discriminatory) and legal tests that are ultimately used in court to determine whether a hate crime has been committed. Models of hate crime law can use either or both the mens rea or actus reus element to attach the hate-element of an offence (e.g. "motivation" of prejudice versus a "demonstration" of prejudice). Laws are also affected by the wording used to encapsulate "hate", including bias, prejudice, hostility and contempt, amongst others. The chapter looks at both the strengths and weaknesses of different models, reflecting on the interpretation of different approaches in the courts across common law jurisdictions. While the chapter offers a "preferred approach" to enacting hate crime legislation, it also acknowledges that due to the political, cultural and historical diversity of jurisdictions and their legal systems across the world there is no single model to legislating for hate crime globally.

In the final chapter I turn to the question of how criminal law can operate within a broader framework of justice that fosters a fairer and more equal society. The social justice liberal approach to criminalising hate advocates for the expansion of criminal law to challenge hate-based conduct in society. However, the extension of criminal law should not be equated with increasing the amount of punishment that is administered by the criminal justice system. This book envisions a changing of lens through which the criminal justice system seeks to respond to criminal wrongdoing. Chapter 7 therefore completes the thesis of the book by outlining a framework of justice mechanisms that are based primarily on restorative (communitarian) ideals that are focused on achieving the aims of restoring the harms of hate at the individual, community and

---

[66] See specifically, Chap. 5.

societal level. It is argued that if the criminal law is to be more than a conduit to inflict pain on wrongdoers, it must be underpinned by a justice system that has as its primary aim the reparation of social injustice. The chapter articulates how such a system might work. Structured around a maximalist approach to restorative justice, I outline how restorative interventions can take a primary role in delivering "justice" that operates above a secondary framework of threatened retributive punishments—applied only as a last resort (thereby maintaining liberal principles of proportionality).

The conclusion reflects back on 40 plus years of hate crime legislation that has expanded exponentially across the world. The key messages of the book are reiterated, noting again that in fully comprehending the complexities of both understanding and addressing "hate crime", a synthesis of political and legal theory is required that is directly informed by criminological and victimological knowledge. The resulting "social justice liberalism" approach that is offered in this book will no doubt have limitations and its instant detractors. The aim is to push the boundaries of what might be achieved were we to expand our criminal justice lens.

2

Social Justice Liberalism

2.1 Introduction

Liberalism as it emerged as the dominant ideology of European democracies throughout the latter part of the second millennium provides for the foundation of most Western contemporary systems of law and justice. The defining feature of liberalism is that it ascribes certain fundamental freedoms to all citizens. Central to the philosophy is individual choice and autonomy to make decisions that allow people to live their lives free from the coercive control of the state.[1] Liberals assert that it is by respecting the individual as a free agent that society can flourish for most if not all of its members.[2] Important to the healthy functioning of a liberal polity is that all citizens are equal before the law. The law must guarantee that no individual or group of people is either privileged by law or discriminated against by the state.[3] As Roberts asserts, a liberal polity aims to ensure that "everybody's interests are fairly (and in that sense *equally*)

---

[1] John Stuart Mill, *On Liberty* (2nd edn, John W Parker & Son, 1860).
[2] Mill 1860 (ibid.).
[3] Ronald Dworkin, *Justice for Hedgehogs* (Belknap 2011).

factored into the policy-making equation, irrespective of birth, colour, creed, class, gender, sexual orientation or other irrelevant personal characteristics".[4] It is by ensuring that *all* individuals are equal, and that their freedoms are protected by law, that the state can foster a fair and just society.

These aspirations continue to shape the legal landscape of many nations, and intranational entities, globally. Yet it has become painfully clear that contemporary liberal governance structures have not provided for the widespread equality and social fairness in society that its original thinkers may have hoped for.[5] Policy making as treating all citizens' interests equally has nonetheless seen some groups of citizens thrive over, and often at the expense of, certain others.[6] It is by no means new to question why a philosophy that is focused on principles of equality and fairness has seen the continued rise in socio-economic inequalities.[7] I do not intend to provide a detailed critique of liberalism and its impacts upon inequality here, indeed such a task is not likely to be possible in a single volume such as this. It is worth, though, providing some contextual discussion on the developments of liberal doctrine and the social inequalities that continue to proliferate in contemporary society as part of the theoretical underpinnings of this book.

Classical liberalism, and its more recent incarnation neoliberalism, have focused heavily on competition between individuals as fundamental to human development and to the betterment of humankind.[8] Although "neoliberalism" is not easily defined as any one single concept,[9] as a doctrine emerging prominently in the 1980s it has emphasised free market

---

[4] Paul Roberts, 'Criminal Law Theory and the Limits of Liberalism' in AP Simester, Antje Du Bois-Pedain and Ulfrid Neumann (eds), *Liberal Criminal Theory: Essays for Andreas von Hirsch* (Hart 2014) 332.

[5] Simon Springer, Kean Birch, Julie MacLeavy (eds), *The Handbook of Neoliberalism* (Routledge 2016).

[6] See for example Steffen Mau, *Inequality, Marketization and the Majority Class: Why Did the European Middle Classes Accept Neo-Liberalism?* (Springer 2015).

[7] Patrick J Deneen, *Why Liberalism Failed* (Yale UP 2019). For a radical perspective that attempts to outline the of neoliberalism and which dismisses all other paradigms of conceptualising crime see Steve Hall and Simon Winlow, *Revitalizing Criminological Theory: Towards a New Ultra-Realism* (Routledge 2015).

[8] Friedrich A Hayek, *The Road to Serfdom* (first published 1976, Routledge 2001).

[9] Rajesh Venugopal, 'Neoliberalism as concept' (2015) 44(2) Econ Soc 165.

competition, deregulation, privatisation and reduced welfarism as fostering societal advancement.[10] Based on the economic ideas of Hayek and others, it emphasises how healthy competition between humans enables elite wealth creators to generate economic prosperity for all, as capital trickles down to "under-performers" but essential workers who complete menial economic tasks.[11]

Certainly, the amount of wealth created within jurisdictions that have focused on neoliberal policies has increased significantly over the past 30–40 years. Yet the trickling down effect has invariably consisted of a sporadic drip with inequalities amongst populations widening, given rise to a social chasm between the have and have nots.[12] Certain groups in society have taken the brunt of much of this inequality. Women, people of colour (referred to often by public authorities as Black and Minority Ethnic Minorities (BAME)), LGBT+ communities[13] and disabled people are all more likely to experience social and economic disadvantages compared with cisgender white men.[14] For instance, UK Government data shows that women continue to earn less than men in *all* sectors of the UK economy.[15] The median gender pay gap in 2018 was 11.9 per cent, growing to over 16 per cent for those working in the public sector. LGBT+ people too are likely to get paid less than their cisgender straight counter parts, with a survey of 4000 LGBT+ people by YouGov suggesting such individuals earn on average 16 per cent less.[16] The same can be said for "BAME" individuals, where there is a gap of 17 per cent for black male graduates' pay, after taking account of differences in average

---

[10] Adam Przeworksi, 'The Neoliberal fallacy' (1992) 3(3) J Democ 45.

[11] Venugopal 2015 (see Footnote 9).

[12] See for example Feargal McGuinness and Daniel Harari, *Income inequality in the UK* (Briefing Paper No 7484, House of Commons Library, 20 May 2019).

[13] Lesbian, Gay, Bisexual, and Transgender. The + signifies a broader range of sexual and gender identities which may fall within this grouping including intersex, asexual and queer people.

[14] Equality and Human Rights Commission, *Is Britain fairer? The state of equality and human rights* (EHRC 2018).

[15] Aleksandra Wisniewska and others, 'Gender Pay Gap: women still short-changed in the UK' *Financial Times* (London, 23 April 2019).

[16] Ben Chapman, 'LGBT+ workers paid £6,700 per year less than straight workers, survey suggests' *The Independent* (London, 2 July 2019).

qualifications and job type,[17] while disabled people's pay packets are significantly lower than their non-disabled counterparts.[18]

The socio-economic divisions that have proliferated within liberal nations have been brought more sharply into focus during the COVID-19 pandemic with data showing that "BAME" individuals were between 10 and 50 per cent higher risk of dying from the disease when compared to White British people,[19] while those living in the most deprived areas died at double the rate of those in the most affluent.[20] The exposition of information about these inequalities has penetrated public consciousness as postmodern society has become newly sensitised to the social issues faced by its citizens and residents. This is in part a progression that is aided, and sometimes inhibited, by the dissemination of (mis)information via the internet and social media. Yet while some political actors have stepped in to reassert the virtues of a more egalitarian vision of society in both Europe and the US, other populists from across the political spectrum have been quick to pounce on the concerns of communities who have become disenfranchised by the status quo. It is these actors who have more recently taken charge in contemporary politics both in Europe and the US. Central to the narratives of these newly influential political characters is the blaming of perceivably corrupt institutions (such as the European Union in the UK context, and the old guard of Capitol Hill in the US context).[21] In both spheres the lambasting of these institutions has been framed within a renewed jingoism that has focused on strengthening a national identity of old.

Donald Trump's 2016 presidential campaign slogan of "make America great again" is illustrative of this approach. Aligned with both "leaders'" rhetoric has been targeted blame, with certain groups in particular

---

[17] Kathleen Henehan and Helena Rose, 'Opportunities Knocked? Exploring pay penalties among the UK's ethnic minorities' (Resolution Foundation, 18 July 2018).

[18] Equality and Human Rights Commission, *Being Disabled in Britain: A journey less equal* (EHRC 2017).

[19] Public Health England, *Disparities in the risk and outcomes of COVID-19* (Public Health England 2020).

[20] Office for National Statistics, *Deaths involving COVID-19 by local area and socioeconomic deprivation: deaths occurring between 1 March and 17 April 2020* (ONS 2020).

[21] Resulting in Brexit for the former, and the election of Trump and ultimately the invasion of Capital Hill by his supporters in the latter.

coming under fire as (partly) culpable for the social woes of society. Political rhetoric targeted at immigrants, Muslims and LGBT+ people, amongst others, has brought each under the spotlight. Donald Trump's labelling of Mexicans as "rapists", his stating that "Islam hates us", that "we're having problems with Muslims coming into the country",[22] and that COVID-19 was the "Chinese virus", were each accompanied by sharp rises in public expressions of hate towards these groups.[23]

In the UK, the British Prime Minister Boris Johnson's declaration of "Britain's Independence Day" back in 2016 marked a new nationalism that has divided the country, communities and families. In the aftermath of the EU referendum, recorded hate crimes rose 41 per cent from the previous year.[24] In the five years since then, recorded hate crime has doubled.[25] Analysis of Crime Survey for England and Wales data has also revealed real-term increases in estimated numbers of Islamophobic and anti-LGBT hate crimes.[26] The toxic language used by political leaders has continued unabated, with newspaper comments made by the Prime Minister comparing Muslim women wearing Burkhas as "bank robbers" and "letter boxes" being followed by a 375 per cent increase in reported anti-Muslim hate incidents.[27] Other comments previously made by him about gay men as "tank-top bum boys" and Black people as "piccaninnies" with "water melon smiles" similarly give others permission to hate.[28]

---

[22] Jenna Johnson and Abigail Hauslohner, '"I think Islam hates us": A timeline of Trump's comments about Islam and Muslims' *Washington Post* (Washington, 20 May 2017).

[23] See for example Karsten Müller and Carlo Schwarz, 'Making America hate again? Twitter and hate crime under Trump' (2018) SSRN; Griffin Sims Edwards and Stephen Rushin, 'The Effect of President Trump's Election on Hate Crimes' (2018) SSRN; Brian Levin and Kevin Grisham, *Special status report: Hate crime in the United States* (Centre for the Study of Hate and Extremism 2016); Yulin Hswen and others, 'Association of "#covid19" Versus "#chinesevirus" With Anti-Asian Sentiments on Twitter: March 9–23, 2020' (2021) 5(1) Am J Public Health 956.

[24] Hannah Corcoran and Kevin Smith, *Hate Crime, England and Wales, 2015/16* (Home Office 2016).

[25] Home Office (2020) *Hate crime, England and Wales, 2020 to 2021* (Home Office 2020).

[26] Mark Walters, 'After years of decreasing hostilities, hate crimes against LGBT+ people are now on the rise' (*International Network for Hate Studies Blog*, 30 July 2019).

[27] Tell MAMA, 'Tell MAMA Annual Report 2018: Normalising Hatred' (Tell MAMA, 2 September 2019).

[28] Stewart Lee, 'Why the joke's on Johnson in a fantasy violence league' *The Guardian* (London, 23 June 2019).

The populist developments in contemporary American and British politics are by no means an aberration of the neoliberal turn of the twentieth century. As Klein points out, crises—actual or curated—are key to extending the tentacles of neoliberal ideology.[29] The "shock doctrine" as she describes it enables certain elites to paralyse the normal rules of democracy thereby bypassing its institutional constraints.[30] We see this most vividly occurring in the context of the Trump administration that sought to railroad policies through by declaring "national emergencies" and by denouncing judicial decisions that were counter to his views.[31] In the UK, a Prime Minister gung-ho on pushing through Brexit by illegally proroguing Parliament to prevent parliamentarians continuing in their democratic roles, subsequently attacked the Supreme Court and its Justices for upholding constitutional law.[32] Such pronouncements serve only to legitimise enmity against both democratic institutions and those people deemed as frustrating the "true" destiny of the country. They too allow elite politicians to erode democratic principles of equality and respect for others; norms that restrain the social control mechanisms of the state.

In responding to the rising tide of hatred promulgating across the globe, this book asks the question, what role (if any) does the criminal justice system have in stemming its upward trend? More specifically, it examines on what basis criminal laws should be used to prevent acts of hatred. The enactment of hate crime legislation is by no means new to liberal jurisdictions and their attempts to combat hate-based violence.[33] However, as outlined in the Introduction to this book there are two significant lacunas in the literature that I believe may have grave consequences for the future utility of such legislation. The first is that there remains little theorisation on the justification of hate crime legislation beyond the conventional debates on harm-culpability and their nexus to

---

[29] Naomi Klein, *The Shock Doctrine: The Rise of Disaster* Capitalism (Penguin 2008).
[30] Philip Mirowski, *Never Let a Serious Crisis Go to Waste: How Neoliberalism Survived the Financial Meltdown* (Verso 2014).
[31] Peter Baker, 'Trump Declares a National Emergency, and Provokes a Constitutional Clash' *The New York Times* (New York, 15 Feb 2019).
[32] BBC, 'Supreme Court: Suspending Parliament was unlawful, judges rule'(London, 24 Sept 2019).
[33] Valerie Jenness and Ryken Grattet, *Making Hate a Crime: From Social Movement to Law Enforcement* (Russell Sage 2001).

retributive and consequentialist punishment theories.[34] That is to say, hate crime laws have been largely understood in terms of a need to increase punishments as a means of recognising the enhanced harms of hate, the increased blameworthiness of hate motivation, and the desire to deter would-be offenders.[35] With little other legal or political justification, hate crime laws have been left open to the criticism that they are simply another example of the neoliberal state extending criminalisation in order to responsibilise individuals, while obfuscating the broader structural causes of hate that the ideology systemically sustains.[36]

If hate crime laws are to fulfil a broader socio-political purpose that support liberal values of equality, dignity, and respect they must be more cogently situated within a theoretical framework that affirms individual freedom while addressing the social injustices that are caused by acts of hatred. Such a framework must be understood as both a political as well as a legal enterprise. This is because hate, and its lethal consequences,[37] is not only about individual injury and offender culpability, but about broader cultural and economic factors that serve to cultivate an unequal society that is marked by social injustice. As such, a legal framework that proscribes hate must be understood, not simply as a means of reflecting enhanced individual culpability, but as a tool to challenge more broadly the social structures that facilitate toxic environments of hate—that is factors that fundamentally undermine key liberal values of equality, dignity and respect of others.

An important question follows: can laws that enhance punishment for hateful individuals, play a role in advancing social justice for commonly

---

[34] Jacobs and Potter, *Hate Crimes: Criminal Law and Identity Politics* (OUP 1998); Frederick M Lawrence, *Punishing Hate: Bias Crimes under American Law* (Harvard UP 1999); see overview of these debates in Jennifer Schweppe and Mark A Walters, 'Hate Crimes: Legislating to Enhance Punishment' (Oxford Handbooks Online 2015).
[35] Frederick M Lawrence, *Punishing Hate: Bias Crimes under American Law* (Harvard UP 1999).
[36] Jon Burnett, 'Britain: racial violence and the politics of hate' (2013) 54(4) Race & Class 5; Zoë James, *The Harms of Hate for Gypsies and Travellers A Critical Hate Studies Perspective* (Palgrave 2020); Doug Meyer, 'Resisting Hate Crime Discourse: Queer and Intersectional Challenges to Neoliberal Hate Crime Laws' (2014) 22(1) Crit Criminol 113; Emma K Russell, 'Punishment in a "tolerant society": interrogating hate crime law reform discourse' (2017) 26:3 Griffith Law Review 315; Dean Spade, *Normal Life: Administrative Violence, Critical Trans Politics and the Limits of the Law* (South End Press 2011).
[37] As outlined below and in Chap. 3.

targeted groups of people? This question is explored more fully in the chapters that follow. In addition, there has been little to no meaningful critique of the different ways that hate crime laws have been enacted and the potentially diverging effects that these discrete approaches have on recording and prosecution practices, conviction levels, and more broadly their effectiveness in preventing hate-based offences in the longer term. For instance, little is known about the different outcomes of creating substantive criminal hate crime offences compared with those states that more simply enact sentencing provisions that enable judges to aggravate sentencing where there is evidence of hate motivation.[38] In Chaps. 5 and 6, I compare diverging models used globally to assess, not only *why* legislatures ought to legislate against hate-based conduct, but importantly *how* they should best go about drafting (reforming) such laws.

First, this chapter conceptualises a liberal framework of law that is firmly anchored to a renewed emphasis on social justice that seeks to uncover and address identity-based inequalities as being fundamental to preventing hate crime. The term "social justice liberalism" is used to frame a system of (criminal) law and justice that seeks to proactively uncover and prevent the individual, community, and cultural harms of hate-based criminality. Far from accepting the "death of social democracy",[39] this book calls for a resurgence in social liberal thinking to counter the rise of both populism and neoliberalism and the multiple forms of hate and prejudice these have given rise to. The following chapters provide both a normative and practical framework on how this could be achieved.

2.2 What Is Social Justice Liberalism?

During the early part of the twentieth century a "new liberalism" emerged as a response to perceived flaws of its classical cousin.[40] New liberals rejected the laissez-faire economic models that resulted in vast inequali-

---

[38] Jennifer Schweppe, Amanda Haynes and Mark A Walters, *Lifecycle of a Hate crime: Comparative Report* (ICCL 2018).

[39] Ashley Lavelle, *The Death of Social Democracy: Political Consequences in the 21st Century* (Routledge 2008).

[40] John W Seaman, 'L.T. Hobhouse and the Theory of "Social Liberalism"' (1978) 11(4) Can J Polit Sci 777.

ties in terms of income and instead advocated a synthesis of the individualism of liberalism and the cooperative moral of socialism.[41] Hobhouse argued for an ethics of social harmony that sought greater redistribution of wealth and of the curtailment of "outspoken individualist selfishness".[42] Under this approach, the advancement of humankind involves both the fulfilment of one's own capacities and the fulfilment of other personalities.[43] In other words, the fulfilment of individuals involves the fulfilment of social capacities. A harmonious social liberal society, it is argued, involves not "merely absence of conflict but actual support. There must be for each, then, possibilities of development such as not merely to permit but actively to further the development of others".[44]

Hobhouse's theory of social harmony was anchored to an egalitarianism that stipulated that every individual has a moral claim to the development of their personality. Every claim must be equal and the individual good can only be "good" if it does not impede the development of others' personality. The development of one class of people at the expense of another "is not fully harmonious. Gain on one side is set off by loss on another. The problem of true social progress is to find the lines on which development on one side does not [impede] development on another, but assists it".[45] In achieving social harmony as equal participation and fruitful development, individuals must be free as possible to direct the development of their personality. To be free is to enjoy self-determination in the absence of external constraints. Where coercion exists the "human faculties" become attenuated and the ultimate aim of collective harmony is diminished.

Importantly, within a social liberal polity individual freedom must be balanced with collective development. Individuals' claims to absolute freedom, that is to do as they please, are only constrained by the equally valued claim of others to do the same. Seaman summarises, "every man in the society of social harmony is to be as free as every other man from

---

[41] LT Hobhouse, *Liberalism* (first published 1911, OUP 1964).
[42] LT Hobhouse, *The Labour Movement* (2nd edn, Fisher Unwin 1905) 69–70.
[43] Seaman 1978 (see Footnote 40) 783.
[44] Hobhouse (see Footnote 42) 69.
[45] LT Hobhouse, *Social Evolution and Political Theory* (first published 1911, Kennikat Press 1968) 83, cited in Seaman 1978 (see Footnote 43) 783.

coercion imposed by others".[46] Individual freedom as development of personality is fundamental to the acceptance and respect for all people, regardless of their identity. Essential to this endeavour is a commitment to "social justice", a contested term in itself, that has traditionally been tied to socialist movements as a means of transforming social order through the socialisation of the means of production (also referred to commonly as distributive justice).[47] However, economic redistribution does not alone adequately address the deeply embedded structural disadvantages of social groups that are linked to group-based identity. Justice requires that *all* individuals are able to express their needs regardless of their personal characteristics and to make their own choices in order to self-realise.[48] Young notes that "when people claim that a particular rule, practice, or cultural meaning is wrong and should be changed, they are often making a claim about social injustice".[49] Social justice, then, is not only about the means of redistributing capital and goods, but has the objective of creating a fair society both economically *and* culturally, within which there are safeguards against individual and group-based discrimination and measures that actively seek to rectify inequality.

Key to cultivating this state of affairs is equal opportunities. Young asserts that "[e]galitarian social justice requires that all human beings be *recognized* as equals".[50] In other words, to be equal one must be "someone whose life matters equally to that of others".[51] Recognition must come before self-realisation can be attained by an individual. The "social" must enable recognition through affirming equal opportunities. For social liberals this is best achieved through equal access to primary goods such as: freedom of movement, free choice of occupation within a milieu of diverse opportunities; powers of offices and positions of responsibility in the political and economic institutions of the basic structure; income and wealth; and the social bases of self-respect. These primary goods must be

---

[46] Seaman 1978 (see Footnote 43) 784.
[47] Per Sundman, *Egalitarian Liberalism Revisited: On the Meaning and Justification of Social Justice* (Uppsala University 2016).
[48] John Rawls, *A Theory of Justice* (rev edn, OUP 1999).
[49] Iris Marion Young, *Justice and the Politics of Difference* (Princeton UP 2011) 34.
[50] Ibid., 165, emphasis in original.
[51] Ibid., 165.

supported by a system of political, social and economic institutions—what Rawls described as the "basic structure"—which collectively ensure that each individual has the same indefeasible claim to a scheme of equal basic liberties.[52]

As with all forms of social governance, social liberalism is not without its critics.[53] Some political theorists have emphasised that equality of opportunity is an illusion as some characters within a "free" society will reach the top of business empires and maintain and control disproportionally large amounts of capital and property while others remain at the bottom of the economic pile.[54] Indeed, social liberalism does not attempt to ensure that economic capital is divided equally (in absolute terms), but rather it aims to cultivate a system where there is greater redistribution of capital, a smaller wealth gap, and the removal of structural barriers to obtaining self-realisation. It acknowledges that people are different with differing capacities and that what is important is the freedom to express individuality while abolishing poverty and maintaining upper limits on levels of wealth. However, for some critics such a system is seen as simply maintaining power divisions whereby the middle-class elites maintain control of capital and, with it, political power.[55] This, they argue, has resulted in entire communities of people who are disenfranchised from society, many of whom turn to criminality as a result.[56]

Despite the plethora of critics ready to expose the many holes that liberalism contains, few are able to offer a normative vision of how these can be filled. For instance, Hall and Winlow assert that in order to understand harm we need to completely reject liberalism, and all other major theories of harm, and move to what they label as a "Ultra-Realist" position. This newly formed theory "is firm in its intent to confront

---

[52] Rawls' first principle of justice, John Rawls, *Justice as Fairness: A Restatement* (Harvard UP 2001) 42.
[53] Within the context of hate studies see for example Zoë James, *The Harms of Hate for Gypsies and Travellers: A Critical Hate Studies Perspective* (Palgrave 2020).
[54] See for example Wendy Brown *Undoing the Demos: Neoliberalism's Stealth Revolution* (Zone Books 2015).
[55] Michael J Thompson, 'The Limits of Liberalism: A Republican Theory of Social Justice' (2011) 7(3–4) Int J Ethics Educ 3.
[56] John Lea and Jock Young, *What Is to Be Done About Law And Order?* (Penguin 1984).

neoliberal capitalism's worldwide zemiological environment full in the face".[57] They do this by drawing on transcendental materialism as a lens through which human subjectivity and the harms they experience should be comprehended. This theory asserts that human possibility is rooted to the body (brain) and through this subjectivity (being) arises. Human beings, it is argued, are hardwired to be transcendental (being more than their material base). However, once an individual is subject to an external environment, they become caught up in a constitutive relationship between their material base and the meaning given to them by the social milieu to which they are presented. Hall and Winlow assert that "when today's liberal-postmodern subject emerges to seek a coherent symbolic order it encounters a system founded on the fundamental *negative belief* that nothing beyond the current system is possible".[58] While I concur with some of Hall and Winlow's criticisms in relation to neoliberalism's grip on individualism and its hollow focus on human competition,[59] I am less convinced that liberalism, more broadly conceptualised, can be wholly rejected as a method through which humans can self-realise and through which social injustice can be addressed. Walklate reflects further in a review of their work that her concern:

> is that here we are being offered an exchange of one way of doing business for another. Moreover, the kind of thinking that underpins this choice has the potential to be as equally dogmatic and lacking in the fluidity, geographical and ethnically informed nuances necessary for [criminology] to lose its shackles of liberalism.[60]

It is a poignant point and one that is particularly relevant to this book. A complete rejection of liberalism, one which offers little by way of conceptualising the ways in which government, law and economy ought to

---

[57] Steve Hall and Simon Winlow, *Revitalizing Criminological Theory: Towards a New Ultra-Realism* (Routledge 2015) 54.

[58] Steve Hall and Simon Winlow, 'Ultra-realism' in Walter S DeKeseredy and Molly Dragiewicz (eds), *Routledge Handbook of Critical Criminology* (Routledge 2018) 53 (emphasis in original).

[59] I concur also with the need for a broader concept of harm than that which conventional liberal frameworks have allowed for, see further analysis below regarding conduct that contributes to oppression as harm worthy of criminalisation, as detailed more fully in Chap. 3.

[60] Sandra Walklate, 'Book Review: Steve Hall and Simon Winlow (2015) Revitalising Criminological Theory: Towards a New Ultra-Realism' (2016) 5(3) Int J Crime Just Soc Democr 111.

be structured, leaves us wondering what justice might look like; especially for those who fall outside of a society dominated by white heteronormative cisgender male "thinking" (whether neoliberal or not).[61]

The main alternative to a liberal framework of understanding harms and the systems of justice is to move towards a socialist model that seeks to dismantle capitalism, and with it, individual liberties. Socialist ideals, though continuously evolving, have conventionally sought to bring about human equality through the equal distribution of economic resources as determined by collective (state) ownership and control over the means of production.[62] The largely empirically unsupported belief asserted by the socialist theorem is that human beings become "equal" where they no longer have to compete for resources. Without the conflicts that arise from such competition, or the social inequalities that are generated from vast inequalities in wealth, class distinctions wither away and individuals of all creeds become one.

While the idealism of socialism, defined crudely as collective ownership of the means of production, is appealing, we must continue to question whether it can be realised without at least some loss of political and human rights. Some post-Marxist scholars have responded to this question by engaging in a "critical redemption" of rights, emphasising the limitations of human rights while simultaneously acknowledging that they play a vital role in protecting oppressed minorities.[63] Such critiques are often outlined in utopian terms whereby the universality of rights are reconceptualised through a normative lens that seeks to completely re-understand how human rights operate. However, it is difficult to see how, in reality, individual rights can be truly "redeemed" whilst dismantling capitalist systems of governance. Ultimately, rights must be limited to achieve anti-capitalist goals. Other post-Marxist political thinkers are more upfront with their deeply embedded scepticism of individual rights: for instance Badiou critiques human rights as the "cult of freedom

---

[61] Though see James 2020 (see Footnote 53).
[62] See for example GA Cohen, *Self-ownership, Freedom, and Equality* (CUP 1995).
[63] See Ben Golder, 'Beyond redemption? Problematising the critique of human rights in contemporary international legal thought' (2014) 2(1) London Review of International Law 77; Ben Golder, 'Foucault, rights and freedom' (2013) 26(1) Int J Semiotic Law 5. See also post-Marxist critiques by Lefort Claude, *The Political Forms of Modern Society: Bureaucracy, Democracy, Totalitarianism* (MIT Press 1986); *Undoing Gender* (Routledge 2004).

(including, of course, freedom of enterprise, the freedom to own property and to grow rich that is the material guarantee of all other freedoms)".[64] Such a critique asserts that individual freedoms cannot be guaranteed if society is to overcome its class-based struggles; those which have resulted in an inequitable division of economic resources.

Ultimately, then, it is difficult to see how a system that emphasises the needs of the "social" can square the circle of protecting all individual rights. The reality is that decisions made by politicians, whether elected or not, about what is good for society will be made by human beings who are susceptible to environmental factors and belief systems that extend well beyond the nefarious aspects of capitalism or neoliberal systems of governance. Of particular concern is whether cultural and identity differences will be respected within a system that relies on a willingness to reject individual freedoms in favour of more collective moral character. Social constructions of difference and the negative stereotypes and hostilities that attach to these are constructed historically over decades, centuries and even millennia, and are imbedded institutionally through practices and systems that reproduce hierarchies of identity. While I have argued elsewhere that socio-economic disadvantage is likely to be connected to many acts of hostilities against minority groups, it is not this factor alone that is causal to oppressive conduct such as hate crimes.[65] For instance, social psychological research has suggested that as numbers of minority group members increase in any given community, the perceived threat of these individuals increases as do the social control mechanisms used to subjugate them (law enforcement, harsher sentences, drug polices, school exclusions, etc.).[66]

Empirical research has provided insight into why and how these identity-based hostilities arise across differing political and economic systems of governance. The central concept of *threat* is key to understanding almost all theories of hate crime causation.[67] Social psychologists com-

---

[64] Alain Badiou, *The Communist Hypothesis* (Verso 2010) 2; see also, Agamben Giorgio, *Homo Sacer: Sovereign Power and Bare Life* (Stanford UP 1998).
[65] Mark A Walters, 'A General *Theories* of Hate Crime: Strain, Doing Difference and Self Control' (2011) 19(4) Critical Crim 313.
[66] Hubert M Blalock, *Toward A Theory of Minority-Group Relations* (John Wiley & Sons 1967).
[67] Mark Walters and Rupert Brown, *Causes and Motivations of Hate Crime* (Equality and Human Rights Commission 2016); Walters 2011 (see Footnote 65).

monly distinguish between "realistic" and "symbolic" threats.[68] Realistic threats consist of tangible conflicts of interest—frequently perceived competition over jobs, housing and welfare distribution between the (majority) ingroup and outgroups (often minority groups or immigrants or disabled people). Symbolic threats are concerned more with the cultural and/or group identity of the ingroup. Members of dominant groups can begin to fear the visibility of those who appear to be "different" as encroaching upon social and cultural norms and values, thereby changing their ways of being.[69] These threats and the violent responses that typically follow them have occurred throughout history, whether within feudal, capitalist, socialist, communist or tribal communities.

A system based on distributive justice may well help to decrease some of the perceived realistic threats posed by minority groups. However, competition for resources cannot alone explain inter-group hostilities.[70] These fears can relate to gender or sexual identity which threatens heteronormative identity ideals, or to religious norms where rituals, dress and beliefs threaten the dominant values and norms of any given society. In one cross-jurisdictional comparative study, attitudes towards immigration were found to be more aligned to sharing group identity, common experiences and heightened empathy, and were less aligned to competition for jobs, housing and welfare benefits; suggesting that perceptions of threat and identity-based antipathies are not always caused by socioeconomic competition between groups.[71]

---

[68] Walter G Stephan and Cookie White Stephan, 'An integrated threat theory of prejudice' in Stuart Oskamp (ed), *Reducing Prejudice and Discrimination* (Psychology Press 2000) 23–46.

[69] David Gadd, Bill Dixon and Tony Jefferson, *Why Do They Do It? Racial Harassment in North Staffordshire* (Centre for Criminological Research, Keele University 2005); Donald P Green, Dara Z Strolovitch and Janelle S Wong, 'Defended neighbourhoods, integration and racially motivated crime' (1998) 104(2) Am J Sociol 372; Larry Ray and David Smith, 'Racist Violence As Hate Crime' (2002) 48(1) Crim Just Matters 6.

[70] Explained more fully below under "cultural imperialism".

[71] Asma Mustafa and Lindsay Richards, 'Immigration attitudes amongst European Muslims: Social identity, economic threat and familiar experiences' (2019) 42(7) Ethn Racial Stud 1050. Of particular relevance to this chapter is that research comparing attitudes towards immigration across European countries found that Sweden (perhaps the most salient example of a social democratic country) was by far the most favourable in their attitudes towards immigrants, with over 80 per cent saying some or many immigrants of all types should be allowed to come and live in Sweden. This can be compared to countries where more neoliberal thinking has taken hold, including the UK where 55 per cent said the same.

We must, then, remain wary of systems of government that promise equality through distributive justice alone. Of greatest concern is that those who do not fulfil a socially constructed view of what is good for the social will inevitably be positioned as antithetical to its collective good.[72] This is likely to disproportionately impact minority groups who are forced to adhere to certain social values that they do not personally endorse, referred to by Dworkin as "endorsement constraint".[73] While for some individuals this may be the acceptance of a political ideology that they disagree with, for others the type of equality that is enforced may be an affront to the very essence of who they are.

Without individual rights to question whether the social good is harmful to certain minority groups within society, there may be little that "outsiders" can do to challenge this. This has become apparent in many so-called socialist or communist states where pluralism has been firmly resisted and a strong national character is promoted whereby all citizens are expected to adhere to a homogenous collective identity. It is outside the scope of this chapter to scrutinise the nuances of such states in detail here, but some brief examples help to illustrate this point. For instance, the Communist Party of China, under the leadership of Xi Jinping is committed to a people-centred approach for the public interest that follows "socialism with Chinese characteristics",[74] whereby the people as "the masters of the country" practise socialist core values based on Marxist communism.[75] The extent to which China truly follows key socialist values is debatable, with the country drawing on elements of neoliberal capitalism in its attempts to grow its economy.[76] It

---

[72] Will Kymlicka, *Multicultural Citizenship: A Liberal Theory of Minority Rights* (OUP 1996) 69–72. See further below discussion under "cultural imperialism".

[73] Ronald Dworkin, 'Liberal Community' (1989) 77(3) California L Rev 479, 486; Kymlicka 1996 (see Footnote 72) 81.

[74] Xi Jinping, 'Secure a Decisive Victory in Building a Moderately Prosperous Society in All Respects and Strive for the Great Success of Socialism with Chinese Characteristics for a New Era' (19th National Congress of the Communist Party of China, 18 October 2017).

[75] As set out under the constitutional law of the People's Republic of China.

[76] Barry Naughton, 'Is China Socialist?' (2017) 31(1) J Econ Perspect 3.

is, nonetheless, accurate to say that the Chinese state tightly controls much of its means of production and places a close focus on communitarian values as central to the way of Chinese life, while fiercely rejecting individualism and plurality within its society.

Despite its commitment to "unite the Chinese people of all ethnic groups",[77] there is little that minority groups can do about exerting their rights to self-realisation, especially where their cultural or ethnic identity diverges from that which is expected of its citizens. For example, there appears to be little room within what Xi refers to as "[t]he patriotic united front"[78] for the Uighurs, a Turkic minority ethnic group that settled in China's Xinjiang region. This minority ethnic group has been subjected to decades of persecution and state-based attempts to dilute the Uighurs' cultural identity.[79] Government policies that promote Chinese cultural unity were used to diminish the density of this group including state-sponsored migration of Han Chinese people into the area from the 1950s to 1970s.[80] The ensuing ethnic tensions and attacks by separatists have resulted in the Uighurs becoming an "ethno-nationalist threat to the Chinese state", leading to tight government control of the area marked by mass surveillance and the suppression of religious activity.[81] In recent years a new system of "re-education camps" has been introduced, labelled by Human Rights Watch as a form of "mass arbitrary detention, torture, and mistreatment".[82] The aim of the centres is to "eradicate… mind thoughts about religious extremism and violent terrorism, and to cure ideological diseases" and it involves stripping detainees of all cultural and religious morals, beliefs and values.[83] The treatment of Uighurs by the

---

[77] Xi 2017 (see Footnote 74).

[78] Xi 2017 (see Footnote 74).

[79] Human Rights Watch, *Devastating Blows: Religious Repression of Uighurs in Xinjiang* (HRW, 12 April 2005).

[80] Human Rights Watch 2005 (see Footnote 79).

[81] Human Rights Watch 2005 (see Footnote 79) 3.

[82] Human Rights Watch, *'Eradicating Ideological Viruses': China's Campaign of Repression Against Xinjiang's Muslims* (HRW, 9 Sept 2018).

[83] Human Rights Watch 2018 (see Footnote 82).

Chinese government has given rise to numerous international claims of genocide.[84]

The failure to give primacy to the liberal principles of individual freedom risks the enabling of systems that directly oppress groups of people who do not fulfil a unitary vision of national identity. Once instituted there may be little that members of society can do to challenge these, certainly legally. A similar state of affairs can be observed in Russia, where Russian identity has historically been based on Slavic Orthodox communitarian traditions.[85] Drakulić's analysis of the fall of the USSR emphasises that a fundamental problem in the centralisation of economic production was that the system was run by men for men. Products needed or desired by women were simply not made and thus the demand for some products was never realised and women's needs were therefore never fully met.[86]

We can observe elsewhere the focus of so-called socialist states on a collective good much to the detriment of LGBT+ communities. Mariela Castro's one-woman mission to bring about greater protections and recognition for the significant LGBT+ community in Cuba has led to some welcomed changes to legal protections for these individuals—including antidiscrimination laws on the grounds of sexual orientation and gender identity.[87] Yet these changes have occurred within a vacuum of state-controlled socialism. Rights are only ever extended to individuals if those rights do not come into conflict with what is perceived to be good for the collective. Rights are not balanced in this regard and determined by a court of law, but by state agencies who are answerable to themselves. The

---

[84] Newlines Institute for Strategy and Policy, *The Uyghur Genocide: An Examination of China's Breaches of the 1948 Genocide Convention* (Newlines Institute, March 2021).

[85] Igor Zevelev, *Russian National Identity and Foreign Policy* (Center for Strategic and International Studies, 12 December 2016).

[86] Post USSR, identities that challenge this orthodox nationalist identity continue to be fiercely resisted. Amnesty International exclaimed that violent racism in Russia was "out of control", Amnesty International, 'Russian Federation: Violent racism out of control' (Amnesty International 2006). The levels of violence directed at LGBT+ people are also of grave concern. Actual numbers are difficult to calculate but there is cogent evidence of systemic torturing of LGBT+ people compounded by law enforcement inaction, and in some cases complicity. Amnesty International, 'Russia: Two years after Chechnya's gay purge victims still seek justice as LGBTI defender receives death threat' (Amnesty International 2019).

[87] Article 42, Constitution of the Republic of Cuba.

last-minute cancellation of an LGBT+ pride event in Havana in 2019 by the authorities due to claims that outside groups might use the event as a "weapon" against the Communist party resulted in a clash between police and LGBT+ people who took part in the "unauthorized" march, resulting in several arrests and claims of violence against participants.[88]

If we are to protect individuals of difference from state-imposed subjugation, individual liberty must be protected while simultaneously instigating legal protections to ensure that all citizens have equal access to the resources that can advance their own self-realisation. In this regard, social liberalism is an attempt to balance the competing ideologies of socialism and liberalism in order to foster a society that respects the interests of both the individual and community. It is a political choice in favour of creating a fairer playing field, through which individuals can self-realise in different ways, with the rights to do this protected by law. The aim is not to ensure everyone gets exactly the same piece of the economic pie, but that they have opportunities to live their lives free from poverty and oppression. The removal of barriers to opportunities is pivotal here and may well involve state ownership of key resources and higher taxation on corporations that generate vast capital sums. However, governments must restrict their total control of economic outcomes in order to ensure the ethical neutrality of the state.[89]

Social liberalism, then, is not just about letting individuals do as they please, but frames freedom within an environment in which doing what one wants is informed and changeable to the ideas and values of others around you. As Kymlicka states, "to inhibit people from questioning their inherited social roles can condemn them to unsatisfying, even oppressive lives".[90] The state owes all its citizens equal concern, meaning that regardless of race, sexual orientation or social class each citizen must

---

[88] Ed Augustin, 'Cuba's gay rights activists take to the streets defiant and proud' *The Guardian* (London, 12 May 2019).
   Beyond these isolated events is empirical evidence that suggests "dark-skinned Cubans" have lower educational levels, lower occupational prestige levels, and lower-income levels, Yesilemis Pena, 'Discrimination without Opposition: Latin America's Racial Permeability and Its Debilitating Effects on Political Mobilization' (PhD Thesis, University of California 2004).
[89] Rawls 1999 (see Footnote 48).
[90] Kymlicka 1995 (see Footnote 72) 92.

be treated by the government with the same level of concern when determining the fate of every individual.[91] Hence, when deciding on a public policy, the government cannot discount the negative impact it will have on some individuals, even if a small minority, and even if the impact on the majority is positive. In addition, the state must also treat each person with equal respect; this Dworkin argues means that governments must treat each person with dignity allowing them to determine their own destiny—or what, he says, "would count as a good life?"[92]

Under such a framework of equality and social justice, the state must seek to ensure that there are not individuals in society that are disadvantaged by the activities of dominant groups. Inequality of outcome can, however, be justified where a policy is aimed at rebalancing inequalities in favour of those who are most disadvantaged in society. John Rawls on the principles of justice asserts that:

> All social primary goods—liberty and opportunity, income and wealth, and the bases of self-respect—are to be distributed equally unless unequal distribution of any or all of these goods is to the advantage of the least advantaged.[93]

Rawls' "difference principle" denotes that social and economic inequality are just if and only if they "are to be to the greatest benefit of the least advanced members of society".[94] Being least advantaged means "suffering more than others from natural and social misfortune". In seeking to promulgate social justice the state must be involved, not just in the fair distribution of opportunity, but in distributing the resources necessary to exploit those opportunities, especially for the most marginalised groups in society.[95] The degree to which society promotes the institutional conditions that are necessary for the development of one's capacities and to the expressing of one's experiences, is the degree to which it promotes

---

[91] Ronald Dworkin, *Justice for Hedgehogs* (Belknap 2011).
[92] Dworkin 2011 (ibid.). The good life is defined broadly by political philosophers as a life worth living. See, Joseph Raz, *The Morality of Freedom* (OUP 2003).
[93] John Rawls, *A Theory of Justice* (Belknap 1971) 303.
[94] John Rawls, *Political Liberalism* (Columbia UP 2005) 6.
[95] Ronald Dworkin, 'What is Equality? Part II: Equality of Resources' (1981) 10(4) Phil & Pub Aff 283.

social justice.[96] Such a principle dictates that a degree of affirmative action may be necessary if we are to lift disadvantaged groups up from the very bottom of society.

What I refer to then as a "social justice liberal" polity must actively seek out injustice if it is to create a society that allows all individuals to flourish, for differences to be expressed and valued, and for both economic and social capital to be distributed more fairly throughout communities. But before the state can use its statutory apparatus to address social injustice, it must first be able to unearth it. It is beyond the scope of this book to identify the multitude of ways that individuals may experience social injustice. Instead, I focus on one of the most salient forms of social injustice that remains pervasive throughout societies globally: that of hate crime. It is with a social justice liberal framework that the criminal law emerges as a *potential* tool within the "basic structure" for addressing this form of social injustice.[97] Yet in order to more fully understand *why* the criminal law should be used to address social injustice, we must first comprehend the numerous and intersecting ways in which hate crime (re)produces the harms that prevent individuals from pursuing a good life.[98]

Such an endeavour is necessary if a careful balance is to be realised between social justice (understood as the proactive realisation of a fair and equal society) and liberalism (understood as individual freedom from the coercive powers of the state). In other words, if the criminal law as a form of social control is to be used to address social injustice, it must be clear in what ways, and to what extent, expressions of hate generate group-based inequality. Such an investigation can be elucidated via an analysis of hate crime as a form of oppression. Iris Young conceptualises oppression as the institutional constraint on a social group's self-development, which is embedded in "unquestioned norms", symbols and in the assumptions that underlie society's rules and regulations. Social groups are described by Young as "a collective of persons differentiated

---

[96] Young 2011 (see Footnote 62 in Chap. 1) 37.

[97] The basic structure refers to "society's main political, social, and economic institutions, and how they fit together into one unified system of social cooperation from one generation to the next", Rawls 2006 (see Footnote 94) 11.

[98] That which goes beyond that of other types of criminal offending. After which, it will be crucial to outline how criminal justice intervention can be used to help prevent hate, and its invidious harms, from proliferating in society (Chap. 6).

from at least one other group by cultural forms, practices, or way of life".[99] Group members often have an affinity with one another through sociality, engaging in communal practices, sharing a locality, and fundamentally by sharing an identity characteristic.[100] It is through shared experiences, social norms and values that individuals develop a sense of group identity.

Those social groups whose norms and values perceivably conflict with the dominant assumptions that underly a society's normative identity ideal can become susceptible to group-based oppression. Young explains that there are five faces to oppression that help to demarcate the intersecting processes through which a groups' access to a "good life" can be diminished, and these include: exploitation;[101] marginalisation;[102] powerlessness; cultural imperialism and violence.[103] In the next chapter I utilise four of these faces of oppression to frame the distinct harms of hate crime; evidencing the phenomenon as a form of social injustice that requires specific legislative attention. Before then, it is helpful to first set out more generally what these four faces of oppression can entail.

2.2.1 Cultural Imperialism

Within contemporary liberal and socialist societies minority (and minoritised) communities are often othered, not simply because they look or act differently, but because they represent a perceived threat to dominant

---

[99] Young 2011 (see Footnote 49) 43. The centrality of group identity and how it effects experiences of hate crime is discussed in detail in Chap. 3, s. 3.1.1.

[100] See Mark A Walters and others, 'Group identity, empathy and shared suffering: understanding the "community" impacts of anti-LGBT and Islamophobic hate crimes' (2020) 26(2) Int Rev Vict 143. Institutional practice may also give rise to social groups, such as where individuals with certain characteristics are excluded from public activities. For example, where women, gay or trans people have been excluded from military service or other vocations.

[101] Young asserts that exploitation occurs where "some people exercise their capacities under the control, according to the purposes, and the benefit of other people" (2011 (see Footnote 62 in Chap. 1) 49). Though relevant to the broader discussion of inequality, I do not emphasise its role here as being key to the criminalisation of hate.

[102] Young refers to this as the process of pushing certain people to the margins of society which consists of the blocking of "opportunity to exercise capacities in socially defined and recognized ways" (Young 2011 (see Footnote 49) 54).

[103] Young 2011 (see Footnote 49) 37.

identity ideals. There are myriad multidisciplinary analyses of how identity and cultural difference is resisted by dominant groups in society.[104] Young's political analysis terms this process as "cultural imperialism" which is defined as "the universalization of a dominant groups experience and culture, and the establishment as the norm… [it] involves the paradox of experiencing oneself as invisible at the same time that one is marked out as different".[105] Hegemonic cultural identity as a representation of humanity is often expressed as a singular experience. Those that fall outside of this dominant cultural experience can become othered as they are stereotyped by dominant groups in typically derogatory and sometimes odious ways.[106] Stereotypes commonly depict others as deviant and potentially dangerous people who actively seek to undermine the cohesion of society. It is these stereotypes and the cultural norms that resist difference which fuel social climates that are hostile towards certain identity groups.

Social psychologists have helpfully explained perceptions of threat through theories such as integrated threat theory (ITT).[107] Building on the work of social identity theory,[108] ITT asserts that people naturally coalesce around identity sameness; this is because humans as social beings seek out other individuals who are likely to share similar experiences of the world around them.[109] Group identity can become central to the way in which we live and plan for our futures; groups often coalesce around racial and ethnic backgrounds, religious beliefs, sexual orientations, gender and gender identities to name but a few. In some cases, one's identity as a member of a group can become fundamental to how they live their lives, including who they socialise with, where and what social practices they are willing to engage in.[110] As I will outline in the following chapter,

---

[104] Within criminology, Perry's use of structured action theory and "doing difference" is a particularly enlightening macro explanation of hierarchies of identity and the violent responses that become systematised within structural processes and practices. See also Walters 2011 (see Footnote 65).

[105] Young 2011 (see Footnote 49) 59.

[106] Barbara Perry, *In the Name of Hate: Understanding Hate Crimes* (Routledge 2001).

[107] Stephan and Stephan 2000 (see Footnote 68).

[108] Henri Tajfel and John C Turner, 'The social identity theory of intergroup behavior' in Stephen Worchel and William G Austin (eds), *Psychology of Intergroup Relations* (Nelson-Hall 1986).

[109] Stephan and Stephan 2000 (see Footnote 68).

[110] Walters and others 2020 (see Footnote 100).

members of the same in-group will often feel greater levels of empathy towards one another, and in relation to minority group identity often experience a sense of "shared suffering" that occurs locally, nationally and even globally.[111]

In creating social in-groups, members will seek out out-group members who are definitely not like them. It is by understanding those who are unlike us, that we can better create a sense of self as both an "individual" and as a member of a group, community or society. Where out-group members move into spaces inhabited by a different identity group, some members will react by perceiving these individuals as a threat, either or both to their physical safety (realistic) or to their groups collective identity (symbolic).[112] In these situations, group members may attempt to resist the social mobility of others through acts of discrimination, the creation and proliferation of negative stereotypes and through violent altercation. In some situations, this invidious social process can occur between two vulnerable groups themselves who see each other's value or norms as undermining their own group identity. For instance, in the UK numerous protests have occurred outside Schools in cities such as Birmingham against the inclusion of LGBT+ relationships being taught within primary schools. Amongst the daily protestors, Muslim participants held up banners reading "Adam and Eve, not Adam and Steve", while misinformation was spread that schools were teaching children about "anal sex, paedophilia and transgenderism".[113]

Though minority group threat can clearly occur across marginalised groups, it is dominant groups in society that wield most power to oppress certain group identities. Racial threat theory studies have consistently shown that where minority ethnic groups increase in size in any given area, social practices and institutions used to oppress and subjugate these individuals increase, whether that be through over-policing tactics, greater levels of punitive sentencing, tougher drug policies or increased

---

[111] Walters and others 2020 (see Footnote 100).
[112] Stephan and Stephan 2000 (see Footnote 68).
[113] Nazia Parveen, 'Council asks judge to ban LGBT lessons protesters from near school' *The Guardian* (London, 18 October 2019).

levels of school expulsion (amongst others).[114] Such cultural practices continue in contemporary British and American society unabated. The disproportionate levels of "BAME" people in the prison estate in both countries are a damning indictment of the oppressive nature of state institutions that continue to discriminate against non-white citizens.[115]

But cultural imperialism cannot be explained by social psychology alone. Political ideology plays a role in cultivating cultural imperialism. Whether this is simply a symptom of social psychological processes or partly causal of how we see our identities in the world is far from settled. What is clear is that the advocacy of certain political ideas can directly result in certain groups becoming the scapegoats of society's woes. Within contemporary British and American society economic competition between groups is exacerbated by elite classes' blaming of certain groups for the socio-economic instability of already marginalised social classes.[116] There is no more vivid illustration of this occurrence than during the Brexit campaign in the UK where a giant poster was unveiled by a leading Leave campaigner showing crowds of refugees along the tag line "Breaking point: the EU has failed us all".[117] The posters were launched in connection to the erroneous assertion that accession of Turkey into the EU would open up British borders to over 80 million mostly Muslim Turks.[118] Within the US context it is exampled through Trump's presidential campaign to build a wall along the US border with Mexico in order to keep

---

[114] Blalock 1967 (see Footnote 66).

[115] See for example Jennifer Bronson and E Ann Carson, *Prisoners in 2017* (US Department of Justice Office of Justice Programs NCJ 252156, 2019); Georgina Eaton and Aidan Mews, *The impact of short custodial sentences, community orders and suspended sentence orders on reoffending* (Ministry of Justice 2019). For example, in the US in 2017, black people are imprisoned at six times the rate of white people (Bronson and Carson, as cited here). In England and Wales, 40 per cent of prisoners aged under 18 were Black or Mixed ethnicity based on 2017–2018 figures (Eaton and Mews 2019, as cited here).

[116] Ray and Smith 2002 (see Footnote 69); Walters 2011 (see Footnote 65).

[117] Sarah Looney, 'Breaking Point? An Examination of the Politics of Othering in Brexit Britain' (SSRN 28 April 2017).

[118] Heather Stewart and Rowena Mason, 'Nigel Farage's anti-migrant poster reported to police', *The Guardian* (London, 16 June 2016).

out "illegal immigrants", the likes of whom the president claimed are "bringing drugs. They're bringing crime. They're rapists".[119]

2.2.2 Marginalisation

Within divided societies, marked by dominance over difference,[120] are the many groups that become pushed to the very outer peripheries of communities. These individuals are likely to become socially and economically marginalised. Marginalisation refers to the process of blocking individuals' "opportunity to exercise capacities in socially defined and recognised ways".[121] To exist on the periphery of society is to become insignificant, neglectable and in many cases invisible.[122] To be marginalised is to experience social exclusion and in turn exclusion from social recognition. Exclusion restricts social participation and reduces the value of individuals in society. Marginalisation serves as a blocking mechanism of the opportunities to exercise one's own capacities in socially recognised ways.[123] Processes of marginalisation are likely to be multiple and collectively they serve to restrict social mobility including successful employment, access to housing and failures to implement reasonable adjustments for disabled people, amongst various others. For instance, in England and Wales, research conducted by the Equality and Human Rights Commission found that 45.3 per cent of disabled adults reported having difficulty accessing services in the areas of health, benefits, tax, culture, sport and leisure compared with 31.7 per cent for non-disabled people.[124] The failure to remove these barriers means that disabled people will

---

[119] Staff, 'Here's Donald Trump's Presidential Announcement Speech *Time* (New York, 16 June 2015).
[120] Perry 2001 (see Footnote 106).
[121] Young 2011 (see Footnote 49) 54.
[122] Sundman (see Footnote 47).
[123] Young 2011 (see Footnote 49) 54.
[124] EHRC 2017 (see Footnote 18) 12.

continue to be mis-recognised as equal citizens and thus they will ultimately fail to achieve self-realisation.

Before people can even access many of the welfare and social or private resources available in society they will need a home. It is concerning then that housing problems are more likely to be experienced by most minority identity groups. A study by the Human City Institute (HCI) revealed that the level of "housing stress" in minority ethnic communities is much greater than for white people.[125] Disabled people too continue to face difficulties in finding appropriate housing, with fewer than 17 per cent of housing authorities having strategies to build homes that are disabled access-friendly.[126] This means that "[d]isabled people face problems in finding adequate housing and this is a major barrier to independent living".[127] Housing problems mean that certain groups of people are more likely to become homeless. The number of minority ethnic people who are homeless has also dramatically increased between 1997 and 2017 from 18 per cent to 36 per cent; double the estimated percentage of "BAME" people who make up the general public.[128] A similar picture can be seen amongst LGBT+ communities, with an estimated 24 per cent of young homeless people identifying as LGBT+.[129]

The social disadvantages faced by these particular groups of people means that fewer individuals make it in the workplace. Those with multiple characteristics are likely to experience "double disadvantage" such as where those who are from a lower social class are also disabled, from a BAME background, and female.[130] For instance, research by the Social Mobility Commission in the UK found that 21 per cent of disabled people who are from working-class backgrounds go on to enter higher level occupations, compared with 43 per cent whose parents had professional

---

[125] Kevin Gulliver, 'Racial discrimination in UK housing has a long history and deep roots' (LSE BPP, 12 October 2017).

[126] EHRC 2017 (see Footnote 18).

[127] EHRC 2017 (see Footnote 18) 72.

[128] Gulliver 2017 (see Footnote 125).

[129] The Albert Kennedy Trust, 'LGBT Youth Homelessness: A UK national scoping of cause, prevalence, response and outcome' (Albert Kennedy Trust 2015).

[130] Social Mobility Commission, *State of the Nation 2018–19: Social Mobility in Great Britain* (TSO 2019).

backgrounds. Similarly, women and those from ethnic minority backgrounds are more likely to experience downward social mobility[131] than their male or white counterparts. Within the justice system, these figures become particularly stark. In England and Wales, minority ethnic individuals are under-represented relative to the population among the police, National Offender Management Service, the judiciary and magistracy.[132]

2.2.3 Powerlessness

The obstacles that are created by pernicious stereotypes and the marginalisation that is created by systemic barriers to self-realisation are likely to result in feelings of powerlessness. Young frames powerlessness mostly in relation to the division of labour. The powerless, she claims, are those who lack authority and power to decide policies or determine results—"they must take orders and rarely have the right to give them".[133] Those without power are therefore reduced in their capacity to gain the status of being a "professional", which brings with it expertise, employment advancement and in turn a strong sense of self.

While powerlessness can be saliently expressed in terms of the division of labour and lack of economic status, it reaches well beyond labour markets affecting all aspects of social life. Sundman refers more generally to powerlessness as individuals lacking "the ability to effect things".[134] People are rendered powerless where there is a lack of both economic and social means to enact change in their lives. Group identity can bring with it privilege without awareness. The power to develop capacities through decision making is easier within systems where identity is no barrier to accessing public goods, including education, health and criminal justice agencies. Identities that are perceived to be a threat to social norms and institutions can be resisted, both consciously and unconsciously. Resistance to accessing public resources will likely mean that there are

---

[131] Meaning an individual is more likely to end up with lower incomes or in lower skilled jobs than their parents.
[132] Ministry of Justice (2019) *Statistics on Race and the Criminal Justice System 2018* (MOJ 2019) 63.
[133] Young (2011) (see Footnote 49) 56.
[134] Sundman 2016 (see Footnote 47) 151.

fewer opportunities for certain individuals to self-realise. Powerlessness is therefore both a social condition as well as a psychological infliction. Institutional barriers render individuals unable to change the social conditions that will enable them to fulfil their individual potential. The sense of powerlessness that this invokes is in turn internalised, thereby becoming part of group consciousness on what is expected in life, and what is achievable. Powerlessness therefore becomes a state of affairs that leaves entire social groups lacking authority and control over the tools required to have a good life.

People can only fully realise their potential if they are able to determine their own path.[135] Of course, not all barriers to realising of self are explainable, at least substantially, by social conditions pertaining to oppression. Individuals also have self-direction; that is the capacity to make decisions that affect their position in society. Ultimately individuals are "free" to make choices about what role they can play in any given society. It is why oppressed communities still observe individuals who, against all odds, break through fortified barriers to become leaders in industry, politics, academia and beyond. Nonetheless, for this to be fully realisable across all group members there must still be *genuine* possibilities for individuals to cultivate self-realisation. The fewer the opportunities and the greater the height of the barriers, the fewer individuals will "make it".[136]

2.2.4 Violence

Cultural imperialism, social marginalisation and powerlessness reinforce the social, economic and cultural conditions for disrespect. That is, the failure to listen to what certain people have to say, to do what they request, or for them to simply be taken seriously. It too means that certain groups of individuals are vulnerable to violence. Most minority groups in society are disproportionately vulnerable to physical and verbal abuse. Research in the UK shows that Black and Asian people, and people with dual or

---

[135] Sundman 2016 (see Footnote 47) 153.
[136] Sundman 2016 (see Footnote 47) 154.

multiethnicity are more likely to be victims of crime than White people,[137] while disabled people are more likely to be victims compared with non-disabled people.[138] Within the US context other data show that Black and Hispanic people are much more likely to be the victims of race-based hate crimes,[139] while in the UK Black and Asian people are most likely to be victims of such crimes in the UK.[140] Vulnerability to violence can be intersectional with multiple minority identities giving rise to increased likelihood and regularity of violence.

The frequency of violence against certain groups creates a climate of fear that penetrates most group members' everyday consciousness. Research by Stonewall (the UK's leading LGBT+ rights charity) surveyed over 5000 LGBT+ people in the UK reporting that almost one in ten LGBT+ people (eight per cent) do not feel safe in the area where they live.[141] Previous research by the same organisation found approximately 40 per cent of LGB people were worried about being the victim of a crime, while 75 per cent of gay and lesbian young people felt that they were more at risk of being assaulted for being gay.[142] Data from the Crime Survey for England and Wales similarly shows that 17 per cent of people with Asian Ethnic background and 17 per cent with Black and Minority Ethnic backgrounds were "very worried" about being attacked because of their skin colour/ethnic origin or religion, compared to only 3 per cent of white adults.[143] Other studies have shown that disabled people feel less safe in their local neighbourhood compared to non-disabled people.[144]

---

[137] Home Office, *Hate Crime, England and Wales, 2017/18 Statistical Bulletin 20/18* (Home Office 2018) 25–26.

[138] EHRC 2017 (see Footnote 18).

[139] Robert A Tessler and others, 'Differences by Victim Race and Ethnicity in Race- and Ethnicity-Motivated Violent Bias Crimes: A National Study' (2021) 36(13–14) J Interpers Violence 6297.

[140] Home Office 2018 (see Footnote 137) 26.

[141] Chaka L Bachmann and Becca Gooch, *LGBT in Britain: Hate Crime and Discrimination* (Stonewall 2017) 14.

[142] Sam Dick, *Homophobic Hate Crime: The Gay British Crime Survey 2008* (Stonewall 2008) 30.

[143] Home Office 2018 (see Footnote 137) 29.

[144] EHRC 2017 (see Footnote 18).

Young notes that despite the frequent and disproportionate levels of violence against minority groups, theories of justice have rarely considered this fact.[145] This is so even though targeted violence is a key component of social injustice. What makes violence a face of oppression is that it is systemic and institutionalised. Violence is not the product of individual pathology but of a wider social milieu that enables and legitimises its use. As such it is not just an individual moral wrong, but an invidious "social practice".[146] The correlation between the renewed political rhetoric and xenophobic discourses on national identity and the rise in hate crimes in the UK and the US are demonstrative of the social contexts within which hate is not only permitted but incited.[147]

2.3 Conclusion

Hate-based violence as social practice cannot be effectively addressed through distributive methods of justice alone. To effectively address the causes of hate crime, institutions need not only be reformed through redistribution of resources or personnel, but also by directly challenging the stereotypes and prejudices that give rise to the perceived threats posed by "difference".[148] Rawls' "difference principle" requires that any economic inequalities be to the greatest advantage of those who are least advantaged. However, if we are to move towards a society where the principles of equality and freedom can be fully realised, we must shift beyond the main focus on economic redistribution of wealth and acknowledge that social inequalities will exist wherever there are group identity differences in society. Social justice liberalism recognises that "difference" *matters*. It requires a society that acknowledges the potential for minority groups to be perceived as economic *and* cultural threats and emphasises the need for these perceptions to be countered as a matter of public policy and state measures that protect communities from the individual,

---

[145] Young 2011 (see Footnote 49).
[146] Young 2011 (see Footnote 49) 62.
[147] Explored more fully in Chap. 3.
[148] Perry 2001 (see Footnote 106); Young 2011 (see Footnote 49).

community and cultural harms of targeted violence. In this regard I am in agreement with Harel and Parchomovsky who assert that "protection against crime is a good produced by the criminal justice system, which, like many other state-produced goods, should be distributed in an egalitarian manner".[149] Ultimately, this requires a state that actively works to ensure that those individuals who experience hate crimes are specifically protected in law to ensure that all individuals have an opportunity to fully participate in society as equals.

There will of course be multiple methods of achieving the goals of a social justice liberal society, including through welfare provision, education, social and public policy, and via human rights law and civil law. However, left out of most discussions on challenging inequality is the use of criminal law. Indeed, there remains a vast lacuna within criminal law philosophy on how criminalisation might help to rectify structural inequalities that disproportionately harm certain identity groups.[150] In the next chapter, I set out how hate crime operates to fulfil each of the four faces of oppression outlined here, and I examine how principles of criminalisation should draw upon a theory of social justice liberalism to justify, shape, and frame the boundary of hate crime as a legal concept.

---

[149] Alon Harel and Gideon Parchomovsky, 'On hate and equality' (1999) 109(3) Yale LJ 507.
[150] Harel and Parchomovsky 1999 (ibid.); Mohamad Al-Hakim, 'Making a home for the homeless in hate crime legislation' (2014) 30 J Interpers Viol 1755.

3

Social Justice Liberalism and the Criminalisation of Hate

3.1 Introduction

There are varied pathways for the process of criminalising conduct within liberal states, which tend to draw on a number of common moral and ethical considerations.[1] Theorists of "liberal criminal law", if such a thing can be said to exist, have typically focused on individual liberty as "the primary unity of ethical concern".[2] Traditionally, the creation and enforcement of criminal laws has held the purpose of furnishing the boundaries of individual freedom, curtailing only those conducts that are harmful or that restrict the interests of others.[3] One would expect at the very least that criminal laws protect against conducts that seek to undermine certain liberties, such as freedom from violence, persecution and false

---

[1] For pathways see for example McNamara L and others, 'Understanding processes of criminalisation: Insights from an Australian study of criminal law-making' (2021) 21(3) Criminol Crim Just 387. For moral and ethical considerations see for example AP Simester, Antje Du Bois-Pedain and Ulfrid Neumann (eds), *Liberal Criminal Theory: Essays for Andreas von Hirsch* (Hart 2014).

[2] Paul Roberts, 'Criminal Law Theory and the Limits of Liberalism' in AP Simester, Antje Du Bois-Pedain and Ulfrid Neumann (eds), *Liberal Criminal Theory: Essays for Andreas von Hirsch* (Hart 2014) 332.

[3] Joel Feinberg, *The Moral Limits of the Criminal Law: Harm to Others* (OUP 1984).

imprisonment (e.g. assaults, rape, homicide, slavery, human trafficking) as well as public security and safety (harassment, stalking, public order offences). We would also expect that it should prevent invasion of bodily autonomy (e.g. assaults without injury, sexual offences), while ownership of property, central to liberalism, is likely to play a key role in liberal criminal law frameworks (e.g. theft, fraud, burglary).

What role, though, is there for the criminal law in promoting broader liberal principles of equality, non-discrimination, pluralism, freedom of expression, and "equal concern and respect"?[4] Roberts notes that conducts that strike at the fundamental equality norm such as racially motivated violence and misogynistic harassment are good candidates for criminalisation under a liberal framework of law.[5] However, such a position has been vehemently resisted by other so-called liberal thinkers. Classical liberal commentators have consistently asserted that legislation aimed at preventing hate-motivated crimes is an illiberal endeavour; as per its attempt to punish hateful expressions (i.e. freedom of expression) and individual character (including freedom of thought).[6] Here lies a tension in liberal criminal legal theory between the criminal law's role in promoting liberal principles (i.e. freedom from targeted violence) and its potentially contradictory purpose of restricting other individual liberties (i.e. freedom of expression). At the other end of the political spectrum are criticisms that the use of criminal law to address the social problem of hate crime reduces it to individual acts committed by culpable private agents. This has the potential effect of responsibilising the propagation of identity-based hostilities at the micro level; meaning that the structural and institutional causes of hate crime remain underchallenged.[7]

In order to reconcile these seemingly fundamental contradictions, it is important that a liberal theory of criminalisation be grounded in an account of the nature and aims of a polity in political theory. Part I of this

---

[4] Ronald Dworkin, *Justice for Hedgehogs* (Belknap 2011).
[5] Paul Roberts (see Footnote 2) 332.
[6] James B Jacobs and Kimberly Potter, *Hate Crimes: Criminal Law and Identity Politics* (OUP 1998); Heidi M Hurd, 'Why liberals should hate "hate crime legislation"' (2001) 20 Law & Phil 215; see further exploration of this debate below.
[7] Doug Meyer, 'Resisting Hate Crime Discourse: Queer and Intersectional Challenges to Neoliberal Hate Crime Laws' (2014) 22(1) Crit Criminol 113.

chapter outlines a justification for the criminalisation of hate that is framed on social justice liberalism.[8] The theoretical framework outlined in Chap. 2 and further here seeks to maintain, and balance, the centrality of individual liberty with the proactive goal of preventing targeted conduct that oppresses entire communities of people. It is through this framework that I seek to extend the conventional lens of criminalisation theory by conceptualising the harms of hate as individual, community and cultural impacts that impair the interests and capacities of certain groups of people to participate fully in society. In underpinning the foundation of hate crime laws through a framework of social justice liberalism, Part II of this chapter sets out a detailed examination of how such offences fulfil the connecting criteria of oppression outlined in Chap. 2.

Centring the role of the criminal law in preventing hate crime inevitably responsibilises individual transgressors for their hate-based conduct. However, as this chapter outlines, this does not mean that hate crime legislation fails to address the structural and institutional causes of hate and prejudice. Hate crime laws aim also to (partly) reverse the historical marginalisation of oppressed groups by refocusing law and its enforcers on protecting groups that the state has, itself, been implicated in violently oppressing. The rule of law means that such laws apply equally to private citizens *and* to state actors; meaning that those who harass, abuse or attack those deemed as "different" are *all* subject to the same laws. Moreover, within an international framework of human rights laws that imposes duties on states to protect citizens from hate speech and hate crime, any failures of state agencies to adequately police, investigate and sentence hate crime offences can amount to an infringement of those rights.[9] What has been referred by some as "coercive human rights" means that almost all states have a duty to address hate crime using criminal law and/or criminal sanctions.[10]

---

[8] As outlined in Chap. 2.
[9] See for example European Union Framework Decision on Racist and Xenophobic Crime (2008/913/JHA); ECtHR, *Nachova and Others v. Bulgaria*, No. 43577/98 and 43579/98, judgment of 6 July 2005.
[10] See Natasa Mavronicola and Laurens Lavysen (eds) Coercive Human Rights: Positive Duties to Mobilise the Criminal Law under the ECHR (Hart Publishing 2020).

Finally, Part III of the chapter explores how hate crime laws may play an important norm creating role that assists in challenging pervasive social acceptances of hate-based conduct; prejudices that penetrate both communities and state institutions. Here, the role of law in potentially reducing hate-based violence is highlighted, emphasising both empirical research and correlational data that links legislation with reduced levels of hate crime.

It is by analysing why and how hate crimes harm liberal societies that we are able to set out its boundaries as a concept.[11] It is important to emphasise at this stage of the book that a distinction is to be made between the principles and concepts that underpin the criminal law and those which furnish the utility of retributive or punitive penalties. While it is common for scholars to conflate criminalisation with punishment, such that to criminalise is to inflict pain on offenders, the utility of criminal law need not be coalesced with punitivism so readily. Indeed, the aim of hate crime laws within a social justice liberal framework is not to turn "the cannons of the punitive machine against the powerful", as articulated by Aviram,[12] but instead it is to advocate a framework of criminal law that marginalises[13] punishment through a synthesis of community-based restorative interventions to address the harms of hate (Chap. 6). It is through this normative framework of law and criminal justice that I argue states can best promote social justice for the most marginalised communities in society.

3.2 Part 1: Framing the Criminalisation of Hate as Social Justice Liberalism

While there is no single theory underpinning the criminalisation of conduct, conventionally it has been agreed that for conduct to fall within the ambit of the criminal law it must firstly be considered to be a public

---

[11] Outlined in greater detail in Chaps. 4, 5 and 6.
[12] Hadar Aviram, Progressive Punitivism: Notes on the Use of Punitive Social Control to Advance Social Justice Ends, 68 Buff. L. Rev. 199 (2020).
[13] As will be outlined in Chap. 7, the maintenance of punishment as an ultimate threat is utilised within a system that centres restorative justice and community-based solutions to criminal conduct.

3 Social Justice Liberalism and the Criminalisation of Hate 55

"wrong" and secondly its proscription is deemed "necessary" to prevent it from occurring in society.[14] Within most liberal polities there have been two key theories that have underpinned the determination of what is wrongful conduct for the purposes of criminalisation: the harm principle and legal moralism.[15] Although it cannot be said with any certainty that conduct that is considered to be either harmful to others, or immoral to most people in society, will be included in the criminal law, legal theorists have long argued that conduct must fall within one or both of these for criminalisation to be justified.[16]

A fundamental tenet of classical liberalism is that the state must first and foremost respect individual liberty and personal autonomy. Individuals possess free will and must be allowed to act and behave as they please, free from state interference. Important to any liberal society is that citizens respect each other's right to non-interference unless the actions of one individual harm the interests of another.[17] Mill's famous words summarise this position:

> The only purpose for which power can be rightfully exercised over any member of a civilized community against his will is to prevent harm to others. His own good, either physical or moral, is not a sufficient warrant. He cannot rightfully be compelled to do or forbear because in the opinion of others to do so would be wise or even right.[18]

---

[14] Herbert L Packer, *The Limits of the Criminal Sanction* (Stanford UP 1968); Douglas Husak, *Overcriminalization: The Limits of the Criminal Law* (OUP 2008); RA Duff, *The Realm of Criminal Law* (OUP 2018).

[15] See overview of theorists in Sally R Kyd, Tracy Elliot and Mark A Walters, *Clarkson and Keating: Criminal Law: Text and Materials* (10th edn, Sweet & Maxwell 2020) ch 1); RA Duff 2018 (see Footnote 14).

[16] Feinberg 1984 (see Footnote 3); Husak 2008 (see Footnote 14); AP Simester and Andrew von Hirsch, *Crimes, Harms, and Wrongs: On the Principles of Criminalisation* (Hart 2011).

[17] For a discussion on what amounts to "interests" see Feinberg 1984 (see Footnote 3) 33, 34, 36, 215–216.

[18] John Stuart Mill, *On Liberty* (2nd edn, John W. Parker and Son 1860) ch 1, para 9.

What, though, do we consider as falling within the meaning of "harmful" conduct? Liberal perspectives on criminalisation have tended to take a narrow view on this. Harms that have been deemed worthy of criminalisation are typically defined as "primary harms", such as where there is a direct cause and effect. These types of harms are often measured in terms of the degree to which someone suffers physical or psychological injury.[19] Other laws are used to prevent bodily harm and to protect the bodily integrity of victims.[20]

Beyond these most obvious of harms are thousands, perhaps millions, of discrete acts that can be harmful in some way or another to individuals, communities and society. It is not always clear how we can identify and measure these harms to determine those worthy of legal proscription. Feinberg's influential work provides some assistance, defining harm as "the thwarting, setting back, or defeating of an interest… One's interests… consist of all those things in which one has at stake."[21] An initial question that arises from this description is: what interests do each of us have at stake? Feinberg does not elaborate on this, but Simester and von Hirsch have elucidated further by stating that what is "at stake" is something that constitutes a resource over which a person has a normative claim.[22] A resource, they claim, is an "asset" or a "capability" that subsists over a longer period of time. Resources are capable of contributing to the quality of a person's existence. Simester and von Hirsch argue that that the harm principle is therefore a principle of "resource protection".[23] Rawls' assertion that the state should have as one of its defining roles the safeguarding of the means by which citizens can live good lives is of relevance here.[24] The principle can be employed as a means of "safeguarding people's interests that matter for the quality of their lives".[25] Interests as "capabilities" are essential to protecting an individual's good life, as they

---

[19] See for example Offences against the Person Act 1861 (UK).
[20] See for example Sexual Offences Act 2003 (UK).
[21] Feinberg 1984 (see Footnote 3) 33.
[22] Simester and von Hirsch 2011 (see Footnote 16) 248.
[23] Simester and von Hirsch 2011 (see Footnote 16).
[24] John Rawls, *A Theory of Justice* (Belknap 1971).
[25] Simester and von Hirsch 2011 (see Footnote 16) 249.

refer to a person's capacities to undertake a course of conduct that aids in their attainment of self-realisation.

Conceptualising harm in terms of interests opens its lens to a society where capacities and resources are shaped by individuals' social positionality within society. Yet liberal scholars have given few examples of crimes that might disproportionately affect certain citizens' right to a good life. Von Hirsch, for example, gives the example of a set back of an interest as capacity as the justification of why a "wounding" becomes "mayhem" when injury results in capacities being lost due to arms and legs being maimed. Clearly, though, interests as resources and capacities go well beyond one's physical ability to walk down the street.

Extending the principle of the good life further to include Rawls' "difference principle" we can see what "one has at stake" may depend on the social position that one takes up in society; which as explored in more detail in Chap. 2 and below can be negatively affected by group identity. Interests are not equally shared in society. For some, their interests will generally be well looked after, as their identities ensure that they mostly experience the privilege of equal concern and respect. For others, what is at stake is much more precarious. For instance, an act of hate demonstrated towards a minority (or minoritised) group member risks much more than that which might occur if directed towards someone of a dominant group background.[26]

What role then does criminalisation play in ensuring that there is the "greatest benefit of the least advanced members of society"? Lawrence asserts that hate crimes are more harmful in that the "bias crime victim's injury to autonomy—in terms of his sense of control over his life—and to his personal dignity will exceed that inflicted upon the parallel assault victim".[27] Simester and von Hirsch in referring to the criminalisation of "racial insult" explain further that such speech-conduct is harmful not only as it expresses contempt for someone's identity, but importantly because it has the potential, where such insults become pervasive, to adversely affect individuals' working and social existence.[28] Conversely,

---

[26] Outlined in more detail below in Part 2.
[27] Frederick M Lawrence, *Punishing Hate: Bias Crimes under American Law* (Harvard UP 1999) 63.
[28] Simester and von Hirsch 2011 (see Footnote 16) 248.

when such an offence is committed by an ethnic minority group member against a dominant ethnic group individual it is unlikely to have the same impact. For example, anti-White racist abuse towards someone in Europe or the US is unlikely to adversely affect their working and social existence because the vast majority of people in European or US society are white, and it remains the case that white people are overrepresented in social, economic and political life. The underlining reason for criminalising racial insult is its *disproportionate* impacts on racial *minority* groups. Criminalising racially aggravated offences is therefore an attempt to reverse this disadvantage bringing a greater benefit to disadvantaged members of society and thereby protecting their right to a good life.[29]

Less certain is how personal interests can be measured, and whether the law can or should be tailored to protecting certain individuals whose interests are at greatest risk. I set out below how this can be measured and evidenced for hate crime. Before then, it is important to note that an evaluation of the extent and degree to which conduct is a setback to certain individuals' interests remains only part of the question of what conduct ought to be criminalised. We must also ask whether conduct, though harmful, is nonetheless still socially desirable, or as a minimum tolerable. There are, in fact, numerous activities that are without doubt harmful (e.g. physically injurious) but which are deemed acceptable in certain circumstances (e.g. boxing) or even necessary (e.g. surgery). Determinations of what is harmful, and whether harmfulness is nevertheless permissible, are not without frequent contestation. In making decisions about what is harmful, distinctions are often made as to whether something is harmful, but morally acceptable, or harmful and morally wrongful.[30] For instance, some harms may be perceived as fulfilling a social need (e.g. contact sports,[31] or cosmetic surgery) and therefore are not considered to be wrongful. There are various other situations that

---

[29] Note also that scholars refer to "remote harms" which typically include offences that risk harm (e.g. dangerous driving), those which are dependent on a secondary participant acting in correlation with a primary actor (e.g. inchoate offences); and conjunctive harms (those which rely on multiple people acting a similar way to cause a harm (e.g. pollution offences). I will return to the latter type of remote harm below. See AP Simester and Andrew Von Hirsch, 'Remote Harms and Non-constitutive Crimes' (2009) 28(1) Crim Just Ethics 89.

[30] Feinberg 1984 (see Footnote 3); Simester and von Hirsch 2011 (see Footnote 16).

[31] *R v Barnes* [2004] EWCA Crim 3246.

have caused much disagreement as to whether the criminal law should play a role in preventing conduct perceived as immoral or dangerous to societal wellbeing but which serves an individual interest, such as sexual or aesthetic pleasure (e.g. sadomasochism or body modification).[32]

This complex mix of harm and morality means that legislatures often consider conduct that is harmful to the moral fabric of society when determining whether an activity is *deserving* of legislative proscription. Lord Devlin famously noted that "it is clear that the criminal law as we know it is based upon moral principle. In a number of crimes its function is simply to enforce a moral principle and nothing else. The law, both criminal and civil, claims to be able to speak about morality and immorality generally."[33] We see this line of thinking most saliently in the English case of *Brown*,[34] involving sadomasochistic sexual conduct between gay men. In his House of Lords speech, Lord Templeman opined, "[s]ociety is entitled and bound to protect itself against a cult of violence. Pleasure derived from the infliction of pain is an evil thing. Cruelty is uncivilised."[35]

Whether legal moralism, alone, should permit the criminalisation of conduct is highly questionable.[36] We need only look at the pervasive criminalisation of same sex intimacy (i.e. homosexuality) throughout the world, a result of social disgust and moral disdain against what many still perceive as "evil" and "uncivilised" behaviour, to see that laws based predominantly on moral turpitude can result in the criminalisation of people *for being people*.[37] In such a case, the state itself is implicated in the infliction of harm on specific social groups; in some countries against its own commitment to liberalism.

---

[32] See, *Brown* [1994] 1 AC 212, and *R v BM* (2018) EWCA Crim 560. Both activities are currently deemed criminal despite individuals desiring and/or enjoying them.
[33] Patrick Devlin, *The Enforcement of Morals* (OUP 1965) 7.
[34] *Brown* [1994] 1 AC 212.
[35] *Brown* [1994] 1 AC 212 [237].
[36] RA Duff, *The Realm of Criminal Law* (OUP 2018); See alternatively Michael S Moore, 'Liberty's Constraints on What Should be Made Criminal' in RA Duff, Lindsay Farmer, S E Marshall, Massimo Renzo, and Victor Tadros (eds), *Criminalization: The Political Morality of the Criminal Law* (OUP 2015), 182-212.
[37] Seventy-two countries still criminalise same-sex sexual relations, ILGA, 'Sexual Orientation Laws in the World—Overview', last updated October 2017.

There are myriad other acts that might constitute moral wrongs but for which it would be illiberal to criminalise (e.g. infidelity or embellishing on your Curriculum Vitae). Duff explains that this is "why any sane system of criminal law recognizes a *de minimis* principle."[38] Applying a negative legal moralist perspective Duff notes that:

> We should not criminalize conduct that is not in some relevant way morally wrongful, nor impose criminal liability on those who are not morally culpable, but the wrongfulness of the conduct and the culpability of its agent do not give us positive reason to criminalize it.[39]

For Duff this does not necessarily mean that the main focus of criminalisation should be on harm. He asserts that we can in fact do away with the harm principle and instead conceive public wrongs as they pertain to civil order. Conduct is a public wrong, he argues, if it violates a duty that is owed to a whole community and that affects society rather than only an individual victim. He theorises that citizenship in a polity generates a social bond which gives rise to a sort of fellowship. What makes hate crime (or hate speech) a specific type of "public" wrong is that it amounts to a "denial of fellowship", and as such, these offences create a form of "civic hatred", most saliently understood as a refusal to respect the victim's dignity.[40]

Duff goes on to assert that we should resist the idea of defining what affects society as what "impacts" it, as there is the "problem of determining just what kinds of consequence [are] relevant".[41] However, it is not clear why assessing societal impacts is more problematic than assessing what falls within the scope of "civil order" and when conduct breaches it. Moreover, the failure to consider societal impacts (as outlined below)

---

[38] RA Duff, 'Perversions and Subversions of Criminal Law' in RA Duff, Lindsay Farmer, SE Marshall, Massimo Renzo and Victor Tadros (eds), *The Boundaries of the Criminal Law* (OUP 2010) 88–112, 89.

[39] Duff 2010 (ibid.) 89. For further discussion on types of moral legalism see Duff 2018 (see Footnote 36) ch 2; Simester and von Hirsch 2011 (see Footnote 16); Moore 2015 (see Footnote 36).

[40] Duff 2010 (see Footnote 38) 120ff. See also RA Duff and SE Marshall 'Criminalizing Hate?,' in Thomas Brudholm and Birgitte S Johansen (eds), *Hate, Politics, Law* (OUP 2018) 115–149; see also Marcia Baron, 'Hate Crime Legislation Reconsidered' (2016) 47(4–5) Metaphilosophy 504.

[41] Duff 2018 (see Footnote 38), p. 77.

3 Social Justice Liberalism and the Criminalisation of Hate

risks perpetuating a polity that continues in its omission to proactively uncover, recognise and address social injustices (criminal or otherwise). Recognising that hate crime is an affront to human dignity is important, but it reveals just one aspect of the social harms caused by acts of hate. Conceptualising hate crimes as "civic hatred" does not sufficiently recognise the myriad and egregious harms that, collectively, cement the building blocks of social injustice. Without specifying the intersecting individual and social harms of hate, the state will remain prone to patching up its structural render, thence ignoring that society's foundations have turned rotten. Such a state of affairs means that the social structure is left in a constant state of disrepair, whereby well-meaning state policies are used to patch up (or paper over) the exterior. It is only when civil rights movements, most recently BLM or #MeToo, have exposed some of the gaping chasms left by many years of social injustices that governments have been forced into action. Yet rarely does this involve action through the criminal law. As the most potent of institutions in preventing harmful behaviours, it is lamentable that the criminal law has typically been reluctant in playing a role in preventing the varied harms caused by crimes such as hate crime.

In many respects this is unsurprising. For classical liberals, the role of the state and its interference in human behaviour must be limited in order to protect individual liberty.[42] Paradoxically, for critics of classical and neo forms of liberalism, the criminal law is often viewed as a tool of oppression that responsibilises individuals instead of challenging wider structural inequalities that are causal to criminality.[43] For instance, Spade argues that hate crime laws individualise hate-based violence thereby covering over the institutions that inflict structural violence on marginalised communities.[44] Victims who report crimes into such a system are often met with suspicion, are ignored and in some cases are brutalised by the

---

[42] Douglas Husak, *Overcriminalization: The Limits of the Criminal Law* (OUP 2008).

[43] Including disproportionately implementing hate crime laws against already marginalised groups, see for example 'hate.' Bill Dixon and David Gadd, 'Getting the message? "New" Labour and the criminalization of "hate"' (2006) 6(3) Criminol & Crim Just 6(3) 309; see also Doug Meyer, 'Resisting Hate Crime Discourse: Queer and Intersectional Challenges to Neoliberal Hate Crime Laws' (2014) 22(1) Crit Criminol 113.

[44] Dean Spade, *Normal Life: Administrative Violence, Critical Trans Politics and the Limits of the Law* (South End Press 2011).

police.[45] Meyers additionally asserts that hate crime statutes have reinforced rather than undermined inequality because, as he argues, they have resulted in plea bargaining (within the US context) and added to carceral expansion. He therefore concludes that "progressive political strategies must reject the utility of hate crime statutes".[46]

This book poses an alternative vision which is to reimagine criminal law, not as a source of oppression, but as a means of rectifying it. It is argued that the criminal law is not, in and of itself, a form of oppression. Rather, it is the manner in which it is instructed and applied which can make it so. The overuse of criminal law against already marginalised groups[47] reflects a system of governance that is institutionally biased, and which is rarely countered in a broader political system focused on neoliberal policy making.

Within a system of social justice liberalism, the criminal law must not be used to arbitrarily criminalise groups of people. It must not be applied disproportionately, and it should not be used to obfuscate structural inequalities in favour of emphasising individual responsibility. This is because a social justice liberal criminal law would operate in a broader political system that functions to protect individual rights while proactively seeking to uncover and address social inequality.[48] Criminalisation under such a system is used to proscribe behaviour that not only causes individual injury, but which is *additionally* implicated in social processes that reproduce social injustice. To be clear, this is not to suggest that the criminal law should proscribe *all* discriminatory behaviour or activity that causes all forms of social inequality, but it is asserted that legislators should be permitted to evaluate conduct that is *particularly* harmful to certain groups of individuals' freedom, understood both in terms of their personal interests

---

[45] Leslie J Moran and Andrew N Sharpe, 'Violence, identity and policing: The case of violence against transgender people' (2004) 4(4) Criminol Crim Justic 395; Barbara Perry and D. Ryan Dyck, '"I don't know where it is safe": Trans women's experiences of violence' (2014) 22(1) Critical Criminology 49.

[46] Doug Meyer, 'Resisting Hate Crime Discourse: Queer and Intersectional Challenges to Neoliberal Hate Crime Laws' (2014) 22(1) Crit Criminol 113, 115.

[47] Discussed further below.

[48] To be clear, this is not to suggest that the criminal law should proscribe all discriminatory behaviour or activity that causes all forms of social inequality, but it is asserted that legislators should be permitted to evaluate conduct that is particularly harmful to certain groups of individuals' freedom, understood both in terms of their personal interests as well as their (and others') capacity to participate freely in society.

as well as their (and others') capacity to participate freely in society. Viewed in this way, offenders of hate crime are criminally culpable, not only for setting back an individual's personal interests (e.g. micro-level injuries), but also for consciously (or knowingly, subjectively or objectively) cultivating social injustices against an entire community of people.[49] Fundamental to this approach will be a system of justice interventions that seeks to address the unique harms of hate crime, not by inflicting greater levels of harm on perpetrators as a first response, but through measures that focus on the restoration through community-based dialogical processes that are open to exploring individual, community and institutional forms of responsibility as well as harm reparation.[50] Before we explore how such a system might work, we need first to examine in greater detail hate crime as social injustice.

3.3 Part 2: Understanding the Harms of Hate as Social Injustice

There is now a well-documented body of research on the individual impacts of hate crime.[51] Collectively these studies reveal a truth about the consequences of hate. This is that certain groups experience dispropor-

---

[49] On the levels of culpability for intentional and knowledge of subjugating identity during the commission of hate crimes see Mark A Walters, 'Conceptualizing "hostility" for hate crime law: Minding "the minutiae" when interpreting section 28(1)(a) of the Crime and Disorder Act 1998' (2014b) 34(1) OJLS 47. See further discussion on this when analysing what models of hate crime legislation should be used in Chap. 6, Part 2.

[50] Outlined more fully in Chap. 7.

[51] See for example Matthew D Fetzer and Frank S Pezzella, 'The nature of bias crime injuries: A comparative analysis of physical and psychological victimization effects' (2019) 34(18) J Interpers Viol 3864; Gregory M Herek and others, 'Hate crime victimization among lesbian, gay, and bisexual adults: Prevalence, psychological correlates, and methodological issues' (1997) 12(2) J Interpers Violence 195; Gregory M Herek and others, Psychological Sequelae of Hate-Crime Victimization Among Lesbian, Gay and Bisexual Adults' (1999) 67 J Consulting & Clinical Psych 945; Jack McDevitt and others, 'Consequences for victims: A comparison of bias—and non-bias-motivated assaults' (2001) 45(4) Am Behav Sci 697; Paul Iganski and Spiridoula Lagou, 'Hate crimes hurt some more than others: Implications for the just sentencing of offenders' (2015) 30(10) J Interpers Violence 1696; Jenny L Paterson, Rupert Brown and Mark A Walters, 'Feeling *for* and *as* a group member: understanding LGBT victimization via group-based empathy and intergroup emotions' (2019a) 58(1) Br J Soc Psychol 211; Jenny L Paterson, Rupert Brown and Mark A Walters, 'The short and longer term impacts of hate crimes experienced directly, indirectly and through the media' (2019b) 45(7) Pers Soc Psychol Bull 994; Mark A Walters and others, 'Group identity, empathy and shared suffering: understanding the "community" impacts of anti-LGBT and Islamophobic hate crimes' (2020) 26(2) Int Rev Vict 143.

tionate levels of targeted victimisation, which is more *likely* to cause *greater* and *distinct* levels of harm.[52] Such evidence is, in and of itself, justification for (re)criminalisation of hate crime, as Feinberg has persuasively claimed: "the greater the *gravity* of a possible harm, the less probable its occurrence need to be to justify prohibition" and "the greater the *probability* of harm, the less grave the harm need be to justify coercion".[53] With research showing both that the harms of hate are probable and often grave, the justification of specific criminalisation of the hate-element can be cogently made—even within conventional frameworks of penal theory.

While the commonly used phrase that hate crimes "hurt more"[54] is true—with the qualification that it is the risk of elevated harms that is actually increased—largely absent from analyses on the impacts of hate crime is that the *types* of harm caused by hate crimes are *qualitatively* different to so called parallel offences. Central to the thesis of this book is that the harms caused by hate-based offences are not only heightened, but they are also distinct from those caused by similar non-hate offences. In other words, hate crimes are not just "aggravated" versions of basic offences, in the sense they heighten the *same* harms of parallel wrongs, but are unique types of wrong that result in the setback of interests in specific ways.

Common amongst liberal theorists of hate crime is to assert that the hate-element is an extraneous addition to a criminal offence. The argument made here is that "hate" is a mental state, or thought, which motivates the offender to commit an already criminalised act (e.g. an assault). Jacobs and Potter arguing in this vein stated:

---

[52] See n 256267.
[53] Feinberg 1984 (see Footnote 3) 216. Duff and Marshall refer to this as the "Harm Prevention Principle", RA Duff and SE Marshall, '"Remote Harms" and the Two Harm Principles' in AP Simester, A Du Bois-Pedain and U Neumann (eds), *Liberal Criminal Theory: Essays for Andreas von Hirsch* (Hart 2014) 205–223.
[54] Paul Iganski, 'Hate crimes hurt more' (2001) 45(4) Am Behav Sci 626.

3 Social Justice Liberalism and the Criminalisation of Hate 65

Generic criminal laws already punish injurious conduct; so recriminalization or sentence enhancement for the same injurious conduct when it is motivated by prejudice amounts to extra punishment for values, beliefs, and opinions that the government deems abhorrent.[55]

This, the authors assert, is tantamount to punishing hate speech. Heidi Hurd goes even further by arguing that hate crime legislation punishes an offender not for their actions, but for their character.[56] The offender's hatefulness may be morally wrong but it would, she argues, be illiberal to punish this as it amounts to an infringement upon individuals' freedom of conscience.

Such assertions give rise to what some philosophers have referred to as the "additive fallacy".[57] It assumes that the "hate" and the "crime" are two discrete moral wrongs that are simply added together to justify additional punishment. For instance, Kahan asserts that hate crime offenders are punished twice, once for the commission of a basic crime and again for expressing their "bad values".[58] This, he argues, amounts to an implicit "bad-value added tax" on violence.[59] Yet, such claims fail to comprehend the cumulative impacts that such crimes have on individual interests (i.e. setbacks to capacities and resources). Furthermore, hate crimes cause additional community and societal harms that accrue when both hate *and* crime are combined.[60] In other words, the totality of a "hate crime" is greater than the sum of the parts. These harms can be saliently explicated through an analysis of hate crime as oppression. More specifically, to understand the harms of hate crime we must evaluate empirically its effects as violence, marginalisation, powerlessness and cultural imperialism.

---

[55] Jacobs and Potter 1998 (see Footnote 6) 121.
[56] Hurd 2001 (see Footnote 6); Heidi M Hurd and Michael S Moore, 'Punishing Hatred and Prejudice' (2004) 56(5) Stanford L Rev 1081.
[57] See for example Shelly Kagan, 'The Additive Fallacy' (1988) 99(1) Ethics 5.
[58] Dan M Kahan, 'Two liberal fallacies in the hate crimes debate' (2001) 20 Law & Phil 175.
[59] Kahan 2001 (ibid.).
[60] Others also assert that motive cannot always be conceptualised as a distinct emotion or thought, because the motive behind an action can make the action distinct from similar actions not motivated in a particular way, see Stephen Mathis, 'Motive, Action, and Confusions in the Debate over Hate Crime Legislation' (2018) 37(1) Crim Just Ethics 1.

3.3.1 Hate as Violence

Research suggests that hate crimes tend to be more violent than non-hate motivated offences. Analysis of data from the Crime Survey for England and Wales, a survey of over 55,000 households in England and Wales each year about experiences of crime, has shown that violence against the person accounts for 45 per cent of hate crime incidents compared with only 18 per cent of overall CSEW crime.[61] Further, 17 per cent of hate crimes result in injury compared with 9 per cent of non-hate crimes.[62] Research in the US also suggests that hate motivated assaults are more likely to be accompanied by serious forms of injury than non-hate assaults, with some research showing the former results in higher hospital admission rates.[63] For instance, Fetzer and Pezzella analysed National Crime Victimization Survey (US) data and found that when compared with non-bias assaults, the odds of sustaining a serious physical injury were 23 per cent greater when the assault was motivated by bias.[64] Steven Messner et al.'s analysis of National Incident Based Reporting System (NIBRS) data has similarly showed that hate crime victims are almost three times more likely to be seriously injured by assault compared with assaults where no bias motive is present.[65] Additionally, Cheng and colleagues' analysis of US FBI data found that homophobic hate crimes were more likely to be physical in nature (as against property) and were more likely to be correlated with more serious forms of violent offending.[66]

The violence involved in hate motivated murder cases can be particularly egregious and it is common for such offences to involve

---

[61] Home Office, *Hate Crime, England and Wales, 2019 to 2020* (Home Office 2020).
[62] Home Office 2020 (ibid.).
[63] Jack Levin and Jack McDevitt, *Hate Crimes: The Rising Tide of Bigotry* (Plenum 1993) 11; see also Brian Levin, 'Hate Crime: Worse by Definition' (1999) 15(1) J Contemp Just 6; Edward Dunbar, 'Race, Gender, and Sexual Orientation in Hate Crime Victimization: Identity Politics or Identity Risk?' (2006) 21(3) Violence Vict 323.
[64] Fetzer and Pezzella 2019 (see Footnote 51).
[65] Steven F Messner, Suzanne McHugh and Richard B Felson, 'Distinctive Characteristics of Assaults Motivated by Bias' (2004) 42(3) Criminol 585, 605.
[66] Wen Cheng, William Ickes and Jared B Kenworthy, 'The Phenomenon of Hate Crimes in the United States' (2013) 43 J Appl Soc Psychol 761, 789.

3 Social Justice Liberalism and the Criminalisation of Hate 67

torture.[67] Cases such as: Bijan Ebrahimi, who was badly beaten before being set on fire; Jody Dombrowski, whose head and face were stamped on so brutally that teeth records were required to identify his body and Brent Martin, whose murderers took turns during a £5 bet to see who could knock him unconscious, Martin was punched and kicked until his body became lifeless, are but just a few examples of the extreme violence that is perpetrated on people of "difference".[68] There are many other examples that illustrate the grotesque lengths to which some offenders will go to express their contempt and hatred of others.[69]

As noted above, the violence of hate cannot be understood simply in terms of "aggravated" physical violence. While it is true that not every single hate crime will involve violence, the fact that hate-based criminal conduct is more likely to involve severe forms of physical injury shows that this type of crime is a distinct social problem, one that is deserving of special attention in law. Nevertheless, critics have asserted that because not *all* hate crimes cause more physical harm, legislation that enhances the punishment of all hate crimes remains unjust.[70] It is asserted that new legislation is unnecessary because where greater levels of injury are inflicted there are already serious violent offences against the person on the statute book that can be prosecuted.[71] However, this interpretation of criminalisation fails to recognise the role that the criminal law plays in reducing the risk of serious harms. As noted by Feinberg above, if hate-based conduct increases the probability of physical injury and if those injuries are of a graver kind, then the criminal law has a legitimate role in specifically regulating such behaviour. This is why an armed robbery or aggravated burglary is considered more serious than the basic offence of robbery or burglary, even though in some cases victims of these basic offences may be impacted to a greater degree than those where the

---

[67] Equality and Human Rights Commission, *Hidden in Plain Sight: Inquiry into Disability-related Harassment* (EHRC 2011).
[68] Further details of these cases can be found in Neil Chakraborti and Jon Garland, *Hate Crime: Impacts, Causes and Responses* (Sage 2015).
[69] See for example Stevie-Jade Hardy and Neil Chakraborti, *Blood, Threats and Fears: The Hidden Worlds of Hate Crime Victims* (Palgrave 2020).
[70] Mohamad Al-Hakim and Susan Dimock, 'Hate as an Aggravating Factor in Sentencing' (2012) 15(4) New Crim LR 572.
[71] Ibid.

offender used a weapon. It is also why the carrying of a knife in a public place is a criminal offence in some jurisdictions, despite such conduct involving no physical harm at all.[72]

It is not just physical violence that is of concern to our inquiry into criminalising hate. In the early literature on hate crime it was often asserted that hate crimes will likely cause enhanced emotional trauma.[73] Doubting these claims, Jacobs and Potter in 1998 proclaimed that "[t]hese assertions depend on empirical assumptions that seem dubious and have not been substantiated".[74] Over 20 years later and there is now a large body of empirical research, employing randomised sampling and secondary analyses of national victimisation surveys, that has evidenced not only how hate crime victims are more likely to experience certain emotional traumas compared with non-hate crime victims, but also how victims are likely to experience certain traumas in ways that are unique to this type of victimisation.

Evidence that hate crime victims are more likely to experience certain emotional traumas can be found in CSEW data, where it has been revealed that 36 per cent of hate crime victims were very much" affected emotionally compared with 15 per cent for all CSEW crime.[75] Twice as many hate crime victims had experienced a loss of confidence or had felt vulnerable after the incident (40 per cent compared with 19 per cent), while more than twice as many hate crime victims had suffered feelings of fear, difficulty sleeping, anxiety or panic attacks or depression compared with victims of overall CSEW crime.[76]

---

[72] See for example Criminal Justice Act 1988 (UK), section 139 "Offence of having article with blade or point in public place".

[73] Arnold Barnes and Paul H Ephross, 'The Impact of Hate Violence on Victims: Emotional and Behavioral Responses to Attacks' (1994) 39(3) Social Work 247.

[74] Jacobs and Potter 1998 (see Footnote 6) 90.

[75] Home Office 2020 (see Footnote 61).

[76] Home Office 2020 (ibid.). See also Fetzer and Pezzella 2019 (see Footnote 51); Iganski and Lagou 2015 (see Footnote 51).

The Centrality of Group Identity and Perceptions of Threat in Understanding Emotional Harm

While multiple studies have evidenced the enhanced levels of emotional harms likely to be experienced by hate crime victims, few have evaluated quantitatively *why* this occurs.[77] The Sussex Hate Crime Project (SHCP) was one of the largest studies globally on the impacts of hate crime and was conducted in the UK over a five-year period.[78] Over 3000 people participated in a total of 21 separate studies which examined different aspects of both the direct and indirect (community) impacts of anti-LGBT and anti-Muslim hate crime.[79] Unlike most other studies on the impacts of hate crime, the researchers tested for variables that are predictive (and in some studies causal) to these impacts. The researchers found in all of the studies the emotional responses to hate were intrinsically linked to the *group identity* of the victim. Drawing on Social Identity Theory and Intergroup Emotions Theory (IET), the authors hypothesised that the individual reactions to incidents of hate would likely be directly affected by each person's shared common identity trait; those which shape group members' interests and experiences in wider society.[80] Groups can be both formal or informal, large or small, and include, for example, racial and ethnic groups, religious groups and people who share similar sexual or gender identities. While group identities do not necessarily define who someone is in totality, the different and intersecting identities that each individual possesses will likely play a significant role in shaping their sense of self.

The researchers (including this author) used both quantitative (including cross-sectional and longitudinal surveys and experiments) and qualitative (semi-structured interviews) methods to examine the different

---

[77] Though many have explored this qualitatively, theorising that this relates to the attack on identity that is likely to damage an individual's sense of self, which in turn destabilises their ontological security, see for example Herek 2004 (see Footnote 51).
[78] Jenny Paterson and others, *The Sussex Hate Crime Project: Final Report* (University of Sussex 2018a).
[79] Focusing specifically on anti-LGBT and anti-Muslim hostilities.
[80] Diane M Mackie and Eliot R Smith, 'Intergroup Emotions' in Mario Mikulincer, Phillip R Shaver, John F Dovidio and Jeffry A Simpson (Eds), *APA Handbook of Personality and Social Psychology, Vol 2 Group Processes* (APA 2015) 263–293.

impacts of hate crimes on LGBT+ and Muslim people.[81] The authors found in each of their studies that reactions to hate incidents were correlated (and in some cases casually connected) to a perception of *threat* that such incidents pose. These threats are related to physical threats (such as fearing for one safety) and, distinctly, to symbolic threats (threats to group identity and ways of life). It is these perceptions of threat that predict (cause) a number of emotional reactions, most prominently anger and anxiety. However, the studies also found a third common type of feeling experienced by manty victims of hate crime, that of shame.[82] Shame occurs where hate crime victims feel they are (partly) to blame for their own victimisation and, consequently, that they deserve to be punished for being "different".[83] This means that unlike parallel crimes, the hate-element of a crime can be internalised within victims and processed as a form of stigma that serves to diminish their own sense of self. This, in turn, destabilises individuals' sense of ontological security, meaning the world around them becomes a less safe and secure place. It is perhaps unsurprising then that other researchers have shown that rates of suicidal ideation are much higher amongst victims of hate crime.[84]

Shared Suffering

The SHCP found that it was not just direct victims who experienced these negative emotional behavioural consequences. Intergroup emotional theory proposes that by sharing a group identity, individuals will likely form emotional and cultural attachments to the group and its members. Thus, events which are positive or negative for the group (or its members) can be felt acutely by others as if it is happening to them and so can affect how they think and feel. The more salient the group identity,

---

[81] Paterson, Brown and Walters 2019a (see Footnote 51); Paterson, Brown and Walters 2019b (see Footnote 51); Walters and others 2020 (see Footnote 51).

[82] Though to a lesser degree than anger and anxiety.

[83] Gregory M. Herek, 'Beyond "Homophobia": Thinking about Sexual Stigma and Prejudice in the Twenty-first Century' (2004) 1(2) Sexuality Research and Social Policy, 6; Monique Noelle, 'The Ripple Effect of the Matthew Shepard Murder: Impact on the Assumptive Worlds of Members of the Targeted Group' (2002) 46 American Behavioral Scientist, 27.

[84] Matthew L Williams and Jasmin Tregidga, 'Hate crime victimization in Wales: Psychological and physical impacts across seven hate crime victim types' (2014) 54(5) Brit J Criminol 946.

the more important and meaningful group events and external incidents that affect group members' interests.

Hate crimes serve as symbolic messages to entire communities of people with the aim, or at least consequence, of instilling a sense of threat amongst those who share similar characteristics.[85] Research has shown that crimes involving brutal forms of violence can be particularly impactful, increasing levels of fear in other group members.[86] The reporting of hate crimes by local and national media can heighten the levels of threat experienced by certain minority groups who fear that they too could be next.[87] Despite these findings, Al-Hakim and Dimock have asserted that there is a "weak correlation between impacts on persons other than the victims and bias motivation" making it an "implausible… justification for treating hatred as a formal aggravating factor in all cases."[88] However, the SHCP found anything but weak correlations in their 21 separate large scale quantitative surveys and experiments. They have reported that group members are more likely to experience a heightened perception of threat after hearing or reading about hate crimes against another group member that in turn results in similar emotional reactions experienced by direct victims, including anger, anxiety and in some cases feelings of shame.[89] The constant fear of targeted victimisation is compounded by the frequency with which individuals experience indirect victimisation, inevitably permeating the consciousness of entire groups that they must be alert to the possibility of targeted violence at all times (known as hypervigilance).[90]

As with direct victims, key to understanding these *indirect* harms was the group identity of individuals. Walters et al. examined the meaning of group identity through a number of qualitative in-depth interviews with members of LGBT+ and Muslim communities. They outline how and why hate crimes can affect group members within identity groups from

---

[85] James Weinstein, 'First Amendment Challenges to Hate Crime Legislation: Where's the Speech?' (1992) 11(2) Crim Just Ethics 6; Lawrence 1999 (see Footnote 27).

[86] Noelle 2002 (see Footnote 83); Barbara Perry and Alvi Shahid, '"We are all vulnerable": The in terrorem effects of hate crimes' (2012) 18(1) Int Rev Vict 57.

[87] Paterson, Brown and Walters 2019b (see Footnote 51).

[88] Al-Hakim and Dimock 2012 (see Footnote 70).

[89] Paterson, Brown and Walters 2019b (see Footnote 51).

[90] Perry and Alvi 2012 (see Footnote 86); Walters and others 2020 (see Footnote 51).

the local, national and even international context. In summary, the authors found that indirect harms of hate crimes are experienced at differing degrees depending on the strength of collective identity, as it is expressed through socialising with group members locally, participation in cultural and identity-based practices (e.g. attending mosque, frequenting LGBT+ venues), or simply by sharing an identity trait.[91] Importantly, the researchers found that while hate crimes that occur in their local neighbourhood gave rise to the strongest reactions, incidents which occur globally could also have direct and distinct impacts on their emotionality. This, it is explained, occurs because of a more deeply felt empathic connection that individuals had for members of their same identity group; these connections were strengthened most saliently where individuals experienced a sense of "shared suffering", the result of facing similar (frequent) incidents of hate that were connected directly to their group identity.

Figure 3.1 below shows the results from the Sussex Hate Crime Project on levels of empathy (based on Likert-type scale) for empathy towards victims having read about a hate crime versus a similar non-hate crime.

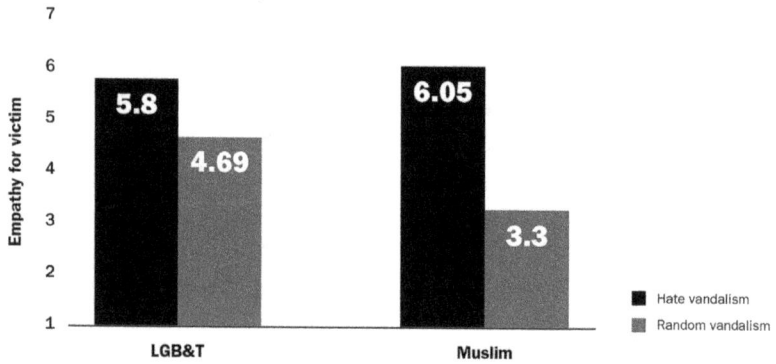

Fig. 3.1 Empathy for victims of hate motivated vs. random acts of vandalism. (Adapted from Paterson and others 2018a (see Footnote 78) 25)

---

[91] Walters and others 2020 (see Footnote 51).

3.3.2 Hate as Marginalisation and Powerlessness

Behavioural Impacts

The substantial body of victimological research on hate crime provides persuasive evidence of its distinct physical and emotional harms. Studies have consistently showed that hate crime incidents are likely to be more violent in nature than non-hate offences, and victims are more likely to be affected at an emotional and psychological level. Yet the effects of hate crime run deeper still, affecting entire social groups' capacity to participate freely and equally in society. The marginalising effects of hate-based conduct are most profoundly experienced where acts of hatred become pervasive throughout a community or society. For example, von Hirsch reflects that racial insult as an isolated speech-act[92] may cause mere offence, but when commonly expressed it has the "potential of restricting victims' opportunities to participate in the community's working and social life".[93] This is because the commonality of hate-based conduct serves to remind groups of people about their (lack of) safety in the community and this forces group members to take certain actions to avoid targeted victimisation.

The marginalising effects of hate crime incidents might be referred to by what Simester and von Hirsch define as "conjunctive harms". These are harms that occur when multiple people do the same thing at a similar time. Let us take the example of polluting a stream. If one person throws their waste into a stream, the volume and flow of water quickly dilutes the waste and no real damage is caused to the wildlife swimming in the stream. In such a case, it cannot really be said that the dumper has had any tangible impact on the wellbeing of the river's organisms and hence the wrongfulness of their conduct appears minimal. However, if multiple people begin to dump their waste in the river, the water quickly becomes poisoned and fish and fauna in the stream will be directly harmed and even killed. Simester and von Hirsh assert that the original dumper's own

---

[92] See further discussion on speech-act theory in Chap. 5.
[93] Andrew Von Hirsch, 'Harm and Wrongdoing in Criminalisation Theory' (2014) 8 Crim L & Phil 245, 247.

contribution is individually wrong "in virtue of its participating in the collective wrong... [s]ince the ultimate harm is collectively caused, the immediate wrong that causes it is a collective one."[94]

While the conjunctive harms of hate crime may appear difficult to calculate with any certainty, we can measure these by quantifying the behavioural consequences that such crimes have on group members' capacity to participate freely and equally in society. The Sussex Hate Crime study was able to show empirically that victimisation has a number of behavioural consequences that directly thwart the "interests" of targeted groups in this regard. As noted above, the project found that hate crimes resulted in elevated perceptions of threat amongst group members linked both to their sense of security and their rights *as* LGBT or Muslim people. These realistic and symbolic threats directly resulted in three distinct emotional responses: anger, anxiety and shame. However, across the various studies the researchers also showed that each of these emotional reactions were linked to distinct types of behavioural responses. For example, feelings of anger were predictive of group members participating in proactive behaviours, most uniquely joining "rights-based groups" and posting rights-based statements on social media. Anxiety on the other hand predicted avoidant behaviours, some of which are common with other types of crime such as leaving home less often, seeing friends less regularly, and avoiding certain places and locations.[95] More uniquely, though, the research also showed that group members were less inclined to reveal their identity (such as LGBT hiding their sexual or gender identities); individuals also stated they would dress differently and change their appearance, while some would not show affection to their partner in public (such as holding hands). Feelings of shame had particularly significant impacts on an individual's interests. The study found that it was connected to all types of behaviour that were researched, including individuals seeking out greater security and hiding their identity.[96] Each of these behavioural harms were experienced not only by direct victims,

---

[94] AP Simester and Andrew Von Hirsch, 'Remote Harms and Non-constitutive Crimes' (2009) 28(1) Crim Just Ethics 89, 103.

[95] Paterson, Brown and Walters 2019b (see Footnote 51).

[96] It was also the only emotion that predicted a desire to retaliate against perpetrators, suggesting that hate crimes may in some instances give rise to inter-group hostilities.

but by indirect victims too—for example those who knew of a victim in their local neighbourhood or who read about a victim in a news article.

The distinct impacts uncovered by the study revealed the extent to which hate crimes can restrict *all* group members' capacity and resources to participate freely in society. James similarly notes in relation to anti-Gypsy and Traveller hate that "[t]he incapacity for [community members] to function, let alone thrive, in a contemporary society that maligns them has resulted in their social and economic exclusion."[97] The economic costs of victimisation highlighted by James should not be underestimated. Emotional consequences such as anxiety and depression and behavioural responses such as staying at home for fear of being abused can have dire financial costs. In Walters' study of ongoing hate abuse in London, he found that some victims had lost their job as a result after missing work due to the health problems associated with their ordeal, and in one case because a neighbour barricaded her into her apartment so she could not leave.[98] Others incurred financial costs associated with their victimisation, such as repairing damaged property, while for many victims they had wished to move away from their home to avoid abuse but were unable to do so because of a lack of social housing options. Other victims spoke of persistent false complaints made by their neighbours to housing associations, which they believed were racially or homophobically motivated, resulting in threats of eviction from housing officers.[99]

Such a state of affairs is enabled where hate-based conduct becomes prolific and where incidents go underchallenged. The result is a social milieu within which certain social groups experience the constant fear of targeted violence. The threat manifests not just as one against physical safety but to one's ability to express one's rights as a black, Muslim, gay, trans or disabled (etc.) person. The resulting precarity of a group's social positionality is a form of societal misrecognition, as individual members begin to perform their identities in a way that is non-threatening to

---

[97] Zoë James, *The Harms of Hate for Gypsies and Travellers A Critical Hate Studies Perspective* (Palgrave 2020) 51.
[98] See also, Jack McDevitt and others, 'Consequences for victims: A comparison of bias—and non-bias-motivated assaults' (2001) 45(4) Am Behav Sci 697, 710.
[99] Mark A Walters, *Hate Crime and Restorative Justice: Exploring Causes, Repairing Harms* (OUP 2014a) ch 3.

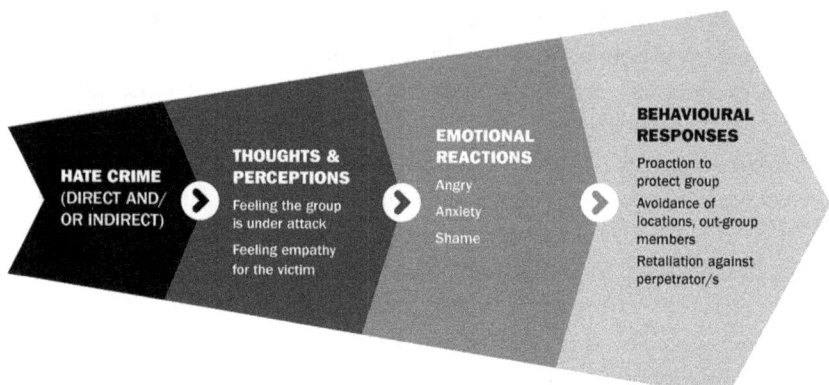

Fig. 3.2 Flow chart illustrating the process of hate crime harms. (Adapted from Paterson and others 2018a (see Footnote 78) 30)

mainstream identity ideals.[100] In doing so they are forced into a performativity that rejects their essence of self in favour of an identity that embodies dominant normalcy. Such behaviours are intrinsically oppressive, harming not only the emotional wellbeing of direct and indirect victims, but their economic stability as well. In doing so, hate crimes can significantly diminish an entire group's capacity to pursue the good life (Fig. 3.2).

Institutional Harm

A society that fails to recognise the distinct harms of hate crime is a society that is likely to repeat these harms via the practices and processes of its public institutions. That is because "the system" is set up to respond to crimes as "primary harms". It does not take as its starting point the prevention of harm as social injustice. It is unsurprising, then, that law enforcement agencies are often ignorant of the wider social structures that affect victims of hate. If state agencies do not comprehend the harms of hate crime as both individual violence *and* societal marginalisation

---

[100] See more generally, Charles Taylor, 'The politics of recognition' in Amy Gutmann (ed), *Multiculturalism* (Princeton UP 1994) 25–73.

3 Social Justice Liberalism and the Criminalisation of Hate

they are at risk of perpetuating both. For example, CSEW data has shown that that victims of hate crime are less likely to think the police have treated them fairly or with respect, compared with victims of CSEW crime overall.[101] Unsurprisingly, CSEW data also shows that hate crimes victims are more likely to be very dissatisfied (27 per cent) with the police handling of the matter compared with overall CSEW crime (17 per cent).[102]

Previous research by the author has revealed the breadth of failures that occur when statutory agencies respond to hate crime, from victims facing insensitive responses to their claims, disbelief and even direct forms of bias.[103] The SHCP also explored perceptions of the criminal justice system in relation to hate crime. It found that in general, respondents did not believe the police or the Crown Prosecution Service were effective in dealing with hate crimes. Notably, amongst Muslim participants those who had had contact with the police by reporting a hate crime perceived them to be less effective at dealing with such crimes, indicating that the police may have exacerbated their experience of victimisation.[104] For some communities the distrust of police means that individuals will not report incidents at all, or when they do come into contact with services they will hide their identity to avoid facing discrimination.[105]

A case example helps to illustrate the marginalising effects of hate and the powerlessness that victims often experience in its aftermath. The murder of Bijan Ebrahimi, briefly mentioned above, was the culmination of many years of abuse, which had been largely ignored by local authorities. The inquiry into Ebrahimi's death revealed that he had made 85 telephone calls to his local police force. In 73 of these calls, Ebrahimi, who had a learning disability, had reported incidents involving racial abuse,

---

[101] Data shows that victims of hate crime thought the police treated them fairly in 67 per cent of cases, compared with 81 per cent of cases for CSEW crime overall, Home Office, *Hate Crime, England and Wales, 2017/18 Statistical Bulletin 20/18* (Home Office 2018) 28.

[102] Home Office 2020 (see Footnote 61); see also Neil Chakraborti, Jon Garland and Stevie-Jade Hardy, *The Leicester Hate Crime Project: Findings and Conclusions* (University of Leicester 2014).

[103] Walters 2014 (see Footnote 99) ch 5; see also Chakraborti, Garland and Hardy (2014) (ibid.) 64ff; Stevie-Jade Hardy and Neil Chakraborti, *Blood, Threats and Fears: The Hidden Worlds of Hate Crime Victims* (Palgrave 2020).

[104] Paterson and others 2018a (see Footnote 78).

[105] James 2020 (see Footnote 97).

criminal damage and threats to kill. Yet the police failed to record a crime on at least 40 of these occasions. Instead of investigating Ebrahimi's allegations as hate crimes, the police had largely dismissed him as being a nuisance.[106] In one incident preceding his murder, a neighbour had broken into Bijan's home and had beaten him whilst shouting racist abuse. Bijan called the police and by the time they arrived an angry mob of neighbours had gathered outside of his home chanting "paedophile". However instead of arresting the culprit, Bijan was instead detained for breach of the peace. Hardy and Chakraborti report that his complaints were dismissed by the police who had had regarded him as a "pest", an "idiot" and a "pain in the ass".[107] An independent report into the events leading up to his death subsequently found that he had been treated with disrespect and even contempt by some police officers, and that both the council and the police's lack of care towards Ebrahimi was a result of "institutional racism".[108]

Beyond the inaction of statutory agencies to take hate crime seriously, are the incidents involving individual officers towards marginalised community members. It is beyond the scope of this book to explore this in detail here, but it is worth highlighting that a social justice liberal criminal law should not only focus its attention on individual culpability of offenders as members of the public, but on the conduct of officers who serve us via agencies such as the police. For many years now empirical research has uncovered the disproportionate use of criminal justice measures against certain communities (especially people of colour). Disproportionately high levels of imprisonment, arrests, and the use of stop and search suggest that racial bias is playing a significant role in the

---

[106] David McCallum, 'Safer Bristol Partnership Multi-Agency Learning Review Following The Murder of Bijan Ebrahimi' (Safer Bristol Executive Board 2014).

[107] Stevie-Jade Hardy and Neil Chakraborti, *Hate Crime: Identifying and Dismantling Barriers to Justice* (Centre for Hate Studies, University of Leicester 2016) 10.

[108] McCallum 2014 (see Footnote 106). See also another case in 2007 involving ongoing disablist abuse towards a family with various learning disabilities and the failures across statutory services to take their experiences with the seriousness they required. A mother (Fiona Pilkington) of two children set fire to her car with herself and her daughter inside, killing them both. Independent Police Complaints Commission, *IPCC report into the contact between Fiona Pilkington and Leicestershire Constabulary 2004–2007* (IPPC 2009).

criminalisation of minority ethnic individuals.[109] Where there is clear evidence that an individual has been stopped illegally due to racial bias (false imprisonment) and personally searched (assaulted) such incidents should no longer be treated as a matter of internal discipline but as criminal matters concerning hate crime legislation. For an assault that demonstrates hostility towards someone because of their racial background, is not only an abuse of power, but it is crime motivated by prejudice. Where there is evidence, as there has previously been,[110] that an entire institution has become institutionally biased, it may too be time for the criminal law to extend its powers to encompass group liability.[111]

Hate crimes do not occur within a social vacuum. Too often incidents make up part of a process of ongoing victimisation that is compounded by the failure of state agencies to recognise the needs of victims or the actions of institutions which signify bias. Combined, these failures ultimately result in the marginalisation of many minority group individuals who end up feeling powerless to improve their circumstances. Far from being remote harms, there are few more salient examples of how others' conduct can limit the opportunities for certain members of society to self-realise.

3.3.3 Hate as Cultural Imperialism

In Sect. 3.2.1 I referenced Simester and von Hirsch's example of polluting of a river as a conjunctive harm to help explain the marginalising behavioural effects of hate-based conduct. Linked to this idea of environmental pollution is the impacts that iterative expressions of hate can have on the societal norms and values that shape people's attitudes and behaviours

---

[109] See for example David Lammy (chair), *The Lammy Review: An independent review into the treatment of, and outcomes for, Black, Asian and Minority Ethnic individuals in the Criminal Justice System* (TSO 2017).
[110] William Macpherson, *The Stephen Lawrence Inquiry: Report of an Inquiry by Sir William Macpherson of Cluny* (Cm 4262-I, TSO 1999).
[111] Such as in the case of corporate criminal liability.

towards people of difference.¹¹² In this sense hate crime can be understood as a form of "cultural harm". Palmer defines cultural harm as:

> a type of harm which manifests in the normalization of attitudes and practices deemed negative… normalization in this context [refers] to a process by which attitudes, practices and/or ways of being become accepted as routine, unremarkable or at least understandable aspects of everyday life.¹¹³

Whether legislatures can legitimately criminalise these more remote harms should be a matter of determining the gravity of the harm that can occur and the likelihood of others in any given polity performing such acts in a contemporaneous manner. Here, Young's concept of oppression as cultural imperialism helps to enrich our analysis by comprehending hate, not just as a rejection of principle, but as a phenomenon that serves to buttress a hostile environment towards difference.¹¹⁴ As a violent form of oppression, hate crimes position othered identities as inferior. Jeremy Waldron expounds upon such an idea in relation to permissive antilocution, which he states:

> creates something like an environmental threat to social peace, a sort of slow-acting poison, accumulating here and there, word by word, so that eventually it becomes harder and less natural for even the good-hearted members of the society to play their part in maintaining this public good.¹¹⁵

I have written elsewhere about the socio-structural and individual conditions that are causal to hate-based violence.¹¹⁶ Drawing on the work of Perry who focuses on structured action theory,¹¹⁷ together with theories relating to socio-economic strain and self-control theory, I assert that

---

[112] Jack Levin and Gordana Rabrenovic, 'Hate as Cultural Justification for Violence' in Barbara Perry and Brian Levin (eds) *Hate Crimes: Volume One: Understanding and Defining Hate Crime* (Praeger 2009).

[113] Tanya Palmer, 'Rape pornography, cultural harm and criminalization' (2018) 69(1) NILQ 37, 39.

[114] Iris Marion Young, *Justice and the Politics of Difference* (Princeton UP 2011).

[115] Jeremy Waldron, *The Harm in Hate Speech* (Harvard UP 2012) 4.

[116] Mark A Walters, 'A General Theories of Hate Crime: Strain, Doing Difference and Self Control' (2011) 19(4) Critical Crim 313.

[117] Barbara Perry, *In the Name of Hate: Understanding Hate Crimes* (Routledge 2001).

socio-cultural classifications of identity difference, when combined with socio-economic conditions that result in economic marginalisation, collectively help to create environments from within which certain Others become scapegoats for broader structural and socio-economic societal inequities.[118] These toxic environments produce individuals who experienced unacknowledged internalised rage that resurfaces and is projected on to the socially constructed other;[119] with individuals experiencing low-levels of self-control being most likely to engage in forms of targeted violence.[120]

As such, hate crime is not just a matter of individual violence, that contains distinct forms of both individual and community impact, but it is a specific type of criminality that cultivates and fortifies a cultural imperialism that actively resists identity difference. In this sense, it is asserted that the hate-element of "hate crimes" is a form of cultural harm that fuels a vicious cycle of violence aimed at oppressing the perceived threat of dangerous Others.

The concept of cultural harm has been invoked by others to defend the criminalisation of various socially corrosive conduct. For instance, McGlynn and Rackley have argued that criminalising the possession of extreme (rape simulation) pornography could be justified under the harm principle as a form of cultural harm.[121] McGlynn and Rackley assert that the enactment of legislation should aim to change "the cultural and social environment in which sexual violence is marginalised, in which rape conviction rates are at an all time low and in which pornography is becoming (if possible) even more ubiquitous".[122] The authors note that despite the Government's original consultation paper justifying the proposed legislation on such grounds this approach changed following opposition from "arch liberals" who argued that such a type of harm could not be ade-

---

[118] James (2020) also writes of the "symbolic harms" caused by the language and ethos of neoliberalism (323) 57ff.
[119] Larry Ray, David Smith and Liz Wastell, 'Shame, Rage and Racist Violence' (2004) 44(3) Brit J Criminol 350.
[120] Walters 2011 (see Footnote 116).
[121] Clare MS McGlynn and Erika Rackley, 'Criminalising extreme pornography: a lost opportunity' [2009] 4 Crim LR 245, 257.
[122] McGlynn and Rackley 2009 (ibid.) 257.

quately measured and "[u]ltimately ...[the Government] fell back on the easy tradition of the conservative-moralistic and disgust-based arguments which consume the [Obscene Publications Act]".[123]

It is certainly difficult to measure with any certainty the extent to which certain behaviours become culturally normalised, and in turn to what extent they are causally connected to other types of harmful behaviour. A recent study by Wiedliztka and others found that offline hate crime was predictive of online hate speech.[124] They assert that this is likely to be a result of what they refer to as "compound retaliation", which explains how offline hate crimes reported by media and social media compound (reinforce) intergroup hostilities, providing further permission for others to express hatred online. Other researchers have found that online hate is likely to predict offline hate crime.[125] Whether offline or online precede each other, what is clear is that public expressions of hate are likely to be mutually reinforcing, thereby exacerbating identity-based hostilities in society.

This vicious cycle can be particularly damaging where enmity against certain groups is expressed by politicians. For instance, Palmer asserts that the political rhetoric surrounding the EU referendum contributed to "the cultural scaffolding which support[ed] the manifestation of racism and xenophobia in material harms such as discrimination and hate crime".[126] As mentioned in the previous chapter, the EU referendum was a salient example of how speech, campaign posters and newspaper columns served to normalise racist and xenophobic attitudes in the UK. The activities of some Leave campaigners helped to depict white working-class Britons as victims and immigrants as both an economic and security threat.[127] Senior government ministers made countless announcements

---

[123] McGlynn and Rackley 2009 n (339) 258.

[124] Susann Wiedlitzka and others, 'Hate in Word and Deed: The Temporal Association Between Online and Offline Islamophobia', J Quant Criminol (2021): https://doi.org/10.1007/s10940-021-09530-9.

[125] Though others have found the reverse with online hate predicting offline hate crime, see for example Matthew L Williams and others, 'Hate in the Machine: Anti-Black and Anti-Muslim Social Media Posts as Predictors of Offline Racially and Religiously Aggravated Crime' (2020) 60(1) Brit J Criminol 93.

[126] Palmer 2018 (see Footnote 113) 41.

[127] Ibid.

3 Social Justice Liberalism and the Criminalisation of Hate

that were the UK to remain it would be swamped by immigrants from Turkey who would soon join the EU, while also linking higher rates of criminality and gun ownership in Turkey as posing a security threat to British people.[128]

Unsurprisingly, in the aftermath of the referendum, recorded police data showed an immediate spike in hate crime incidents of 41 per cent compared with the same month a year previously.[129] Further analysis of police data by the Home Office found that there was "a rise in racially or religiously aggravated offences during the EU Referendum campaign, from April 2016, to a peak in offences after the result, in July 2016."[130] Other researchers have also found a direct correlation between increases in reported hate crime and Brexit.[131] Research conducted for this book of police records in greater London found that it was not only the number of reported incidents that rose during and post the referendum but also the number of investigations that resulted in a positive criminal justice outcome (outcomes included, *inter alia*, accused charge/summoned, caution, community resolution, prosecution not in public interest). Analysis of this data showed that six months prior to the month of referendum there were 860 cases with an apprehended suspect and a criminal justice outcome; this number increased to 1087 for the six months after (a 26 per cent increase). Further analysis of the full investigatory details (which include victim statements, suspect statements and police officer notes) uploaded to the crime reporting system (CRIS) showed that certain terms relating to Brexit and to immigration,

---

[128] In reality Turkey was nowhere near accession to the Union. Daniel Boffey and Toby Helm, 'Vote Leave embroiled in race row over Turkey security threat claims' *The Guardian* (22 May 2016).
[129] Hannah Corcoran and Kevin Smith, *Hate Crime, England and Wales, 2015/16* (Home Office 2016).
[130] Aoife O'Neill, *Hate Crime, England and Wales, 2016/17, Statistical Bulletin 17/17* (Home Office 2017) 7.
[131] Daniel Devine, 'Discrete Events and Hate Crimes: The Causal Role of the Brexit Referendum' (2021) 102(1) Soc Sci Quart 374.

Table 3.1 Words/slurs appearing in the Metropolitan Police Service's police crime reporting information system before and after the EU referendum

Slur/words	Six months pre-referendum	Six months post-referendum	Increase
Brexit	5	194	+3780%
EU	45	191	+324%
Foreigner	84	155	+85%
Immigrant	85	140	+65%
Terrorist	174	213	+22%
P*ki	1102	1293	+17%

including the word "Brexit" itself and "EU", appeared much more frequently within these details post-referendum (Table 3.1).[132]

This is not to suggest that pejorative political rhetoric should be criminalised based on an estimation of its cultural harm.[133] However, the symbiotic nexus between hate crime and hate-based political rhetoric does provide additional justification for a liberal state to use the law to challenge public expressions (speech or conduct) of racism, homophobia and other forms of prejudice. Legislation must provide a counter narrative to the social norms that serve to legitimise such behaviours and which give permission to hate.[134] A society that seeks to promote social justice should expect, as a minimum, for the state to challenge expressions of identity-based bias and prejudice through public policy, and where appropriate through legal regulation (Fig. 3.3).

---

[132] Data was collated as part of the study "Policing Hate Crime: modernising the craft, an evidence-based approach" led by David Weir. Note that hate speech online also skyrocketed with research conducted by the think tank DEMOS showing over 5000 xenophobic tweets sent during a two-week period leading up to the EU referendum. Carl Miller and others, *From Brussels to Brexit: Islamophobia, Xenophobia, Racism and Reports of Hateful Incidents on Twitter* (Demos 2016). In the US context, Trump's anti-Muslim tweets have similarly been evidenced as predicting real life spikes in Islamophobic violence on the streets, see Karsten Müller and Carlo Schwarz, 'From Hashtag to Hate Crime: Twitter and Anti-Minority Sentiment' (2020) SSRN.

[133] Though some forms of hate speech are rightly proscribed globally, Viera Pejchal and Kimberley Brayson, 'How Should We Legislate against Hate Speech? Finding an International Model in a Globalized World in Jennifer Schweppe and Mark A Walters (eds), *The Globalization of Hate: Internationalizing Hate Crime* (OUP 2016).

[134] See further discussion on educative deterrence in Part 3.

3 Social Justice Liberalism and the Criminalisation of Hate

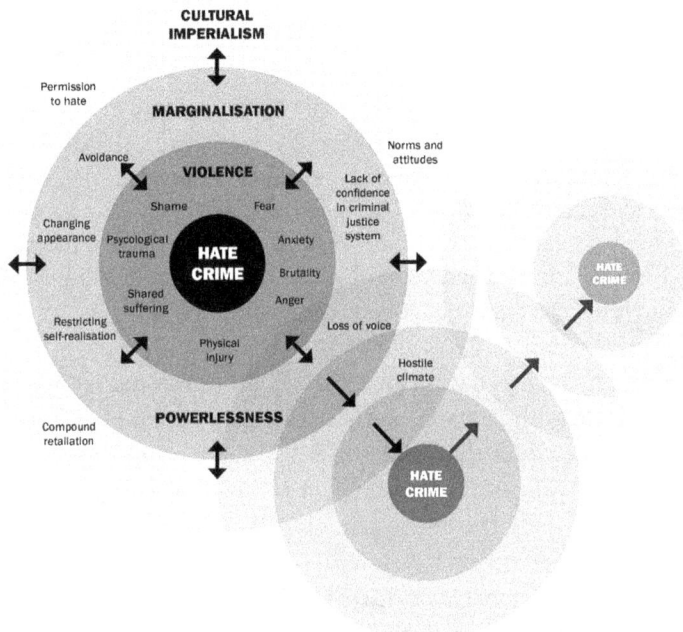

Fig. 3.3 The distinct harms of hate crimes

3.4 Part 3: The Moral Wrongfulness of Hate and the Law's Role as Educative Deterrence

At the start of this chapter I referred to Duff's negative legal moralist account which asserts that immoral behaviour is an insufficient ground for criminalisation, but it is a necessary one before harmful conduct can be proscribed. The wrongfulness of hate crimes should by now be clearly marked out by their oppressive consequences. That is to say, the cumulative impacts of hate crimes should in themselves clearly show that they are distinct wrongs which require specific criminal proscription. However, crimes connected with hate or prejudice can also be considered as distinctly morally reprehensible as they express certain values that are an affront to what a social justice liberal polity stands for.[135] Writing in the US context, Lawrence reflects that:

> [hate] crimes violate not only society's general concern for the security of its members and their property but also the shared values of equality among its citizens and racial and religious harmony in a heterogeneous society. A [hate] crime is therefore a profound violation of the egalitarian ideal and the antidiscrimination principle that have become fundamental not only to the American legal system but to American culture as well.[136]

Moral outrage towards hate crimes reflects the perceived wrongfulness of such behaviour both as particularly harmful to individuals and communities, and as conduct that undermines society's commitment to liberal principles and values.[137] The state plays a central role in expressing reprobation as it yields the most potent power in denouncing public wrongs.[138] The law, as proxy for state, has a legitimate role not only in recognising the distinct harms caused by hate crime, but in expressing condemnation for it. A court conviction for a specific criminal offence (as against the court invoking a sentencing provision during a sentencing hearing[139]), communicates to the public about "what is required of them as citizens".[140] Repeated applications of hate crime (criminal) laws serve to furnish the boundaries of socially acceptable behaviour.

Waldron argues, in relation to hate speech, that criminalisation goes one step further than censuring in that it vindicates the dignity of members of targeted groups.[141] Similarly, by criminalising hate-based conduct the law gives social standing to those who have erstwhile been oppressed

---

[135] As outlined in Chap. 2.

[136] Frederick M Lawrence, 'The punishment of hate: toward a normative theory of bias-motivated crimes' (1994) 93(2) Michigan L Rev 320, 347.

[137] See also Chara Bakalis, 'The victims of hate crime and the principles of the criminal law' (2017) 37 LS 718.

[138] RA Duff, *Punishment, Communication and Community* (OUP 2001) 80.

[139] I explore in greater detail what a social justice liberal system of sanctions might look like in Chap. 7.

[140] Duff 2001 (see Footnote 138) 80.

[141] Waldron 2012 (see Footnote 115).

3 Social Justice Liberalism and the Criminalisation of Hate

within society and historically by the state. Conceived in this way the criminal law is much more than simply a conduit to inflict punishment on wrongdoers, for it is capable of speaking to citizens about the values and principles of the normative community.[142] The re-criminalisation of hate crime assists in a process of norm creation, whereby it supports positive norms (i.e. acceptance of "difference") by publicly condemning violent forms of oppression.[143] The creation of special categories of protection (i.e. race, religion, sexual orientation, etc.) brings specific attention to the validity of these certain groups as *deserving* of special redress.[144] In doing this, legislatures are directly challenging social attitudes that give rise to biases against these groups. The criminal law in this regard not only denounces hate-based conduct but aims "to help reconfigure perceptions of such groups as deviant, dangerous or illegitimate Others".[145]

Duff argues that the ultimate aim of the criminal law is to persuade members of society to "refrain from criminal wrongdoing because they *realize* that it is wrong".[146] In other words, the law has an educative role in that it raises greater awareness as to specific wrongfulness of hate-based conduct. While Duff does not go as far as to assert that the criminal law has a role to play in norm creation, it can be argued that by repeatedly denouncing crimes as "hate crimes" the law helps to shape a social milieu where targeted violence becomes morally condemnable. Incrementally, the importance of respecting marginalised identity traits seeps further

---

[142] Klaus Günther, 'Criminal Law, Crime and Punishment as Communication' in AP Simester, Antje Du Bois-Pedain and Ulfrid Neumann (eds), *Liberal Criminal Theory: Essays for Andreas von Hirsch* (Hart 2014), 123–139.

[143] Note that I do not advocate the use of punishment enhancements for hate crime, but instead support the synthesis of hate crime laws with non-punitive measures, see Chap. 6.

[144] Though it is acknowledged that the neutral terms to include marginalised groups (e.g. "race", instead of "minority ethnic group") means that the law does not always specify specific groups who disproportionately experience violence, marginalisation and powerlessness. See, Valerie Jenness, 'Contours of hate crime politics and law in the United States' in P Iganski (ed), *The Hate Debate: Should hate be punished as a crime?* (Institute for Jewish Policy Research 2002) 15–35. The question of which groups are selected for protection is examined in detail in the next chapter.

[145] Gail Mason, 'The symbolic purpose of hate crime law: Ideal victims and emotion' (2014a) 18 Theo Crim 75, 79.

[146] Duff 2001 (see Footnote 138) 81 (emphasis added).

into the public consciousness.[147] This is not to suggest that people necessarily become more embracing of identity differences, but are likely to become less willing, at least, to publicly express forms of hatred because it becomes a norm that to do so is socially unacceptable.

There is some qualitative evidence to support such an assertion. Gadd and Dixon's focus groups with young offenders found some evidence to suggest that hate crime laws in England and Wales impacted would-be offenders, who though still willing to vocalise their dislike for certain ethnic groups, were conscious of the fact that to act on this in a criminal context would result in them being labelled as "racist" and that they would get into "serious trouble".[148] A potential deterrent effect was therefore identified both in the label given to hate crime offenders and how seriously the police would likely take any physical action taken by them.[149]

It is certainly not always clear whether the law helps to shift attitude and behaviour or whether changes in law reflect evolving attitudes of a people. However, some further tentative inferences may be drawn from the correlations between changes in law and the numbers of estimated hate crimes that occur in society. For example, by reviewing British Crime Survey/ Crime Survey for England and Wales data, which globally, is one of the most robust estimations of total hate crimes within a single jurisdiction, we can view the trends in hate crime before and after the enactment of certain hate crime laws. Below I outline the full data and timeline of legislative changes in England and Wales, looking at race hate crimes. This is selected as the data on race hate crimes goes back to before the legislative changes and remains the most prolific type of hate crime in the UK (Table 3.2).

The data reveals that the estimated number of race hate crimes decreased by 73 per cent between 1999 and 2020. Overall crime levels[150]

---

[147] As to the role of expression and law, see Elizabeth S Anderson and Richard H Pildes, 'Expressive Theories of Law: A General Restatement' (2000) 148(5) U Pa L Rev 1503.

[148] Bill Dixon and David Gadd, 'Getting the message? "New" Labour and the criminalization of "hate"' (2006) 6(3) Criminol & Crim Just 6(3) 309.

[149] Though it should be noted that the authors were less persuaded that the enhanced penalties were a dissuasive factor in would-be offenders' choice not to act on their prejudices.

[150] Excluding fraud and computer misuse.

3 Social Justice Liberalism and the Criminalisation of Hate

Table 3.2 Legislative developments in criminalising (race) hate crime in England and Wales

Year/s	Legislative/policy change	Estimated race hate crimes
1995	–	390,000
1998	Racially aggravated offences introduced under ss. 28–32 Crime and Disorder Act 1998.	–
1999	The publication of the Macpherson Report on the Stephen Lawrence murder inquiry recommends a perception-based definition for recording race hate crimes.	280,000
2001	The Anti-terrorism, Crime and Security Act 2001 adds new religiously aggravated offences to the Crime and Disorder Act 1998. The Crown Prosecution Service publishes its first Racist Incident Monitoring Annual Report in 2001.	-
2002–2004	ss. 145 Criminal Justice Act 2003 introduces new sentencing provisions requiring judges to enhance sentences for any crime aggravated by racial hostility. s. 146 of the same Act includes aggravation based on three other characteristics: religion, sexual orientation, disability.	206,000
2004–2005	ss. 145 and 146, CJA come into force in April 2005.	179,000
2006	The Racial and Religious Hatred Act amends the Public Order Act 1986 proscribing the stirring up of religious hatred.	–
2008	National recording of five strands of hate crime (race, religion, disability, sexual orientation and transgender) is introduced for police forces across England, Wales and Northern Ireland. The Criminal Justice and Immigration Act 2008 amends the Public Order Act 1986 proscribing the stirring up of sexual orientation hatred. The Crown Prosecution Service publishes its first annual hate crime report on prosecution and conviction rates for all five strands of hate crime.	–
2009	UK Government publishes its first cross-Government Hate Crime Action Plan.	–
2011–2013	Legal Aid, Sentencing and Punishment of Offenders Act 2012 adds transgender identity hostility under s. 146 of the CJA 2003.	154,000
2012–2014	A second Government Hate Crime Action Plan is launched.	106,000

(continued)

Table 3.2 (continued)

Year/s	Legislative/policy change	Estimated race hate crimes
2014–2016		104,000
2016–2018	A third Government Hate Crime Action Plan is launched.	101,000
2017–2020	Sections 145 and 146 are consolidated in the new Sentencing Act 2020, s 66.	104,000

dropped by 63 per cent during this same period,[151] suggesting that crimes (especially violence) are falling in general. As this data shows the rate of reduction is slightly higher for hate crime over this period of time. For example, between 1999, the year after racially aggravated offences were enacted, and 2002 the number of race hate crimes reduced by 26 per cent from 280,000 to 206,000 per year. During the same period, crime rates in general dropped by 16 per cent.[152]

There will of course be myriad explanations for the drop in hate crime over this period, other than changes in law and public policy.[153] It is also clear that hate-based activities have moved online where entire communities of people engage in vitriolic abuse of certain social groups.[154] As I have also demonstrated above, other social variables, including changes in political rhetoric and so-called trigger events (such as terrorist attacks) can cause sudden spikes in both hateful attitudes and the crimes that often accompany them. Indeed, the most recent data suggests a small increase in race hate crimes occurred between 2016 and 2020,[155] coinciding with the EU referendum campaign and later the implementation of Brexit.

Nonetheless, there is some reason to believe that the law may have had a positive impact on addressing the social problem of hate crime. Research

---

[151] Office for National Statistics, *Crime in England and Wales: year ending June 2020* (ONS 2021).

[152] Office for National Statistics, *Crime in England and Wales: year ending June 2018* (ONS 2019).

[153] Further time series analysis would provide more scientific evidence of any link between changes in law and rates of hate crime in the UK context.

[154] Carl Miller and others, *From Brussels to Brexit: Islamophobia, Xenophobia, Racism and Reports of Hateful Incidents on Twitter* (Demos 2016).

[155] From 101,000 to 104,000, see Table 3.2.

by Levy and Levy used time series analysis to examine the nexus between state legislation and policies on gay and lesbian rights and reported hate crime incidence.[156] The authors highlight that in the US when the Defense of Marriage Act was enacted, that specifically denied to same-sex couples all the benefits and recognition given to opposite-sex couples, recorded hate crimes against LGBT+ people were increasing. On the contrary when same-sex marriage was legislated for in 2003, the Supreme Judicial Court of Massachusetts reported that hate crimes dropped by 30 per cent.[157] Significantly, Levy and Levy's study found that the criminalisation of hate was correlated with reductions in hate crime. If accurate, it means hate crime laws *may* serve as cultural scaffolding that helps to prevent hate crime.

3.5 Conclusion

Whether hate crime laws in their current forms are having the desired effect of reducing hate crime is still very much open to debate. This book asserts that only where hate crime is conceptualised as social injustice will the law and its institutions be truly able to ensure that commonly victimised groups in society are protected from targeted violence.[158] Law as social justice liberalism demands recognition of hate-based crimes as one of the most odious forms of oppression. Indeed, it would be inaccurate to comprehend hate crimes as simply being more serious versions of basic offences (e.g. an aggravated assault). This is because hate crimes serve to terrorise entire communities of people, resulting in heightened feelings of

---

[156] Brian L Levy and Denise L Levy, 'When love meets hate: The relationship between state policies on gay and lesbian rights and hate crime incidence' (2017) 61(1) Soc Sci Res 142.

[157] Levy and Levy 2017 (see Footnote 156).

[158] Beyond the preventive power of the law is the support that it can offer commonly targeted groups. Research has found that legislation increases reporting rates to the police, meaning that more hate crimes come to the attention of the authorities, Ryken Grattet and Valerie Jenness, 'Transforming Symbolic Law into Organizational Action: Hate Crime Policy and Law Enforcement Practice' (2008) 87(1) Social Forces 501. The legislative framework also ensures that the police officially record incidents, and both the police and the Crown Prosecution Service provide data quarterly and annually on their performance in relation to investigating, prosecuting and convictions for hate crime offences. Home Office, *Hate Crime, England and Wales, 2019 to 2020* (Home Office 2020).

anger, anxiety, vulnerability and shame. Beyond the immediate direct and indirect psychological harms caused by hate are the broader long-term behavioural impacts, including people changing their appearance and avoiding physical locations in order to evade violence. These restrictive behavioural consequences serve to marginalise individuals who feel ostracised from society and often alienated by the state agencies tasked with protecting them. Without a strong message to counter the proliferation of hate, incidents will likely leave a cultural mark, fulfilling a normative role which serves to stigmatise people for their difference. If the law as social justice liberalism is to properly criminalise hate crime, it must recognise that it is a *distinct* type of offending that *disproportionally* affects certain groups in society, and which causes *unique* individual, community, and cultural harms—each of which thwarts the interests of certain social groups restricting their capacity and resources to self-realise. The criminalisation of hate, then, is not only about recognising that hate crimes "hurt more" but that they hurt in ways that are causal to social injustice. To understand hate crime is to understand the role that social, structural and cultural forms of oppression play out in the lives of entire groups of people because of their (multiple) identity/ies.

The use of hate crime laws to address identity-based violence is not distributive, in the sense that it directly assists in the redistribution of wealth and property, but rather it aims to prevent individual and social harms that restrict equal opportunities. Of course, such laws cannot be framed singularly as achieving the objective of social justice alone. They must be situated within a more extensive framework of law and policy that seeks to readdress social inequalities and which proactively addresses structural disadvantage.[159] Governments that use the criminal law as a singular means of addressing hate crime risk paying lip service to the needs of targeted communities. Without structural and institutional reform, such laws risk also being used disproportionately against those they are aimed at protecting.[160] Hate crime law as social justice liberalism can only make a difference to marginalised groups if it operates alongside

---

[159] See Ralph Henham, *Sentencing Policy and Social Justice* (OUP 2018).
[160] Bill Dixon and David Gadd 2006 (see Footnote 148); Jon Burnett, 'Britain: racial violence and the politics of hate' (2013) 54(4) Race & Class 5.

3 Social Justice Liberalism and the Criminalisation of Hate

a policy domain that promotes equality as opportunity through, for example, the implementation of anti-discrimination laws, equal marriage rights, inclusive education initiatives, public health measures, amongst others. Importantly, the way in which hate crime laws are enforced and the measures that are used by the criminal justice system post-conviction become pivotal to the success of hate crime laws as a form of social justice (see Chap. 7).

As Young explains, "[o]pportunity is a concept of enablement rather than possession; it refers to doing more than having."[161] In this sense, hate crime laws must be framed as ensuring that people of difference are more readily enabled to participate in society free from the constant fear of targeted violence. Hate crime laws must serve as a direct attempt by the state to rebalance the historical wrongs that groups of people have suffered.[162] The power of the law, its enforcement, application, and communication *helps* to ensure that "hate", as a form of identity-based threat, is censured and is prevented from being a source of re-reproducing social injustice. In Chap. 7 I will go on to examine how the criminal law can further social justice where it is backed by justice interventions that emphasise communitarian ideals (such as restorative justice), as against those that focus on enhanced punitive penalties. Before then, the next chapter theorises how legislatures can determine which social groups are deserving of the law's special protection.

---

[161] Young 2011 (see Footnote 114).
[162] Alon Harel and Gideon Parchomovsky, 'On hate and equality' (1999) 109(3) Yale LJ 507.

4

Redrawing the Boundaries of Hate Crime: What Characteristics Should Be "Protected" in the Criminal Law?

4.1 Introduction

If the enactment of hate crime legislation serves to address social injustice, what social groups are deserving of its special protection? This question continues to challenge policy makers and legislatures globally. In the US, where modern hate crime statutes were first enacted, different group characteristics have been included at both state- and federal-level legislation.[1] The Hate Crime Statistics Act 1990 was the first piece of federal legislation that required the Attorney General to collect data on hate crimes motivated by race, ethnicity, religion, disability and sexual orientation bias. In 1994 Congress enacted the Hate Crimes Sentencing Enhancement Act, which required the US Sentencing Guidelines Commission to enhance penalties for crimes motivated by bias against a victim's race, colour, national origin, ethnicity, religion, gender, ethnicity and sexual orientation. However, federal jurisdiction initially extended

---

[1] Note that the first "modern" hate crime statute enacted in the US was the Civil Rights Act of 1968 which prohibited interference with federally protected rights by way of violence or threats of violence because of a person's race, colour, religion or national origin. Scholars have debated whether "hate crime" laws existed before then, with some suggesting that first appeared during the creation of the US constitution, see discussion in Nathan Hall, *Hate Crime* (Routledge 2013) ch 2.

only to race, colour, national origin and religion, meaning that crimes motivated by bias towards a victim's sexual orientation, gender or disability could only be pursued if the federal government obtained jurisdiction in some other way.[2] This limitation of jurisdiction was changed by the Matthew Shepard and James Byrd, Jr. Hate Crimes Prevention Act 2009, which extended the reach of federal law to cover sexual orientation, gender or disability. State legislators have also taken diverging approaches to legislating for hate crime, using different models of legislation and including different protected characteristics.[3] There are currently 47 States in the USA with hate crime statutes. All of these states include hate based on race, religion, and ethnicity, while 34 cover disability, 34 sexual orientation, 30 gender, 22 transgender/gender identity, 14 age; 6 political affiliation and 3 (and additionally Washington, D.C.) protect homelessness.

Most countries in Western and Northern Europe have now legislated for different types of hate crime. In England and Wales, for instance, the first hate-based offences were introduced in 1998 and included only "racially aggravated" crimes.[4] Other characteristics were later added in piecemeal fashion, with new laws including religiously aggravated crimes in 2001,[5] and later sexual orientation, disability and transgender-based hostilities were added to separate sentencing provisions.[6] Other Western European countries have legislated against hate crimes motivated by prejudice or hostility towards (amongst other characteristics) individuals' marital status, birth, fortune, age, current and future state of health (e.g. Belgium[7]).

---

[2] Jordan Blair Woods, 'Hate crimes in the United States' in Nathan Hall and others (eds), *The Routledge International Handbook on Hate Crime* (Routledge 2015) 153–162, 155.
[3] Woods 2015 (ibid.); Frederick M Lawrence, *Punishing Hate: Bias Crimes under American Law* (Harvard UP 1999). Discussed in further detail in Chap. 5.
[4] Crime and Disorder Act 1998, ss 28–32. Race hate speech offences were included before this in the Race Relations Act 1965, s 6, later amended by the Public Order Act 1986. The legislation was amended again by the Racial and Religious Hatred Act 2006 to include racial hatred and by the Criminal Justice and Immigration Act 2008 to include sexual orientation hatred.
[5] Amended by the Anti-terrorism, Crime and Security Act 2001, s 39.
[6] Criminal Justice Act 2003, s 146 (now found in s 66 of the Sentencing Act 2020).
[7] Criminal Code (Belgium) 1999, art 405.

The internationalisation of hate crime through various supranational bodies has also seen the concept quickly "migrate" and be integrated into legislative frameworks in jurisdictions beyond Western Europe and the Global North.[8] In Eastern Europe, class (Czech Republic),[9] language (Croatia[10]) or financial or social status (Estonia)[11] have been covered. Beyond Europe, countries in South America and the Caribbean have more recently introduced laws that cover political opinion (Chile[12]), genetic factors, cultural identity, clothing, opinion, and economic condition (Peru[13]), and other beliefs and political persuasions (Sint Maarten[14]). In Africa, hate crimes laws have been introduced that cover "tribal" hatred,[15] while a draft bill in South Africa includes age, albinism, culture, migrant or refugee status, HIV status, amongst other characteristics.[16] Further east, regional group or caste is covered in India,[17] while ideology is included in East Timor.[18]

The fragmented manner in which hate crime laws have been enacted across the world has meant that there is no single coherent framework for legislating against such crimes. The lack of any criteria or common principles has meant that inclusion of specific groups within statutes has occurred on an ad hoc basis; most commonly after significant political pressure by interest groups has led to politicians initiating new laws,[19] or where supranational bodies have worked with member states to promote

---

[8] Jennifer Schweppe and Mark A Walters (eds), *The Globalization of Hate: Internationalizing Hate Crime?* (OUP 2016); Joanna Perry, 'The migration and integration of the hate crime approach in India' (2020) 11(1) Jindal Global Law Rev 7.

[9] Criminal Code (Czech Republic) 2009, art 42.

[10] Criminal Code (Croatia) 1997, art 87(21).

[11] Criminal Code (Estonia) 2001, § 151.

[12] Criminal Code (Chile), art 12(21).

[13] Criminal Code (Peru), art 46.

[14] Criminal Code (Sint Maarten), art. 2:63 with 2:60.

[15] Criminal Code (Angola), art 149.

[16] (Draft) Prevention and Combating of Hate Speech Bill ss.3, 6.

[17] Criminal Code (India), art 153A.

[18] Criminal Code (East Timor), art 52(2)(e). For a list of characteristics covered by jurisdictions globally see Appendix A.

[19] James B Jacobs and Kimberly Potter, *Hate Crimes: Criminal Law and Identity Politics* (OUP 1998); Valerie Jenness and Ryken Grattet, *Making Hate a Crime: From Social Movement to Law Enforcement* (Russell Sage 2001).

international standards in tackling discrimination and inequality.[20] Legislative change has also occurred as a result of high profile "symbolic victims". Matthew Shepard and James Byrd (USA) are a case in point, while in the UK racially aggravated offences were established in the wake of the murder of Stephen Lawrence, a young black man brutally stabbed and killed in central London in 1993.[21]

With victim groups obtaining protection subject to political intervention, it is unsurprising that different jurisdictions include a diverging range of characteristics within their legal codes. The slow and often cumbersome process of legislative change has meant that calls for the inclusion of new characteristics have either been rejected or sometimes ignored.[22] This has resulted in some institutions within criminal justice systems taking it upon themselves to extend the scope of "hate crimes" beyond what has been proscribed by the legislature.[23] What has emerged are different approaches to applying the concept of hate crime, not only across jurisdictions, but within them as well. One major concern with this approach is that the concept is likely to become nebulous. Understanding what hate crime is can therefore be jurisdiction, or even meso-location specific. Furthermore, by continually extending the law to include new groups, questions ultimately arise about whether the potency of hate crime as a distinct type of crime becomes diluted; thereby compounding the uncertainty that already exists amongst the public, as well as those institutions tasked with responding to hate-based offending.[24]

---

[20] Such as the Office for Security and in Europe's human rights agency, the Office for Democratic Institutions and Human Rights. Piotr Godzisz, 'The Europeanization of anti-LGBT hate crime laws in the Western Balkans' (2019) 71 Crime Law Social Ch 291.

[21] Paul Giannasi, 'Hate crimes in the UK' in Hall and others 2015 (see Footnote 2) 105–116.

[22] For example, the Law Commission for England and Wales recommended in 2014 that sexual orientation, disability and transgender identity should be included under the CDA, then six years later in 2020 the Commission conducted a new consultation on hate crime legislation and recommended again that characteristics should be included under the statute. The government has yet to implement its recommendations.

[23] For instance, within the English policing context the College of Policing's (n.d.) guidance on hate crime states, "Agencies and partnerships are free to extend their own policy response to include the hostilities that they believe are prevalent in their area or that are causing the greatest concern to the community".

[24] Neil Chakraborti, Jon Garland and Stevie-Jade Hardy, *The Leicester Hate Crime Project: Findings and Conclusions* (University of Leicester 2014).

Neglected within the extant literature on victim groups has been a discussion on the differences, both in theory and practice, between including identity characteristics under laws that create new substantive hate crime offences, and those which provide for sentencing provisions that create powers for the court to enhance penalties.[25] There has been a tendency within the policy domain to conceptualise hate crimes within a single framework, and to focus on criminological definitions to mark out its boundaries.[26] Yet in order to determine who should be protected by different types of hate crime laws, it is essential to understand why we have such laws. The previous chapter outlined how law as social justice liberalism requires the uncovering of social inequalities that are harmful to entire groups of people. Hate crimes, it is argued, are *distinct* criminal wrongs that have specific individual, community and cultural harms that serve to thwart the interests of entire social groups. The marginalising effects of hate are particularly egregious because they disempower group members, thereby restricting their equal participation in society.

This chapter redraws the boundaries of who ought to be classified as a hate crime victim through the lens of social justice liberalism, as developed in Chaps. 2 and 3. In doing so it challenges current discourse on hate crime victim categories, which has focused predominantly on criminological explanations of hate while failing to adequately synthesise these theoretical frameworks with political and legal theory.[27] It is argued that for hate crime as a concept to survive as a comprehensible legal or criminological concept, it must be firmly grounded in a normative political framework that articulates *why* we as a society ought to criminalise it. From here, we can then set out (broadly defined) criteria that help to create flexibility in the concept's applicability, while maintaining consistency and clarity in its reach. Without a theoretical framework that sets out why we should legislate for hate and what rules are central to its codifica-

---

[25] See detailed discussion in Chap. 5, and examples in Appendix A.
[26] See for example Neil Chakraborti and Jon Garland, 'Reconceptualizing hate crime victimization through the lens of vulnerability and "difference"' (2012) 16 Theo Crim 499.
[27] See exceptions, Chara Bakalis, 'The victims of hate crime and the principles of the criminal law' (2017) 37 LS 718; Jennifer Schweppe, 'Defining characteristics and politicising victims: A legal perspective' (2012) 10 J Hate Stud 173.

tion as a type of crime, the boundaries of the concept will inevitably splinter. As and when this happens, the credibility of the concept and its role in challenging social injustice may be undermined.

4.2 Part 1: Redrawing the Boundaries of Hate Crime: Determining Victim Group Criteria for Criminalisation

The vexed question of who is "deserving" of inclusion under hate crime laws has resulted in a number of differences of opinion in the academic community.[28] One of the first to explore this question was Lawrence who argued that determining which characteristics should be protected in law should be based, firstly, on whether there is a group of people with identifiable members, and secondly whether there is an ideology or "world view", a result of which the group is mistrusted. If the answer is yes to these two questions, legislators must then ascertain whether there is evidence that implicates the group in "social fissure lines"; explained as divisions that run deep into the social fabric and culture of any given society.[29] These divisions are most saliently evidenced by uncovering histories of oppression and persecution that certain groups of individuals have experienced over time.

Such an approach appears, on face value, to be a just way of selecting protected characteristics. However, Chakraborti and Garland have argued that the identification of an exhaustive list of "identity groups" potentially masks the fact that many victims of hate do not belong to a single community and that prejudices will often intersect across identities. Instead, they argue that in understanding who is most susceptible to hate crime victimisation, we should focus our attention on the concepts of "vulnerability" and "difference". Evidence that certain individuals are particularly susceptible to disproportionate levels of abuse and are more vulnerable to its impacts helps us to determine which groups of people

---

[28] For a recent review of the literature on this area, see Bakalis 2017 (ibid.).
[29] Lawrence 1999 (see Footnote 3) 12.

are suffering most from targeted victimisation.[30] Harel and Parchomovsky have previously used a similar approach drawing on what they refer to as the "fair protection paradigm".[31] The paradigm draws on the concept of vulnerability, which depends on the expected costs of crime for a person. Harel and Parchomovsky assert that the "expected costs of crime can be calculated by multiplying the probability of a crime by the size of the harm caused by the crime".[32] They note that the primary challenge for the paradigm is "to determine which differences in the vulnerability of different victims are relevant to the distribution of protection against crime and which are not".[33] They conclude that a comprehensive outline of this is beyond the scope of their paper and it is therefore left unclear what vulnerabilities should be challenged by the criminal law and which ones should not.

Chakraborti and Garland prefer a vulnerability approach to selecting who should be protected under hate crime laws as they argue that it reduces the likelihood of creating hierarchies of hate through designating certain groups as "deserving" of legislative protection, while other victims of targeted abuse fail to gain recognition by the legislature.[34] They go on to highlight how many hate crimes involve factors that are not directly about power and subordination of identity, such as where there is an opportunity to victimise an "easy target", or in situations where individuals lash out in the heat of the moment out of frustration. Chakraborti and Garland argue that by conceptualising hate as a process of subordination relating to power, other types of targeted abuse (e.g. violence against homeless people, or against sub-cultures) can be ignored, while violence within minority groups based on prejudice is also potentially excluded altogether.

Developing this approach further, Mason argues that the current focus on identity groups has allowed victim groups to lobby governments for special inclusion, meaning that those groups with less political capital

---

[30] Chakraborti and Garland 2012 (see Footnote 26). See also Alon Harel and Gideon Parchomovsky, 'On hate and equality' (1999) 109(3) Yale LJ 507.
[31] Harel and Parchomovsky 1999 (ibid.).
[32] Harel and Parchomovsky 1999 (see Footnote 30) 526.
[33] Harel and Parchomovsky 1999 (see Footnote 30) 529.
[34] Chakraborti and Garland 2012 (see Footnote 26).

remain marginalised and unprotected in law. Instead, Mason argues that policy makers must focus on protecting victims who are vulnerable to disproportionate levels of abuse and who can make legitimate claims to "affirmation, equality and respect" based on their "difference"—or what Mason refers to as a "politics of justice".[35] This would entail the legislature firstly identifying groups vulnerable to targeted abuse, and then making an assessment as to which victim groups have a "justifiable or legal claim to social acceptance or state affirmation for the attribute that makes them different", thereby allowing the state to form a "boundary around forms of difference that warrant legal protection".[36]

Other scholars have argued against the use of vulnerability as a key determining factor of hate crime as it places victims in a position of innate weakness. Most closely linked to the theory developed in this book is Al-Hakim's focus on the idea of "disadvantage".[37] By this he means that attention must be paid to whether a group of individuals are experiencing disadvantage in relation to "genuine opportunity for secure functioning".[38] This approach draws on the idea of "development", which relates to the cultivation of "the type of political, social, and economic environment that is conducive for allowing an individual to choose the type of life he or she has reason to value".[39] Those groups who can be classified as experiencing a disadvantage in relation to their claims to political, social and economic freedom have a legitimate claim to special protection under hate crime legislation. In some respects, this approach is similar to Mason's theorisation of vulnerability, difference and the "politics of justice". Both argue that certain groups must be experiencing some form of

---

[35] Gail Mason, 'Victim attributes in hate crime law: Difference and the politics of justice' (2014b) 54 Brit J Criminol 161, 175. Mason argues for example that protection of paedophiles under hate crime laws cannot be justified even if they are vulnerable and perceived to be different as they cannot make a legitimate claim to protection on the basis of equality.

[36] Mason 2014b (ibid.) 176.

[37] Mohamad Al-Hakim, 'Making a home for the homeless in hate crime legislation' (2014) 30 Journal of Interpersonal Violence 1755.

[38] Mohamad Al-Hakim 2014 (ibid.), citing Jonathan Wolff and Avner De-Shalit, *Disadvantage* (OUP 2007) 9.

[39] Al-Hakim 2014 (see Footnote 37) 1174.

targeted victimisation and that they must have a legitimate claim to furthering their claims for "rights" and "social justice". However, diverging from the main claims of this book is that both Al-Hakim and Mason argue that inclusion under hate crime legislation should be untethered from group identity. This it is argued is necessary if we are "to challenge the arbitrary and politicized hierarchy of victimhood".[40]

Linked to claims of rights is the concept of equality. Bakalis argues the principle of equality should be at the heart of determining hate crime victim status. She proposes that the list of characteristics protected in equality law[41] should be replicated in hate crime law as they have "already been identified as requiring the coercive power of the law to eradicate discrimination against them".[42] Bakalis asserts that hate motivation is more morally reprehensible because it purposefully undermines equality in society, which she argues is what gives hate crime its distinctive legal character. Once these characteristics are identified from the "equality enterprise", additional evidence is required to show that individuals with these characteristics are the targets of hate crime; thereby satisfying the principle of minimum criminalisation.[43]

Finally, Schweppe takes the approach to inclusion to its most liberal position, arguing not for the selection of groups based on vulnerability, disadvantage or inequality but instead for any individual to be considered as a victim of hate crime judged on a case by case approach by jurors who can establish victimhood based on whether hostility was directed against the victim because of their personal characteristics, which are linked to an "identifiable social group".[44] Schweppe asserts that where a group of people are experiencing discrimination in society, the law must be flexible in recognising these individuals as potentially being the victims of hate crime. Failure to employ this broader approach risks "the criminal justice system discrimin[ating] arbitrarily between social groups".[45]

---

[40] Mason 2014b (see Footnote 35) 175.
[41] Such as those addressed by the Equality Act 2010 in the UK.
[42] Bakalis 2017 (see Footnote 27) 14.
[43] Bakalis 2017 (see Footnote 27) 735.
[44] Jennifer Schweppe, 'Defining characteristics and politicising victims: A legal perspective' (2012) 10 J Hate Stud 173, 187.
[45] Schweppe 2012 (ibid.) 191.

Each of the contributions to theorising victim protection are valuable to the ongoing debate as to who should be included under hate crime laws. However, while each of the main concepts of equality, vulnerability and disadvantage provide useful insight into the dynamics of targeted victimisation, each have practical and theoretical limitations. I start with why the concept of why equality ought not to be a determinative criterion for inclusion.[46] My rejection of equality as a determinative criterion for inclusion may at first glance appear perplexing to the reader, especially as this book has prefaced the criminalisation of hate as an important mechanism in achieving a more equal society. Yet while this is one of the ultimate aims of criminalising hate, it is argued that such a principle cannot, in and of itself, determine who ought to be included under hate crime law—at least not in terms of enacting substantive hate crime offences.[47] Rather, equality is a guiding principle which must be viewed in relation to the normative position of the criminal law. It is here that the "liberalism" in "social justice liberalism" comes more into focus. This book has so far proffered positive reasoning for criminalisation based on an interpretation of the harm principle which includes social injustice as it manifests through four faces of oppression. It has focused less on liberalism's central tenet of liberty and instead advocated a theory of criminal law that plays an active role in unearthing and transforming social injustices. However, in achieving such an aim, a system of social justice liberalism must ensure that a fair balance is maintained between the rights of individuals to be free from state interference and the rights of groups of people to be free from structural oppression. How then can the criminal law of hate crime strike such a balance?

To begin there must be a differentiation between *guiding* and *determinative* principles in constructing hate crime laws. This is essential considering the consequences that criminalisation can have on individuals who are convicted of a hate crime. The first determinative principle for criminalising hate is tied to one of liberalism's key concepts, that of freedom.

---

[46] Harel and Parchomovsky 1999 (see Footnote 30); Bakalis 2017 (see Footnote 27).

[47] That is laws that create offences in the criminal law marked out as identity-based crimes (e.g. racially aggravated assault). Sentencing provisions that apply to the sentencing stage of the legal process only do not directly "criminalise" hate and therefore may be subject to slightly different theoretical and practical considerations.

Any move towards extending the ambit of substantive hate crime offences in order to account for the wider and intersectional experiences of bias must carefully evaluate the potential consequences of specifically criminalising certain forms of hate-based conduct; not least because these will carry specific criminal labels and potentially enhance penalties. The additional restrictions to freedom that new hate crime offences carry can only be justified where they are balanced against a second determinative principle, that of harm. Even under my extended version of the harm principle as outlined in Chap. 3, the state must evidence the distinct harms that require newly enacted offences. To criminalise conduct based on concepts such as equality alone would be to restrict liberty, not based on evidence of harm, but because "hate crimes" are an affront to principle. In other words, an offender of hate crime could be labelled and punished more (in some cases up to 400 per cent more)[48] for breaching a societal value. While the breaching of liberal principles such as equality may be a guiding principle for recriminalisation, it is argued that the heavy hand of the criminal law ought only ever be used to challenge measurable harms to others.

Such a stance is important within a system of law that aims to protect against overcriminalisation. Conventionally, liberals are "penal minimalists",[49] with criminal law being used as a mechanism of social control of last resort.[50] In protecting the interest of all citizens' liberty, law makers must make use of the law only where all other social methods have been exhausted. While this book advocates a proactive and potentially expansionist vision of criminalisation, the principle of minimal criminalisation remains relevant. This may on first reading sound like somewhat of an oxymoron. To be clear, the aim of this book is to extend the lens through which the criminal law views harm, but within these newly defined boundaries principles of restraint remain central to

---

[48] For example racially aggravated assault under section 29 of the Crime and Disorder Act 1998 (England and Wales) sets a maximum sentence of two years' imprisonment compared with six months for non-bias assault.
[49] Paul Roberts, "Criminal Law Theory and the Limits of Liberalism" in AP Simester, Antje Du Bois-Pedain and Ulfrid Neumann (eds), *Liberal Criminal Theory: Essays for Andreas von Hirsch* (Hart 2014) 339.
[50] Douglas Husak, 'The criminal law as last resort' (2004) 24 OJLS 207.

confining the legal concept of hate crime. Any extension to the criminal law for hate crime must only occur where the legislature is confident that the harms it is proscribing are *distinct* from what is already regulated by criminal rules, and that the mischief that it is attempting to prevent is one that can be effectively prevented by law.

As examined in the previous chapter, legislatures can better understand hate crime's distinct wrongfulness through a lens of social justice that seeks to uncover evidence of group-based oppression, explained as violence, marginalisation, powerlessness and cultural imperialism. In Chap. 3 I outlined the body of research on how hate crimes cause these intersecting forms of social injustice. It was emphasised that hate crimes not only hurt more, but they have distinctive impacts as a result of the physical and symbolic threats that incidents pose to individuals' group identities. It is these threats that predict discrete types of individual, community and cultural harms; many of which relate directly to the victim's identity (e.g. shame, internalised stigma, changing appearance and mannerisms in order to fit in). I argued that it is these harms which thwart the interests of specific groups, thereby restricting their capacity and resources to participate equally in society.

It will likely be that many of the characteristics already protected under a jurisdiction's anti-discrimination (i.e. civil) laws will go arm in arm with their criminal law counterparts (e.g. race, religion, sexual orientation amongst others) as it is likely that those who experience discrimination because of their identity will experience the same types of threats and distinct harms that occur when they are targeted for criminal victimisation. Nevertheless, legislatures must resist simply selecting characteristics based *solely* on whether they have been identified as identity traits that should be protected in civil areas of life. Bakalis arguing on the contrary states that "[i]f a characteristic has been deemed to be sufficiently persecuted or subjugated that it requires civil law protection under the Equality Act 2010, then it is justifiable in principle to extend this protection through the criminal law".[51] However, the civil law requirements to protect against discrimination within certain aspects of social and economic life (such as employment) are not the same mischiefs that the criminal

---

[51] Bakalis 2017 (see Footnote 27) 734.

law is aiming to address. To conflate the civil and criminal law in this way serves to confuse the aims of anti-discrimination laws and hate crime laws, which may have severe consequences on citizens' freedom. While the former may heighten our awareness to likely patterns of discrimination that extend beyond civil life, it cannot automatically provide sufficient evidence that such groups are experiencing the distinct types of harm that I have outlined as being linked to hate crime. For instance, the inclusion of pregnancy within hate crime legislation because it is listed in the Equality Act 2010 would result in new criminal offences with additional penalties being enacted without proper calculation as to whether there is a social issue of pregnancy motivated violence that is resulting in a form of group-based oppression.[52] It is for these reasons that the criminal law must not start from the position of inclusivity and work backwards to justify additional criminalisation and punishment.

Similar limitations apply to the concepts of vulnerability and disadvantage. While each is a laudable attempt in creating a more inclusive and open approach to protecting victims, it is asserted that each fails to give primacy to what makes hate crime a distinct legal and criminological concept: *group identity*. For instance, Chakraborti and Garland's reconceptualisation of hate crime through the lens of "vulnerability" and "difference",[53] as expanded by Mason, seeks to move away from the use of specific identity groups as part of defining hate crime so as to ensure that the concept is more inclusive to the myriad forms of hate-based conduct in society. Although this approach offers a potentially more inclusive method of uncovering the targets of hate and hostility, it is difficult to see how the relationship between vulnerability and "difference" can be properly understood without situating "difference" in the context of group identities. Only through the identification of groups of people who are suffering from targeted abuse can we identify where the targeting of "difference" has become a particular social problem that requires specific

---

[52] Bakalis argues that a further principle of minimum criminalisation would be used to determine whether it is "necessary" for a characteristic that is included in equality legislation be included in hate crime law. Here legislators should ask simply whether people are targeted by criminals on the basis of the particular characteristic in question. Bakalis 2017 (see Footnote 27) 735. Yet this still does not show whether the group experiences distinct harm from being targeted.
[53] Chakraborti and Garland 2012 (see Footnote 26).

criminalisation. Indeed, all of the seemingly extraneous factors that Chakraborti and Garland highlight as frequently being causal to hate incidents do not derogate from the role that group identity plays in targeted victimisation.

It is unsurprising that many of these incidents frequently arise during messy complex interpersonal conflicts that involve multiple causal factors (both personal and situational).[54] Indeed, understanding the complex mix of causal mechanisms will be key to addressing such conflicts and assisting victim recovery.[55] However, in defining an incident as a "hate crime", the group identity of the victim remains central, not only to explaining a pivotal causal element of the offence, but for the purposes of law in understanding the distinct impacts that incidents cause to victims and communities. As I have outlined elsewhere, even where an offender is involved in a messy dispute and lashes out in the heat of the moment, they will be aware, if only fleetingly, that the most potent way to hurt the victim is to denigrate the victim's identity "difference".[56] Indeed, it would take a very unusual situation for an adult offender to be unaware that racist language (e.g.) used during the commission of an offence has a subjugating effect on the victim and others like them. Hence, no matter what the situational context, if an offender chooses to use the victim's identity to denigrate them, they will have engaged in a process that stigmatises someone for being "different".

Ultimately, then, hate crimes are about subordination and power that relates to group identity, whether the conduct involves intentional violence against black or gay people or opportunistic abuse of disabled people because they are seen as an easy target.[57] Any violence or intimidation where someone is abused *because* of their identity reinforces structural processes that serve to marginalise and disempower people because of who they are. Even within some minority groups there will be sub-identities that pertain to power and hegemony within that group. Hate

---

[54] Mark A Walters and Carolyn Hoyle, 'Exploring the everyday world of hate victimisation through community mediation' (2011) 18 Int Rev Vict 7.

[55] Mark A Walters, *Hate Crime and Restorative Justice: Exploring Causes, Repairing Harms* (OUP 2014a).

[56] Mark A Walters, 'Conceptualizing "hostility" for hate crime law: Minding "the minutiae" when interpreting section 28(1)(a) of the Crime and Disorder Act 1998' (2014b) 34 OJLS 47.

[57] Barbara Perry, *In the Name of Hate: Understanding Hate Crimes* (Routledge 2001).

crime is not exclusive to majority group attacks on minority groups in society, but to the "hegemony of the perpetrator's group" towards "usually" marginalised and stigmatised groups.[58] There is little to suggest that hegemonies cannot exist within groups, nor that certain members within it cannot be stigmatised.

A similar limitation occurs in relation to Al-Hakim's use of disadvantage. Although disadvantage illustrates how certain individuals experience structural inequalities which restrict their opportunities for securing functioning, it does not provide an adequate framework for setting out *how* the boundaries of hate crime should be defined. This is because disadvantage does not explain fully how victims of hate crime experience harm *differently* to non-bias offences, other than to suggest victimisation compounds pre-existing social and economic disadvantage. There are many forms of victimisation that compound socio-economic disadvantage. What makes "hate crime" distinct is that this disadvantage occurs because of group identity, and only by examining group identity can we fully comprehend the discrete and myriad ways in which hate-based conduct thwarts the interests of entire groups of people. In other words, while individuals who are targeted because of their vulnerability or who are disadvantaged socially and economically may well be victims of hate crime (e.g. where a perpetrator perceives a victim to be vulnerable or disadvantaged due to a bias towards their group identity), not all targeted victimisation is committed by reason of group identity. Where individuals are targeted for victimisation because of a characteristic that does not make up a group identity it is asserted that they are not a victim of a hate crime. This does not mean targeted victimisation is not worthy of special legislative and policy attention within a system of social justice liberalism, to the contrary. However, not all targeted victimisation should be automatically conflated as "hate crimes", where it is agreed that the purpose of hate crime as a legal concept is to prevent offences that disproportionately affect groups of people *because* of their group identity.

It is worth reemphasising that the vast majority of hate crime victims will be vulnerable to crime and will experience disadvantage as result of it.[59] However, these are concepts that guide our understanding of the

---

[58] Perry (2001) (ibid.).
[59] As explained in Chaps. 2 and 3.

harms of hate, and are not determinative principles for inclusion. In determining what characteristics should be included in hate crime law a liberal polity must start first with protecting individual liberty and only where there are observable harms to others should we turn our attentions to the criminal law.

4.2.1 Criteria for Determining What Characteristics Should Be Included in Hate Crime Laws

The Law Commission for England and Wales has proposed a three-stage test for inclusion of characteristics in hate crime legislation.[60] The first stage is to determine whether there is a "demonstrable need" to include a characteristic based on "evidence of the prevalence of the criminal targeting of the characteristic group based on prejudice or hostility".[61] This is followed by the criterion of "additional harm", requiring "evidence that criminal targeting based on hostility or prejudice towards the characteristic causes additional harm to the victim, members of the targeted group, and society more widely". The final criterion is "suitability", which requires an assessment that inclusion would "prove workable in practice, represent an efficient use of criminal justice resources, and is consistent with the rights of others".[62]

The Commission drew significantly on an unpublished draft of this chapter in determining their criteria.[63] However, several important distinctions remain in my own criteria that are outlined below. Firstly, the Commission rejected the inclusion of "group identity" as a determinative criterion, noting that it is a "difficult concept to assess objectively". While that may be true in some cases, as I have explained above and in Chap. 3, collective identity remains central to understanding what makes hate crime unique. It is no more nebulous than other constituent elements of the phenomenon, including determining what is and is not an "offence", measuring psychological and physical impacts, and determining whether

---

[60] Law Commission, *Hate Crime Laws: Final Report* (Law Com No 402, 2021) 77.
[61] Law Commission (2021) (ibid.).
[62] Law Commission (2021) (ibid.).
[63] Law Commission, *Hate Crime Laws: A Consultation Paper* (Law Com CP No 250, 2020).

someone holds any given characteristic. Without group identity we are unable to properly measure the "additional harms" that the Commission proposes as their second criterion. As I have shown in detail in Chap. 3, it is the collective element of identity which gives rise to the perception of threat that predicts certain emotional and behavioural reactions which are causal to social marginalisation. These are not just "additional" harms but are unique impacts that require careful attention and address. Removing group identity from any equation of defining hate crime, therefore, removes the key element of what makes it a distinct type of crime.

What follows is criteria based on a social justice liberal approach to determining what characteristics ought to be included in hate crime law:

1. *Prevalence*: Is there evidence of hate-based criminal conduct that is being targeted towards individuals because of their "group identity"?

   - In answering this first question, the legislature should ask: is there a shared characteristic amongst individuals that gives rise to a sense of collective identity?
   - Are individuals commonly targeted as victims because of this shared characteristic?

2. *Harm*: Does the hate-based criminal conduct produce a *distinct* type of wrong (beyond that which is already criminalised)?

In answering this second question, a number of sub-questions can be explored:

- Violence:
   - Does the conduct cause enhanced levels of physical or psychological harm to direct victims?
   - Does the conduct cause indirect harms experienced vicariously by other group members?
   - Does the conduct have impacts which are qualitatively different to those of similar non-hate-based wrongs?[64]

---

[64] For example perceptions of threat, emotions such as shame, and behaviours such as avoidant behaviour, changing appearance, ameliorating identity traits to "fit in".

- Marginalisation and powerlessness
    - Does the conduct have the potential to marginalise group members by affecting behaviours that disempower individuals to participate fully in society?
- Cultural imperialism
    - Does the conduct have the potential to cause cultural harm by fostering norms and attitudes that are hostile towards the identity group in question?
- Legal moralism
    - Does the conduct undermine democratic mores and principles such as equality, respect and dignity?

If all or part of these questions are answered in the affirmative, a third question must be settled:

3. *Necessity*: Is it necessary to introduce new laws as a means of preventing/challenging this type of hate?

In answering this question, the legislature should ask:

1. Are there any competing human rights that outweigh the benefits of criminalisation?
2. Are there good reasons to believe criminalisation would have a counter effect?
3. Are there any procedural or practical concerns that outweigh the value of (re)criminalisation?[65]

---

[65] For example laws may already be in place that target a specific type of targeted crime, such as sexual offences, or the offence of coercive and controlling behaviour (i.e. domestic violence). The Law Commission for England and Wales has recommended exclusion of gender or sex hostility in hate crime legislation based on concerns that it would over-complicate these already complex laws, thereby potentially reducing further the conviction rates of gendered crimes. Law Commission (2021) (see Footnote 60) 201–204.

Legislatures must endeavour to answer most if not all of these main questions before adding "characteristics" to substantive hate crime offences.

The criteria do not require that a characteristic relate to a minority group nor that it is immutable to the group's members. Legislators must be alive to the fact that group-based oppression can occur regardless of whether an identity is unchangeable or that members of the group are small or large in size.[66] In some jurisdictions minority racial groups may hold dominant social, political and economic positions, meaning majority ethnic groups remain most prone to the harms of oppression.[67] Even within nations where racial or ethnic majority status provides certain social privileges, some individuals located in socio-economically deprived communities can still become vulnerable to victimisation due to their ethnicity, religious beliefs or gender.[68]

Whether hate crime laws should apply in the contexts of a majority group victim can be determined by reference to the criterion of harm and group identity. For example, the decision to protect against disablist crime can be determined based on evidence that disability can make up part of an individual's group identity, which when targeted gives rise to distinct harms. This can be compared to non-disabled people who are not commonly targeted because of their identity, and if they were targeted because of this the effects would not give rise to the distinct harms of social injustice. A more inclusive and flexible approach may be needed for some characteristics (such as race and ethnicity) whereby group-based oppression may occur between and within communities.

---

[66] For example, the subjugation of women through misogyny can be referred to as the minoritisation of women: Marian Duggan and Hannah Mason-Bish, 'A feminist theoretical exploration of misogyny and hate crime' in Irene Zempi and Jo Smith, *Misogyny as hate crime* (Routledge 2021); Mark Austin Walters and Jessica Tumath, 'Gender "Hostility", Rape, and the Hate Crime Paradigm' (2014) 77(4) MLR 563.

[67] See for example the racial history of South Africa.

[68] Mark Austin Walters, 'Why the Rochdale Gang Should Have Been Sentenced as "Hate Crime" Offenders' [2013] 2 Crim LR 131.

4.3 Part 2: Evidencing Distinct Harms: In Defence of Identity Politics

Central to the endeavour of (re)criminalising hate will be evidencing its distinct harms. The magnitude of harm caused by conduct is often difficult to measure.[69] One of the most cogent ways of evidencing the harms of hate has been through an historical exposition of the systematic and institutional abuse endured by certain groups of people.[70] Some of the most salient examples of such histories have been: anti-black racism, including racial segregation, discrimination and violence going back to slavery and beyond; antisemitic persecution, including the genocide of Jews during WWII; widespread Islamophobia and the rise in Islamophobic attacks post 9/11; the criminalisation of homosexuality and torturous treatment of LGB people (including during the Holocaust); the acknowledgement of pervasive targeted victimisation or killing of disabled people (including during the Holocaust); and, more recently, the social isolation, stigma and vitriolic abuse experienced by transgender individuals.[71]

There need not be a long or deep history of hate and hostility against a group of individuals, but it will be important that there is evidence to show that certain groups are being subjected to sustained and pervasive forms of targeted victimisation. The Law Commission for England and Wales has suggested that prevalence can be determined by assessing data on: "absolute prevalence", that is the total amount of criminal behaviour that is targeted based on hostility or prejudice towards the characteristic; by "relative prevalence", that is the amount of criminal behaviour that is targeted based on hostility or prejudice towards the characteristic, as compared with the size of the group who share the characteristic;[72] or by

---

[69] Harel and Parchomovsky 1999 (see Footnote 30) 527.
[70] Lawrence 1999 (see Footnote 3).
[71] See Neil Chakraborti and Jon Garland, *Hate Crime: Impacts, Causes and Responses* (Sage 2015) for an outline of the historical contexts of all of these.
[72] This would represent a relative estimate of prevalence and would capture the proportionate frequency of criminal targeting.

"severity", that is identifying whether certain social groups experience more severe types of crime, such as violence with injury, compared with the general population.[73]

Measurement will not be an exact science. Large quantitative surveys and intricate experiments, using longitudinal design and control groups, while highly useful are by no means necessary in evidencing these three types of prevalence. Evidence can come from multiple domestic and international sources. Politicians, civil society groups, NGOs, academics and the general public all have an important role to play in this regard.[74] Public consultations,[75] parliamentary inquiries, All-Party Parliamentary Groups Inquiries, criminal justice inspections, NGO reports, academic research, the lobbying efforts of interest groups and the work of journalists are all vital in uncovering the various forms of oppression that pervade every corner of society. Indeed, the European Court of Human Rights has consistently held that information provided by NGOs on the risks of targeted crimes against specific communities should be used by state authorities to help prevent incidents from occurring.[76] The collective work of all of these stakeholders in evidencing the harms of hate need not occur within single locations. Evidence collated internationally by supranational bodies provides tangible and comparative information that reveals the nature and dynamics of hate that will be directly relevant to individual jurisdictions.[77] Indeed the globalisation of the concept of hate crime means that there is now an expansive body of research work produced by international NGOs[78] and academics working across international networks that provides a cogent evidence base from which legislatures globally can draw from.[79]

---

[73] Law Commission 2020 (see Footnote 63) 197.

[74] Joanna Perry, 'A shared global perspective on hate crime?' (2015) 27(6) Crim Just Policy Rev 610.

[75] Such as those recently completed by the Law Commission for England and Wales; Northern Ireland, Scotland and Ireland.

[76] See for example *Identoba and Others v. Georgia* App no 73235/12 (ECtHR, 12 May 2015), cited also in Joanna Perry, 'The migration and integration of the hate crime approach in India' (2020) 11(1) Jindal Global Law Rev 7.

[77] See for example the extensive evidence on hate crime produced by the European Agency for Fundamental Rights (FRA); and the OSCE's Office for Democratic Institutions and Human Rights.

[78] See for example the work of Human Rights Watch.

[79] See for example the International Network for Hate Studies, extensive library of research.

Civil society groups and NGOs, both domestic and international, have in particular been key to highlighting the experiences of marginalised groups in society.[80] The coalescence of groups of people by identity traits who collectively campaign for civil rights is commonly referred to as identity politics. Such groups were pivotal to the enactment of hate crime legislation both in the US and UK during the 1980s and 1990s.[81] Some commentators were heavily critical of the way in which these interest groups helped to shape hate crime legislation.[82] Early critics of identity politics commonly asserted that the focus on identity was divisive and stifled free speech preventing mainstream commentators from criticising overly sensitive racial minority groups. Walters highlights how leading sceptics of identity politics were primarily white straight men who typically cited other white straight men in their lambasting of its so-called invidious effect on the liberal polity.[83] We may well wish to give pause on the cogency of a line of critique about minority group politics where the overwhelming criticism comes primarily from hegemonic elites.

Notwithstanding the "political correctness gone mad" brigade that has so often vociferously denounced the attempts of interest groups to highlight minority group experiences of oppression, there have been scathing criticism of identity politics from the left.[84] Criticism of identity politics has also appeared within the field of hate studies itself.[85] Several scholars have highlighted how certain identity-based lobby groups have garnered political power that has enabled them to pressure legislatures to make changes to the law, leaving those groups with less political clout without a voice.[86] Mason has noted how those groups that can evoke the most

---

[80] Rosalind Brunt, 'The politics of identity' in Stuart Hall and Martin Jacques (eds), *New Times: The Changing Face of Politics in the 1990s* (Lawrence & Wishart 1989) 150–159.
[81] Jacobs and Potter 1998 (see Footnote 19); Jenness and Grattet 2001 (see Footnote 19).
[82] See for example Jacobs and Potter 1998 (see Footnote 19).
[83] Suzanna D Walters, 'In Defense of Identity Politics' (2018) 43(2) Signs 473.
[84] Steve Hall and Simon Winlow, *Revitalizing Criminological Theory: Towards a New Ultra-Realism* (Routledge 2015).
[85] Zoë James, *The Harms of Hate for Gypsies and Travellers: A Critical Hate Studies Perspective* (Palgrave 2020).
[86] Neil Chakraborti, 'Framing the boundaries of hate crime' in Hall and others 2015 (see Footnote 2) 13–23; Hannah Mason-Bish, 'Beyond the silo: Rethinking hate crime and intersectionality' in Hall and others (see Footnote 2) 24–33; Gail Mason, 'The symbolic purpose of hate crime law: Ideal victims and emotion' (2014a) 18 Theo Crim 75; Jen Neller, 'The need for new tools to break the silos: Identity categories in hate speech legislation' (2018) 7 Int J Crim Just Soc Democr 75.

compassion from the broader public are likely to be granted special victim status, while others that struggle to gain credence as to their personal experience of vulnerability, or who appear too "strange or distant", have struggled to gain legislative protection. This, she asserts, has "led to the emergence of a judgemental hierarchy of victimisation that narrowly defines which groups count as legitimate hate crime victims, leaving some victims of targeted violence out in the cold".[87]

This hierarchical outcome for group inclusion, it is argued, has ultimately meant that some vulnerable groups have been excluded from the hate crime paradigm. Even where groups are included, this does not necessarily mean that identity "difference" is accepted by dominant hegemonies. Neller notes that identity politics has produced "subjects through identity categories, which can be criticised for reinforcing problematic distinctions… [that] classify everyone in relation to a singular biased standard (white, able-bodied, heterosexual, cisgender, male, citizen, and so on)".[88] This, she asserts, risks groups being marked as "others", who require special measures in order to be treated equally with those who occupy the centre of society. The danger is that applying liberal norms of equality (as a form of sameness) may result in marginalised groups being brought into the political fold only for them to conform to the identities of the dominant group.[89] In other words, one must question whether identity politics challenges the maintenance of the status quo, or simply brings a group on the periphery inwards.

The development of identity politics as a method of both identifying social injustice experienced by certain groups and mobilising communities to demand change has certainly not been without an abundance of critics.[90] One must question, though, where would these marginalised groups be without the capacity to coalesce and demand equal participation,

---

[87] Mason 2014a (ibid.) 79.

[88] Neller 2018 (see Footnote 86) 78.

[89] Such as where gay people are given equal access to marriage, which may be viewed as an historically heterosexual and patriarchal institution. See for example Claudia Card, 'Gay divorce: Thoughts on the legal regulation of marriage' (2007) 22 Hypatia 24.

[90] See for example Wendy Brown, *States of Injury: Power and Freedom in Late Modernity* (Princeton UP 1995), who argues that group political identities that are founded in reaction to marginalisation are often interested in promulgating their own subordination because their very existence as an identity group depends on it. See also James 2020 (see Footnote 85).

not just as formal but as substantive equality? The reality is that social movements matter.[91] Way before neoliberal ideology captured the political imagination, identity was central to the civil rights movements of the twentieth century, from race equality, LGBT+ pride, to first wave feminism. More recently, the Black Lives Matters movement that began in the US and the global #MeToo movement have brought to the fore the marginalising experiences faced by people of colour and women alike, and in turn have resulted in changes to law, policy as well as the knowledge and perceptions of broader society.

The grass root groups that fuel these movements participate in a democratic process that represents the needs and experiences of some of the most marginalised groups in order to create social change. This process is ongoing and not without its own limitations. For instance, social movements that ignore diversity and intersectionality within the groups that they attempt to lift up risk perpetuating, rather than changing, the isolation of the least powerful.[92] Human suffering occurs where people are ignorant of each other's socially constructed experiences of the world. It is this lack of understanding and empathy about other people's experiences that leads to hate and prejudice towards certain groups that are seen only for their "difference". Social groups must remain sensitised not only to their own suffering but to that which is connected to multiple and intersecting identities. Melo reflects "[w]hen it comes to unravelling and attempting to remedy the subjective elements of human suffering, we are necessarily reliant on the experience of others when we have not experienced something ourselves".[93]

The solution to reducing hate-based conduct is not to strip people of their identity, in the hope that all people will come together and see each other only for their humanity. On our journey towards a post racial, sexual identity and gender society there is still much learning to be done on the role that identity plays in people's lived experiences of the world.

---

[91] See for example Christie L Parris and Heather L Scheuerman, 'How Social Movements Matter: Including Sexual Orientation in State-Level Hate Crime Legislation' (2015) 38 Res Soc Mov Confl Change 229.

[92] See for example Alison Phipps, *Me, Not You: The Trouble with Mainstream Feminism* (Manchester UP 2020).

[93] Dan Melo, 'The Case for Identity Politics' Areo (23 October 2018) 4.

Bridging empathic divides between groups of people cannot be achieved solely by focusing on our shared humanity, for it remains the case that identity shapes our experiences of being human. Identity politics thus helps to ensure that disparities in treatment, including disproportionate experiences of violence and abuse, are brought into focus and that the stories of those who suffer are shared across society.

Important to this endeavour is that identity difference is not only understood but celebrated as an important aspect of social liberal society. Identity politics has not remained static in this regard. In the latter part of the twentieth-century identity politics moved beyond calls for equality as assimilation, to that of acceptance and celebration of "difference". Kruks reflects:

> what makes identity politics a significant departure from earlier, preidentarian forms of the politics of recognition is its demand for recognition on the basis of the very grounds on which recognition has previously been denied: it is *qua* women, *qua* blacks, *qua* lesbians that groups demand recognition… The demand is not for inclusion within the fold of "universal humankind", on the basis of shared human attributes; nor is it for respect "in spite of" one's differences. Rather, what is demanded is respect for oneself *as* different.[94]

Young concurs with this view, arguing for a politics of difference that should be understood as resisting unjust structural inequalities through the assertion of cultural pluralism. While early identity-based interest groups campaigned for recognition of rights on the basis that minority individuals were no different from everyone else, civil rights movements have quickly progressed to demand recognition of difference.[95] Young explains that the very process of political organisation to fight institutional discrimination and societal prejudice during the 1960s and 1970s fostered cultural expression through action, such as group meetings, literature, music and street celebrations. She provides the example of how lesbian and gay liberation sought not merely equal rights but the affirmation of

---

[94] Sonia Kruks, *Retrieving Experience: Subjectivity and Recognition in Feminist Politics* (Cornell UP 2001) 85.

[95] Iris Marion Young, *Justice and the Politics of Difference* (Princeton UP 2011) ch 6.

lesbian and gay people as communities of people with distinct needs and experiences. The birth of gay pride marches in the Global North unashamedly celebrated LGB culture as political difference, and not merely as different behaviour. It continues to do so to this very day, becoming globalised and ever more inclusive of different LGBT+ identities.

Myriad other movements engage in rights advocation as cultural and political plurality, whether that be the transnational SlutWalks of the early 2010s, the Black Lives Matter campaigns of the mid-2010s, or the #MeToo movement in the latter 2010s. Each bring to the body politic a demand for rights and destigmatisation through an unapologetic expression of difference that challenges the acceptance of dominant norms that marks individuals out as deviant others. These movements express identity, not as essentialist characteristics, but as relational traits that are marked out as "different" based on situational and contextual variables.[96] That is to say that the politics of difference, as it relates to group identity, is not about essentialising a common bodily characteristic that is deserving of respect; rather it is engaged in demonstrating how otherness is constructed through hegemonic norms that operates to oppress certain communities. Thus, the fight is not to be accepted as "normal" vis-à-vis dominant cultural identity, but to create spaces in liberal society that embrace cultural and identity-based diversity.

The involvement of identity groups in the development of hate crime law forms part of an inclusive democratic process that involves identifying the inequalities in society based on group differences in order to bring about social change. The role of interest groups in identifying and mobilising difference is, I believe, central to the betterment of a liberal polity that is focused on promoting social justice. The process of advancing social justice must be a discursive one. It is only by engaging in meaningful intergroup contact that we can expect our (political) neighbours to really see us.

This is not to suggest that identity politics is without legitimate criticism. However, its main problems lie not in its conceptual framework as a force for change, but in the way it *might* ultimately be practised; or perhaps more accurately the way certain governing structures force it to be played out. A neoliberal politics that focuses on competing interests in

---

[96] Young 2011 (ibid.).

advancing human interest produces a political environment that forces interest groups to compete with each other for resources.[97] Such a situation benefits no-one and can result in a zero-sum game where little is gained beyond a sense of resentment that some groups have more than others. However, in reality, identity politics rarely plays out in such a crude way. Within the US and UK context, interest groups are constantly engaged in work that highlights the experiences of myriad victimised groups. They coalesce to inform policy makers, they share resources and they lobby governments to ensure that group-based needs are recognised and catered for in practical ways. For example, the Independent Advisory Group on Hate Crime to the UK Government is made up of representatives from civil society organisations from across multiple group-based organisations. This group plays a pivotal role in shaping the Government's Hate Crime Action Plan which sets out the aims and objectives of the government in tackling hate crime. The London Mayor's Office for Policing and Hate Crime Stakeholder Reference Group has a similar makeup,[98] as does the Crown Prosecution Service's Hate Crime External Consultative Group.

Rather than competing for "rights", these groups have worked together to create social change, most prominently by highlighting individual group experiences of oppression *and* the common needs of different marginalised groups. They too frequently illuminate how intersectional experiences of hate crime require an understanding of hate and prejudice as involving multiple identities. The result of these groups has been manifold. For instance, the Hate Crime Stakeholder Reference Group has seen changes to the ways in which hate is tackled outside the framework of punitive hate crime laws, including new programmes using restorative solutions to address hate crime.[99] Other charities are working on generating counter narrative work on social media platforms to challenge hate

---

[97] James 2020 (see Footnote 85).
[98] Previously called the London Hate Crime Reduction Board.
[99] Mayor's Office for Policing and Crime (MOPAC), *A Hate Crime Reduction Strategy For London 2014–2017* (MOPAC 2014).

speech online, while several organisations have worked with justice agencies on education work.[100]

This is not to suggest that identity politics as participatory policy making is perfect. The role of interest groups on these consultative groups is subject to political actors remaining supportive of minority group participation in public policy making. Nonetheless, the identity-based model developed most prominently in the UK where civil society organisations are invited to participate in public policy decision making for hate crime has clearly become an effective tool to promote social equality. It has achieved this by emphasising the needs of identity difference which has in turn been reflected in policy and law. Such participatory processes, far from paying lip service to the needs of oppressed groups, are actively challenging the cultural imperialism that has been traditionally maintained through conservative forms of governance.

4.3.1 What Is the Alternative to Identity Politics?

Those who are quick to denounce the role that these identity-based interest groups play in shaping hate crime law and policy have offered very little by way of a fairer alternative to legally recognising individuals as "hate crime" victims. Those alternative approaches that have been proffered suggest that rather than groups being given "special protection", the government should simply legislate to ensure that an open-ended or non-exhaustive list of identities or prejudices are covered by law.[101] However, this would ultimately mean that either (mainly white male) judges will be left to interpret what is "hate crime", or a selection of 12 lay jurors. For example, as discussed above, Schweppe argues that jurors could determine, case by case, whether a crime was committed against the victim on the basis of a "defining characteristic".[102] She asserts that "[t]he criminal

---

[100] See Mark Austin Walters and Rupert Brown, *Preventing Hate Crime: Emerging Practices and Recommendations for the Improved Management of Criminal Justice Interventions* (University of Sussex 2016).

[101] See examples below.

[102] Jennifer Schweppe, 'Defining characteristics and politicising victims: A legal perspective' (2012) 10 J Hate Stud 173, 187.

law has proven itself capable of identifying core personal characteristics through the operation of the defence of provocation".[103] This, she argues, means that jurors are already called upon to make decisions about identity characteristics in criminal cases. Though this is a laudable attempt at making hate crime law more inclusive, a distinction must be made between a jury's role in applying defences in criminal law and theories of criminalisation and the labelling of offences. While juries may have a legitimate role in determining whether a defence in law applies based on the facts (which may include considering a defendant's characteristics), it does not necessarily follow that jurors, as finders of fact, should be left with an open-ended remit to decide when a basic criminal offence should become a "hate crime" (unless there is a specific law, e.g. racially aggravated assault, that they can apply the facts to). Under such an approach, juries would not be determining whether hostility is an aggravating factor that affects sentence (as judges frequently do in hate crime cases), they would be making decisions as to which individuals they believe should be labelled as a hate crime offender in *law*. If a jury is left to decide which hostilities should give rise to a conviction of hate crime, they would in effect be reclassifying criminal offences—most likely without consistency across different juries. Jurors must only ever apply the law to the facts; they must not take on the role of determining the ambit of the criminal law. That role surely must be left to the legislature.

Furthermore, it is difficult to see how either judge or jury would provide for a more meaningful or inclusive approach to addressing hate crime than identity politics has enabled. On the contrary, judges and jurors are unlikely to receive sufficient information that enables them to comprehend the histories of targeted abuse that certain groups suffer. This is likely to result in juries only applying the provisions to types of hostility that they are most familiar with.[104]

---

[103] Schweppe 2012 (ibid.) 185.

[104] For instance, research by Saucier et al. found that mock jurors (psychology students that were given specific hate-based scenarios) were ready to recognise racial hate crime against non-White people but unwilling to see crimes against women as hate crimes. Donald A Saucier and others, 'Effects of Victims' Characteristics on Attitudes Toward Hate Crimes' (2006) 21 J Interpers Violence 890.

Rights and protections are long fought for, and identity politics remains not only a pivotal part of identifying those most in need of legislative protection but is key to an ongoing conversation between policy makers and justice practitioners as to the evolving needs and experiences of marginalised groups of people. It is true that in many cases prejudices will intersect and the law must be flexible enough to respond to such situations.[105] But in developing flexibility, let us not throw the baby out with the bath water. Six million Jews were murdered during the Holocaust because they were Jewish; 100,000s more were murdered for being disabled. 100,000 more men were imprisoned or sent to concentration camps for being gay. These histories live on, with many thousands of people targeted for being Jewish, disabled and gay every year. It is important that these histories of structural persecution be recognised and specifically challenged by the law.

If some groups have not been included within the scope of hate crime laws because their experiences have been ignored, then politicians, civil society, interest groups and academia must work to give voice to these individuals.[106] One problem with this approach to re-criminalising hate crime is that it is likely to attract the same criticisms levelled against the current framework of laws that it is creating another "hierarchy of hate" within the law.[107] That is to say, the current protected characteristics and any other characteristics which meet the criteria would be additionally protected by the criminal law, while other types of "hate crime"—yet to provide sufficient evidence of pervasiveness and additional harm—would fall only under the "basic" offences, and thus treated less seriously.[108] This is an unfortunate consequence of the way that liberal criminal law works for all conduct. Criminalisation ought to start from the position of protecting individual freedom unless there is evidence that the actions of one person harm those of others. It is the case that all criminal offences (hate-based or not) should meet a certain threshold of wrongfulness before

---

[105] See recommendation in the section 'Characteristics that fall outside of the legislative framework' below.

[106] Joanna Perry, 'A shared global perspective on hate crime?' (2015) 27 Crim Just Policy Rev 610.

[107] Mark A Walters, Abenaa Owusu-Bempah and Susann Wiedlitzka, 'Hate Crime and the "Justice Gap": The Case for Law Reform' [2018] 12 Crim LR 961.

[108] Walters, Owusu-Bempah and Wiedlitzka 2018 (ibid.).

being legally proscribed. If hate crime legislation is to be maintained as a form of specific criminalisation that carries a potent symbolic message of denunciation, it is essential that evidence of specific and distinct harms experienced by a group of individuals is considered by the legislature before each characteristic is included under the law. This does not mean that other people targeted for victimisation should be ignored by the criminal justice system. Rather it may simply mean that some forms of "targeted victimisation" do not fall within the ambit of hate crime legislation.

4.4 Conclusion

The development of laws enacted in response to hate-based offending has occurred in a fragmented and piecemeal fashion which has meant that different groups have been included based largely on political pressures and in the aftermath of the emergence of symbolic victims. The search for a single theoretical framework to determine the inclusion of victim groups remained elusive. Within hate studies scholarship, theorisation of who should be included has been developed predominantly through reference to principles such as equality, disadvantage and vulnerability. Yet few have attempted to synthesise these values and concepts with theories of criminalisation and principles of the criminal law. This is a significant omission given that it is the criminal law that ultimately determines what conduct is a "hate crime". Law as social justice liberalism aims to synthesise political, legal and criminological theory in order to provide a more comprehensive understanding of hate crime, and how the law can properly regulate hate-based conduct. Failure to fully acknowledge the limits of criminalisation risks undermining fundamental principles of liberal democracy.

The desire for inclusion to recognise differing types of prejudice as potentially harmful must not come at the expense of undermining these key principles. In determining which victim groups should be protected under any hate crime law, it is first essential to comprehend the types of harm that are caused by such conduct, that is violence, marginalisation, powerlessness and cultural imperialism, for it is these harms that give hate crime its distinct character. The connecting factor in each of the multilayered harms of hate crime is group identity—both in relation to causation and individuals' reactions and responses to it. It is by understanding that hate crime is an attack on group identity that we are able to more fully comprehend its distinct harms and, in turn, its boundaries as a concept. This does not mean intersecting identities and incidents involving multiple causal factors should be prohibited from the umbrella term of hate crime within criminology or criminal law. Rather it is to remain attuned to the fact that even in the most complex and multifaceted cases of hate-based victimisation, victims' group-based identities remain central to our understanding of what makes a crime a "hate crime".

# 5

Legislating for Hate Crime Globally: Putting "Social Justice" Into Practice, Part 1

5.1 Introduction

Understanding why states ought to criminalise hate crimes and who should be protected by law is fundamental to determining how legislation should be enacted. If legislatures are to truly address the harms of hate crime it is incumbent upon them to devise laws that adequately reflect its distinct wrongfulness. As such, effectively challenging hate, and its egregious harms, requires laws that are constructed in ways that make their application both expeditious and impactful in preventing hate. Without careful deliberation on how such laws should be prescribed there is a risk that statute books will be left to gather dust. Indeed, where hate crime laws are enacted but rarely applied, the symbolic and practical utility of the criminal law will be lost.

5.2 Approach to Data Collection

In this chapter I provide an outline of the different types of hate crime laws that have been enacted globally, as well as a narrower comparative analysis of how legislation is being interpreted and applied across UK and some European jurisdictions. The collation of a global list of hate crime legislation involved extensive searches (and browsing) on legal databases (including subscription: Westlaw, and free: Legislationline and WorldLII) and individual parliamentary websites to identify and then code laws into both "types" and "models".[1] Where legislature websites were poorly maintained further searches were conducted via Google for news items and NGO media reports on new legislation. A number of search terms and Boolean queries using wildcard characters were added to search engines, including: "hate", "bias", "hatred", "prejudice", "contempt", "intoleran*", "discriminat*". This was followed up with searches for likely protected characteristics including: "race", "raci*", "relig", "ethnic*", "orientation" and "trans*".

These terms were then translated into different languages using Google Translate, a multilingual neural machine translation service, and the same searches were conducted on search engines and country legislation websites globally. Laws identified in languages where there was no formal English translation[2] were then professionally translated by translators employed through the Sussex Centre for Language Studies to ensure accuracy when deciphering the types and models of legislation. Searches covered six continents and hate crime legislation was uncovered from all regions.[3] The process of identification was refined gradually as statutes were reviewed and coded.

Deciding which laws had created "hate crime provisions" involved the use of criteria that were shaped by the theoretical framework of this book. Laws were selected based on:

1. whether a provision includes a hate-element (e.g. bias, hostility), that is connected to at least one criminal offence and to specified characteristics, and/or residual group traits, or

---

[1] "Type" refers to area of law and way in which legislation is enacted (e.g. criminal law versus sentencing provisions), while "model" refers to the manner (e.g. legal tests used) in which the legislation proscribes hate-based conduct. See Appendix A. Models are examined in Chap. 6.

[2] Many jurisdictions provide English language versions of statutes/codes, while the OSCE website https://www.legislationline.org/ also provides for many English translations of legislation. Further checks for updated versions of laws listed on this website were carried out via parliamentary websites.

[3] Excluding Antarctica.

5 Legislating for Hate Crime Globally: Putting "Social Justice"... 129

2. where a provision specifies group characteristics that were connected to the commission of the offence,[4] or
3. where the conduct was a criminal manifestation of identity-based prejudice, and/or where specific conduct proscribed was by its very nature, and within the context it is committed, an expression of hate (e.g. drawing of swastikas on public buildings).[5]

Focus was given to legislation that aims to protect against prejudice and targeted victimisation that has the effect of marginalising already stigmatised groups of people. Hence, legislation that specifically criminalised the desecration of religious buildings was excluded from this comparative list where the aim of the legislation, historically, was the maintenance of the dominant religious domination of the state. Statutes that have been enacted (amended) that protect minority religious groups and their institutions were included based on this theoretical framework.

There were significant limitations to the coding process due to limited language skills, technological limitations of translations and the subjective decisions that were made relating to what laws are "hate crime" laws. Therefore, this chapter should only be read as providing an approximation of the different types of hate crime laws used globally; as framed within the book's theoretical lens. The book does not provide an exhaustive list of legislation. Moreover, it has not been possible to gain in-depth expertise of all 190 legal jurisdictions researched for this book. The legal systems used across the world are diverse, and while many commonalities exist between common law and civil law jurisdictions, there will be vast divergences in the manner in which legal frameworks are applied in practice; as they are affected by history, culture and systems of political governance. This means the categorisations that follow must be treated with some caution. While legislation was read carefully and coded based on criteria as set out above, the way in which laws might be applied in practice may differ to how the laws are described below.

---

[4] Note that gender-based crimes were only included in the study where an offence specified an element of animus (e.g. gender hostility or misogyny) or where a provision specified that the offence was committed by reason of sex/gender/gender identity.

[5] Though it should be noted that the drawing of swastikas is not an objective expression of hate, much depends on the context and way it is drawn; as per its use in Hinduism, for example, where it is often used in decoration as part of Diwali.

5.3 Types of Hate Crime Legislation

Since the first enactment of modern hate crime laws in the US, countries across the globe have followed suit in legislating to combat hate-based offences. As was noted in the Introduction to this book, the proliferation of hate crimes has been facilitated through international law and by intergovernmental organisations. The Office for Democratic Institutions and Human Rights (ODIHR), part of the Organization for Security and Co-operation in Europe (OSCE), has been particularly impactful in facilitating the internationalisation of sentence uplifts for hate crime. ODIHR assists its 57 member states "to promote democracy, rule of law, human rights and tolerance and non-discrimination".[6] In 2009 it produced a practical guide on implementing hate crime laws, after member states had agreed at a previous council meeting to combat "crimes motivated by intolerance towards certain groups in society".[7] Goodall identifies Moldova, Bosnia and Herzegovina, and Macedonia as jurisdictions where ODIHR's work has been "decisive" in shaping their domestic legislation for hate crime.[8] Although ODIHR does not officially recommend a single preferred approach to legislating for hate crime, it has—as noted by Godzisz—conducted law reviews for jurisdictions where it has recommended sentence uplift provisions.[9]

Given the internationalisation of hate crime and the active work of intergovernmental agencies in this area it is perhaps unsurprising that the study identified 138 countries, territories and dependencies that have legislated against hate crime.[10] Within some countries there are multiple legal jurisdictions where different hate crime laws have been enacted, for example the US has 50 state jurisdictions plus oversea territories and tribal laws enacted in indigenous reservations. As a result, just over 190

---

[6] https://www.osce.org/odihr/what-we-do, accessed 4 December 2021.
[7] OSCE/ODIHR, *Hate Crime Laws: A Practical Guide* (OSCE/ODIHR 2009); OSCE, Ministerial Council Decision No. 4/03 (OSCE December 2003).
[8] Kay Goodall, 'Conceptualising "racism" in criminal law' (2013) 33 LS 215, 216); see also Piotr Godzisz, 'The Europeanization of anti-LGBT hate crime laws in the Western Balkans' (2019) 71 Crime Law Social Ch 291.
[9] Recommended to Macedonia, Godzisz 2019 (ibid.).
[10] A sample of these is set out in Appendix A.

5 Legislating for Hate Crime Globally: Putting "Social Justice"...

separate legal jurisdictions were identified globally that had enacted hate crime laws. There has by no means been a uniform method of enacting these laws. As we will see below the enactment of such offences can be achieved in numerous ways, while multiple types of hate crime laws are used within many jurisdictions.[11]

Three main types of hate crime legislation were identified within this study, along with four sub-categories. These are categorised as follows:

1. *Substantive offences*: based on whether the legal provision created a stand-alone criminal offence on a statute book or in a penal code. Substantive offences require evidence of a hate-element as a constitutive element of the proscribed crime. Two sub-types of substantive offences were identified:

   - *Aggravated offences*—where a new law creates an aggravated version of a basic offence (e.g. "racially aggravated assault").
   - *Conduct-based offences*—either, where a new law creates a specific crime that does not have a parallel offence because it is by its very nature hate-based (e.g. drawing Nazi symbols on public building). Or, where a crime technically has a parallel offence but the aggravated version of it can only be committed through the hate-element (e.g. use of threatening and abusive language that is racially aggravated).[12]

2. *Sentence uplifts*: based on whether legal provisions provided powers to increase punishments at the sentencing stage of the criminal process. Most sentence uplifts do not relabel the basic offence in law or require

---

[11] See Appendix A. Note that other scholars have applied slightly different categories based on analyses of either a single jurisdiction or small number of countries, see for example Gail Mason, 'Hate crime laws in Australia: are they achieving their goals?' (2009) 33(6) Crim LJ 326; James B Jacobs and Kimberly Potter, *Hate Crimes: Criminal Law and Identity Politics* (OUP 1998) ch 3, who categorise statutes into four types: sentence enhancements, substantive crimes, civil rights statutes and reporting statutes; Lawrence who divides statutes into two categories, "pure bias crimes" and "penalty-enhancement laws", Frederick M Lawrence, *Punishing Hate: Bias Crimes under American Law* (Harvard UP 1999) 92; and the OSCE guide which similarly asserts that there are two types, "substantive offences and "penalty enhancement provisions", OSCE/ODIHR 2009 (see Footnote 7).

[12] Explained more fully below under 2.2.

evidence of a hate-element to prove guilt of a specific criminal offence. However, one sub-type does allow for the hate-element to form part of the particulars of a charge and if proved may be recorded upon conviction.

- *Sentence aggravation*—where provisions provide powers to the court to aggravate sentence but not beyond the pre-existing sentencing maxima for the basic offence. These can give full discretion to a sentencer to determine the penalty or provide prescriptive ranges/levels for them to apply.
- *Penalty enhancements*—where provisions provide powers to the court to sentence beyond pre-existing sentencing maxima for basic offences. These can apply to all or a sub-type of criminal offences.

3. *Hybrid laws*: these take elements of substantive offences and either/or sentence aggravation or penalty enhancements. Legislation typically enables prosecutors to charge a criminal offence and additionally include on the charge that it is an "aggravated offence" or a "hate crime", which then requires the hate-element to be proved at trial (as against at sentencing only). Although not stand-alone offences in law, the offence is still labelled as an aggravated/hate-based on an indictment and will likely appear on an offender's criminal record.

5.4   Substantive Offences

The most common type of hate crime law identified within the study was the substantive hate crime offence. These fell broadly into two sub-categories, with variants found within each of these. The first is where the hate-element has been added to an underlying offence to form new crimes as "aggravated offences" (e.g. "religiously aggravated criminal damage"[13]). A variant of the aggravated offence is where a more serious version of the basic offence is included within a criminal code but which

---

[13] See Crime and Disorder Act 1998 (UK), s 30.

is not labelled as a separate offence (e.g. "grievous bodily injury…perpetrated out of hatred"[14]). The second sub-type is where conduct or activity is in and of itself hate-based and considered worthy of legal proscription because, and only because, it expresses identity-based hostility (e.g. providing "financial or other material support for activities aimed at discrimination against a group"[15]).

5.4.1 Aggravated Offences

In order to create a new substantive hate crime offence, legislatures have typically taken a selection of basic offences and enacted new aggravated versions of these, either under a new statute or more commonly added to an older statute or criminal code. An example is ss. 29–32 of the Crime and Disorder Act 1998 (UK) which lists 11 separate basic offences that can be prosecuted as "aggravated" offences. For example, s. 29 states the following:

Racially or religiously aggravated assaults.

1. A person is guilty of an offence under this section if he commits—

- an offence under section 20 of the Offences Against the Person Act 1861 (malicious wounding or grievous bodily harm);
- an offence under section 47 of that Act (actual bodily harm); or
- common assault,

which is racially or religiously aggravated for the purposes of this section.

The section goes on to set out a maximum sentence for each of the offences which range from 40 per cent to 400 per cent higher than their basic equivalents.

---

[14] Criminal Code (Bosnia and Herzegovina), art 156.
[15] Criminal Code (Sint Maarten), art 157.

Other UK overseas territories and crown dependencies have taken similar approaches to the English and Welsh model,[16] while a slightly different approach is used in other European jurisdictions where instead of creating specific hate-based aggravated offences, an aggravated version of the basic offence is created whereby a hate-element is listed as one of a number of different prescribed forms of aggravation.[17]

US states have also established aggravated versions of already proscribed offences,[18] while others have recriminalised various offences including a hate-element but without specifically referring to them as "aggravated". For example, Oklahoma has enacted the offence of "Malicious intimidation or harassment because of race, color, religion, ancestry, national origin or disability" whereby "[n]o person shall maliciously and with the specific intent to intimidate or harass another person because of that person's race, color, religion, ancestry, national origin or disability".[19] Numerous other states have enacted hate-versions of the offences of intimidation and institutional vandalism thereby creating new stand-alone offences.[20] A similar approach has been taken in some European countries, such as France where there is an offence of physical violence committed because of a protected characteristic,[21] or Hungary where it is an offence for "any person who assaults another person for being a member or a presumed member" of a protected group.[22] For each crime a higher penalty is imposed for the hate-version of the parallel offence.

Another method of aggravating a basic offence in law is used prominently in civil jurisdictions in Europe where instead of creating a new specific "aggravated crime" or hate-based version of a basic offence, a new subsection is simply incorporated into an existing offence which includes

---

[16] See for example Crimes Act 2011 (Gibraltar), Part 7.

[17] See for example the offence of "Aggravated physical assault" under art 272, Criminal Code (Norway) and "Aggravated assault (serious bodily harm)" under art 145, Criminal Code (Spain).

[18] See for example New York "aggravated harassment", NY Penal Law §240.30(3).

[19] Stat. tit. 21 § 850.

[20] Many following the ADL Model of hate crime legislation, see Jacobs and Potter 1998 (see Footnote 11) 33–36.

[21] Criminal Code (France), art 222-13.

[22] Criminal Code (Hungary), art 216(2).

5 Legislating for Hate Crime Globally: Putting "Social Justice"... 135

a hate-element and an enhanced penalty. For example, in Armenia the basic offence of "Infliction of willful heavy damage to health" when carried out with "motives of national, racial or religious hatred or religious fanaticism" carries an increased penalty in law.[23] Given there is no new stand-alone aggravated or hate-version of the parallel offence it is questionable whether such provisions should be included under the category of "substantive offences". Indeed, there is very little to distinguish this sub-category of substantive offence from the penalty enhancement statutes (outlined below). In fact, both require a prosecutor to prove an underlying offence and the hate-element to the trier of fact and both then increase the penalty where the hate-element is proved. It is perhaps why these sub-types of hate crime law are described by Hanek as "specific penalty enhancement" provisions,[24] as against a substantive hate crime offence. However, while these offences are very close in type to a general penalty enhancement provision, a key difference is that the hate-element still makes up a substantive element of the criminal offence as set out in a statute or code, as against the hate-element being layered on top of an offence and proved separately (often at the sentencing stage only). Where the hate-element forms part of a criminal offence it signifies that a more serious offence has been committed in law. It is this key distinguishing factor, and only this, that leads to this type of law being categorised as a sub-type of "substantive offence" as compared to a penalty enhancement provision.[25]

Clearly, legislators have exploited multiple methods of enacting substantive hate crime offences in law. This book emphasises the importance of creating such offences if the state is to recognise hate as a distinct type of criminality; even if legislators do not use the colloquial "hate crime" term in law. However, the use of the word "aggravated" to describe such offences in many jurisdictions may not be the most suitable method either. Questioning whether the word "aggravation" is the best way of codifying hate crimes in law may seem pedantic. However, there is an

---

[23] Criminal Code (Armenia) art 112(12).
[24] Akin to penalty enhancements provisions cited above that apply to specific offences only, for example Wis Stat § 939.645.
[25] It is, though, the weakest sub-type of substantive offences in terms of "fair labelling".

important point to be made here regarding whether such wording fulfils the principle of fair labelling for hate crime offences. While the word and its juxtaposition with basic offences is a simple way to infuse the hate-element in law, it is argued that it does not sufficiently reflect hate crime's distinct wrongfulness. As has been reiterated throughout this book, the hate-element of an offence gives the conduct a unique character, such that it should be labelled as a distinct type of wrong. That is to say, hate crimes are not just basic crimes that hurt a bit more, but are offences that are uniquely harmful.

For this reason, it may be more than "merely semantics" to suggest that the current wording used to proscribe some substantive offences fails to reflect both the moral wrongfulness and the distinct harms that hate crimes embody. A short comparison with other types of crime helps to illustrate this point. For example, sexual assault as a physical assault is not labelled as "aggravated assault" as a means of reflecting its distinct harm. The categories of "sexual assault" and "rape" reflect the distinct nature and harms of these crimes. This is because these crimes reflect more than unlawful personal violence. They are distinct moral wrongs because they transgress bodily autonomy in a way that transcends other forms of assaults.[26] Similarly, domestic violence is labelled as such to denote the domestic nature and the unique consequences that this has on its victims. New legislation has been enacted in jurisdictions that attempt to capture the different ways in which this type of crime is committed, including controlling and coercive behaviour.[27]

In a similar strain, hate crimes should be labelled in law for what they address, that is, "hate crimes",[28] "bias crimes",[29] "prejudice" offences,[30] or perhaps even "crimes against equality of all citizens".[31] For example,

---

[26] Gardner and Shute explain that the wrong of rape is that it amounts to the "sheer use of a person… and… the objectification of a person… is literally dehumanizing". John Gardner and Stephen Shute, 'The Wrongness of Rape' in Jeremy Horder (ed), *Oxford Essays in Jurisprudence, Fourth Series* (OUP, 2000) 205.

[27] See for example Serious Crime Act 2015, s 76 (England and Wales).

[28] As is used, for example, under The Matthew Shepard and James Byrd, Jr. Hate Crimes Prevention Act of 2009, 18 U.S.C. § 249; see also NY Penal Law § 485.05.

[29] See for example Oregon, Or Rev Stat § 166.155.

[30] See for example Hate Crime and Public Order (Scotland) Act 2021, s 1.

[31] As used in Criminal Code (Bulgaria), Ch 3, s 1.

instead of titling an offence "racially aggravated assault" a more fitting classification might be "bias assault" which within the legislation can be defined by different forms of prejudice and bias (e.g. racial, religious, disability). I outline further in the next chapter the different wording used in legislation to determine the threshold of a hate offence, but it is important here to note that the wording used to label actual offences themselves on the statute book is likely to have important symbolic meaning. If hate crimes are to be considered as more than aggravated forms of underlying crimes, they should be described and defined in ways which befit their character and harms.

Whether defined as aggravated or as hate or bias offences, it is important to emphasise that the offence stands alone on the statute books. In jurisdictions where this is the case it stands to reason that legal practitioners are more likely to have heard of them and are more likely to apply the offences in practice. Research by Walters et al. suggests that the hate-element of an offence is more likely to be investigated by law enforcement agencies where the offence is proscribed under the criminal law.[32] This is because the criminal law (as against sentencing provisions) sets out the specific elements of offences that must be addressed by criminal justice personnel. Where the hate-element makes up part of the substantive offence, police officers are more likely to investigate the crime and collate evidence of "bias indicators".[33] This evidence is then more likely to be presented by prosecutors and more readily accepted by the courts as proof that a hate crime has been committed.[34]

The biggest disadvantage to this approach is that legislatures have to create new offences for every type of hate crime that they want to label and punish in law. The CDA (England and Wales) covers just 11 crimes that the legislature has determined requires specific criminalisation. This is largely based on data which showed these were the most common types

---

[32] Mark Walters, Susann Wiedlitzka and Abenaa Owusu-Bempah, *Hate Crime and the Legal Process: Options for Law Reform* (University of Sussex 2017).
[33] For a list of indicators see Walters and others 2017 (ibid.) 80 and OSCE/ODIHR, *Hate Crime Laws: A Practical Guide* (OSCE/ODIHR 2009) 47–48.
[34] See Walters and others 2017 (see Footnote 32); Jennifer Schweppe, Amanda Haynes and Mark A Walters, *Lifecycle of a Hate Crime: Comparative Report* (ICCL 2018).

of offence aggravated by racial hostility.[35] However, there are thousands of offences covered by statute and common law that fall outside of this framework. Where any of these non-CDA offences involve a hate-element the courts can still apply sentencing provisions (enhancements) post-conviction.[36] This dual system of laws means that some hate crimes have much higher sentencing maxima then others, while the fact that different characteristics are covered across the CDA and the Sentencing Act leaves the law open to the criticism that it creates a hierarchy of hate where some types of identity-based prejudice are considered more serious than others.[37]

5.4.2 Conduct-based Hate Offences

The second sub-type of substantive offence can be labelled as "conduct-based" hate offences. This involves the criminalising of conduct that is by its very nature hateful and legislatures have legislated for such offences in four different ways. Before I outline these different approaches, it is worth noting that there is often a crossover here between hate speech offences and hate crime offences. While the vast majority of "hate crimes" involve an underlying offence which when combined with a "hate-element" become a hate crime (e.g. bias assault), there are some acts where the hate-element is, in and of itself, worthy of legislative proscription. This occurs most commonly with hate speech offences where a legislature criminalises verbalised expressions of hate or incitement to hatred. Hate speech crimes do not involve an underlying offence that is aggravated by

---

[35] In a recent review of hate crime laws by the Law Commission for England and Wales the Commission outlines a further list of potential offences that could be reclassified as "aggravated", Law Commission, *Hate Crime Laws: A Consultation Paper* (Law Com CP No 250, 2020); however they do not recommend further inclusion in their final report, Law Commission, *Hate Crime Laws: Final Report* (Law Com No 402, 2021).

[36] Via the Sentencing Act 2020, s 66, outlined further below.

[37] A further disadvantage is this dual system can give rise to what is referred to as "double-counting", whereby a hate-element is counted for the substantive offence and then is uplifted again where a judge has erroneously referred to the sentencing provisions as well, see Mark A Walters, Abenaa Owusu-Bempah and Susann Wiedlitzka, 'Hate Crime and the "Justice Gap": The Case for Law Reform' [2019] 12 Crim LR 961.

5 Legislating for Hate Crime Globally: Putting "Social Justice"... 139

hate, but rather it is the speech itself when hateful that is criminalised.[38] Notwithstanding the separate issue of free speech rights, the distinction between what is "hate speech" and what is "hate crime" has therefore conventionally been to determine whether an underlying basic offence exists, which if aggravated by hate denotes a hate crime, contrasted with speech alone that expresses hate (hate speech).[39]

There is, however, a gap that exists between hate speech and hate crime where speech and action converge, from which hate or prejudice is demonstrated typically in violent form. For instance, the use of threatening and abusive words directed at others in public may fall within the meaning of speech, which triggers separate rights protections, but because the words can have a direct effect upon others (such as feeling physically threatened or distressed) they are also considered as "acts". Under speech-act theory where someone expresses something that is likely to directly cause others to fear for their safety in a public space it is said that the speech becomes performative.[40] The offence of harassment is an example of speech-act, where threatening behaviour (often speech coupled with certain conduct) causes alarm and distress to others. Where conduct (which involves hate speech) is used in certain social contexts it can impact upon the interests of those who are participating in public life (e.g. walking down a public street, shopping in a mall, running in a park). In such situations, an expression of hate can cross the line from hate speech to become a hate crime.[41]

The first way in which legislatures have attempted to criminalise hate-based speech-acts is to "aggravate" basic public order offences. This type of offence can be found in England and Wales where it is a crime to cause

---

[38] Most prominently in European jurisdictions, see Erik Bleich, 'From Race to Hate: A Historical Perspective' in Thomas Brudholm and Birgitte S Johansen (eds), *Hate, Politics, Law* (OUP 2018) 15–33; for an analysis of the different arguments for and against criminalising hate speech see, Alexander Brown, *Hate Speech Law A Philosophical Examination* (Routledge 2015).

[39] See Jennifer Schweppe, 'What is a hate crime?' (2021) 7(1) Cogent Social Sciences, DOI: 10.1080/23311886.2021.1902643.

[40] John L Austin, *How to Do Things with Words* (Clarendon 1962. In the US context sometimes referred to as "fighting words", understood in terms of those words that cause a direct harm to someone or immediate disturbance, Chaplinsky v New Hampshire 315 US 568 (1942).

[41] Schweppe refers to these as "liminal offences" which she argues are neither hate speech offences nor "do they follow the pattern of standard legislative means of addressing hate crime". Schweppe 2021 (see Footnote 39) 9.

"harassment, alarm or distress" through the use of "threatening or abusive words or behaviour".[42] This public order offence can be prosecuted as "aggravated harassment, alarm or distress" where the threatening and abusive behaviour demonstrates, or is partly motivated by, racial or religious hostility.[43] Yet while this appears on the face of it to be a hate crime in the traditional sense (i.e. a basic offence which has an *additional* hate-element) most of these types of offences will *only* be committed when the threatening and abusive behaviour is of a racist or anti-religious nature.[44] In other words, the hate-element does not aggravate a separate basic offence because the expression of hate *becomes* the basic offence. For example, were A to approach B in a public setting and in a hostile manner call that person a racist name the offence of aggravated harassment, alarm and distress will likely be made out. However, if one is to subtract the hate-element (i.e. the racist name-calling) then there is no threatening behaviour, that is, there is no basic offence which can be "aggravated".

Schweppe asserts that where hate-based acts do not involve a pre-existing basic offence—commonly where an offence straddles both speech and conduct—these are better classified as "liminal offences".[45] But I see no cogent reason why conduct, beyond speech-alone, that is worthy of criminalisation and that is hate-based should not simply be classified as "hate crime" and prescribed as such in law. If we begin to exclude certain hate-based criminal conduct from the concept, there is a risk that we deny victims' experiences of violent hatred as being "hate crime victims", while simultaneously narrowing the scope of public policy and legal frameworks that aim to prevent such offending.

A second approach identified within the study was where legislatures identify a very specific act which is considered, in and of itself, one based on bias or identity-based hostility. For example, § 240.31(3) of New York Penal Law states that it is an offence of "aggravated harassment" if someone:

---

[42] Public Order Act 1986, s 5.
[43] Crime and Disorder Act 1998, s 31(1)(c).
[44] See for example *Hammond v DPP* [2004] EWHC 69 (Admin).
[45] Schweppe 2021 n 528).

5 Legislating for Hate Crime Globally: Putting "Social Justice"... 141

with intent to harass, annoy, threaten or alarm another person, because of a belief or perception regarding such person's race, color, national origin, ancestry, gender, gender identity or expression, religion, religious practice, age, disability or sexual orientation... Etches, paints, draws upon or otherwise places a swastika... on any building or other real property, public or private.

The act of "aggravated harassment" under s.240.31(3) is the etching of what is considered to be a hate-based symbol.[46] While technically there is a basic offence of harassment, s.240.31(3) is prescribed in such a way that there would be no basic offence without the hateful nature of the act being proscribed. That is to say, there is no basic offence which is aggravated (i.e. made worse) by hatred as the conduct being proscribed, that is, etching or drawing of a specific symbol on property, does not amount to harassment unless it is of this specific type. In other words, this particular type of conduct has been considered worthy of proscription because, and only because, of its hateful nature.

The third and perhaps most salient method of creating conduct-based hate offences is to proscribe either specific types of conduct, or any acts, that are carried out for the purposes of demonstrating certain forms of hate. The US Civil Rights Act 1968 is an example of this approach which criminalises specified conduct in relation to certain public activities. Section § 245(2) states that it is a crime, "Whoever, whether or not acting under color of law, by force or threat of force willfully injures, intimidates or interferes with, or attempts to injure, intimidate or interfere with... any person because of his race, color, religion or national origin" and because he is or has been engaging in certain public activities (e.g. attending public school or college, enjoying goods, services, facilities including at hotels, motels, restaurants, amongst others).[47] These protections are repeated in state legislation, such as California, and are generally referred to as "stand-alone hate crimes" to signify that they do not carry a parallel or basic offence.[48]

---

[46] Though see FN 10.
[47] Violent Interference with Federally Protected Rights, or Title I of the Civil Rights Act of 1968 § 245.
[48] California Penal Code § 422.6.

Other jurisdictions have proscribed conduct that support others' discriminatory-based activities. In Vatican City, Article 1 (2)(d) of the Vatican City State Law No. VIII, on Complementary Rules in Criminal Law Matters states that it is an offence to provide any form of support to activities directed towards racial discrimination, including by financing them.[49] Again, there is no underlying offence here of financing or supporting activity. The very act of supporting something that has a hate-based (or discriminatory) purpose *is* the offence.

Finally, a broader approach to legislating against conduct-based hate is through the creation of offences that cover either/or speech or acts that are aimed at expressing hate towards certain groups. Broadly speaking these include incitement to hatred offences. While these types of offences tend to fall within the definition of hate speech, as per the typical modus operandi being verbal or written speech that is intended to spread hatred, they can also fall within the definition of hate crime where they include action that is likely to cause hatred. For example, under Article 58 of Mali's Penal Code it is an offence to carry out "**any act** likely to establish or give rise to racial or ethnic discrimination, any speech, **any act** intended to provoke or maintain a regionalist spread".[50] Here there is no specific underlying offence that is aggravated, but simply "acts" that result in discrimination, or as in the case of Mali "regionalism". It is not clear what acts this might include but without further guidance it would appear that any conduct or activity which is deemed to result in these specified forms of bias could fall within the ambit of the offence. This means that otherwise lawful conduct can become criminal where it can be proved that it is likely to give rise to racial or ethnic discrimination or regional spread. These were the broadest and potentially most all-encompassing types of hate crime law observed in the study. Such is their breadth that they

---

[49] See similarly, Criminal Code (Sint Maarten), art 2:63. See also International Convention on the Elimination of All Forms of Racial Discrimination, Article 4(b) "[State Parties] shall declare illegal and prohibit organizations, and also organized and all other propaganda activities, which promote and incite racial discrimination, and shall recognize participation in such organizations or activities as an offence punishable by law".

[50] See also Criminal Code (Mali), art 179. Similarly, various jurisdictions criminalise service or workplace discrimination, for instance in Switzerland it is a criminal offence to refuse to provide a service to another on the grounds of a person's race, ethnic origin, religion or sexual orientation, when that service is intended to be provided to the general public, Criminal Code (Switzerland), art 261 bis.

would not typically satisfy inclusion within a system of social justice liberalism. This is because the lack of specificity in their construction risks either frustrating their application because the proscribed conduct is too vague, or conversely the ambit of such offences is too broad casting the net over any type of discriminatory conduct, with potentially illiberal consequences.

Notwithstanding the need for greater specificity in the final example above, collectively these types of hate crime offences saliently fulfil the obligation of a state that aims to prevent hate-based activities that are causal to social injustice. We see here legislators willing to criminalise conduct in an attempt to prevent activities that have traditionally fallen outside the purview of the criminal law. Categorising such offences as "hate crimes" is contrary to those who have defined it as requiring a pre-existing underlying offence "which is committed with an additional 'hate' element".[51] While it is true that the vast majority of hate crimes will have a parallel basic offence (e.g. assault vis-à-vis bias assault), the defining of hate crime as *necessitating* a pre-codified criminal offence fails to adequately recognise the distinct character of many forms of hate-based conduct worthy of criminalisation. It limits the concept to conduct that already appears on the statute books and in doing so, three problems arise.

The first relates to the central thesis of this book. That is, conventional frameworks of criminal law have failed to identify and uncover the harms which subject certain identity groups to cycles of social disadvantage. This is because the types of harms proscribed in most systems of criminal law are based on a narrow conception of harm, which has historically protected the interests of social elites. To insist on the maintenance of such a framework is to limit the lens through which the law can comprehend the harms caused by hate-based conduct. In fact, it views the harms of hate, not only as secondary to whatever basic offence it must be attached to, but it prevents the state from seeking out new hate-based harms that serve to perpetuate a system of social injustice that continues to oppress various identity groups in society.

Linked to this first problem is a concern relating to fair labelling. Definitions that specify hate crimes as "basic" offences with an additional

---

[51] Schweppe 2021 (see Footnote 39) 7; see also Lawrence 1999 (see Footnote 11) 58.

"hate-element" fail to adequately reflect that the main harm caused by certain types of conduct will be the expression of hate itself. Take the example of etching of a swastika criminalised in New York. The main wrong of this conduct is the symbol that has been etched, which carries with it multi-layered harms as outlined in Chap. 3. The additional harm of say harassment (causing alarm or distress) or of property damage is secondary to these harms. Hence, while the conduct may involve a cost to someone to remove the etching, this harm pales in comparison to the violence, marginalisation, powerlessness and cultural damage that the actual etching of the symbol causes.

A third practical problem occurs where the hate-element is defined as a secondary element of an offence. Research outlined above suggests that where hate is not directly attached to an offence it is more likely to be filtered out of the criminal process altogether.[52] A corollary of this finding is that where hate is not a substantive element of an offence it is less likely to be taken seriously by a criminal justice system. As such, the law ought to codify hate-based conduct in a way that reflects the hate-element as central to the wrong being proscribed in order that criminal justice systems attend specifically to the harms that such crimes cause.

If legislatures are to truly grapple with the extant forms of hate that pervade society, there must be flexibility in moving beyond standard criminal offences in order to uncover the disparate conducts of hatred that impact certain communities, and which perpetuate myriad forms of social injustice. Failure to expand the horizons of what is "hate crime" risks confining it to a conventional framework of law that has historically ignored the individual, community and societal harms caused by acts of hatred.

5.5 Sentence Uplifts

The second main method of legislating against hate crime identified in the study was sentencing provisions that give powers to courts to increase the sentence of a basic offence post-conviction. Such an approach has

---

[52] Walters, Wiedlitzka and Owusu-Bempah 2017 (see Footnote 32).

5 Legislating for Hate Crime Globally: Putting "Social Justice"... 145

been advocated through international law, such as the 2008 EU Council Framework Decision on combating certain forms and expressions of racism and xenophobia by means of criminal law ("the Framework Decision"), Article 4 of which requires Member States to "take the necessary measures to ensure that racist and xenophobic motivation is considered an aggravating circumstance or alternatively that such motivation may be taken into consideration by the courts in the determination of the penalties". This has in turn led to widespread adoption of hate crime laws across Europe aimed at enhancing the penalties of offenders motivated by racism.[53] Hanek notes that the Framework Decision indicates a "strong preference… for [the] adoption of an aggravating circumstance provisions [i.e. sentence uplifts] applicable to all crimes in [a] criminal code".[54] In fact, outside of the EU, the UN Committee on the Elimination of Racial Discrimination (CERD) has also called upon member states to introduce laws that ensure the courts consider racist motivation an aggravating factor at sentencing, while the Council of Europe's ECRI has suggested a preference for such an approach.[55] This study found that legislatures had implemented two main sub-types of sentence uplift.

5.5.1 Sentence Aggravation

This first sub-type of sentencing provision applies across all criminal offences and does not increase basic offence sentencing maxima beyond what is already established in law. For example, where an offender is charged with a basic offence (such as assault), and if convicted, they will

---

[53] Adoption of new hate crime laws has been supported by the EU's Fundamental Rights Agency and the Council of Europe's European Commission against Racism and Intolerance (ECRI) both played key roles in promoting hate crime legislation. See Aleš Giāo Hanek, 'International Legal Framework for Hate Crime: Which Law for the "New" Countries?' in Amanda Haynes, Jennifer Schweppe and Seamus Taylor, *Critical Perspectives on Hate Crime: Contributions from the Island of Ireland* (Palgrave 2020) 467–292. The European Court of Human Rights has also played a significant role in ensuring member states identify and recognised through legislative provisions, see for example *Angelova and Iliev v Bulgaria* App no 55523/00 (ECtHR, 26 July 2007).
[54] Hanek 2020 (ibid.) 476.
[55] See OHCHR (2013) Concluding Observation of the CERD on Ireland, 78th Session, 2011; ECRI General Policy Recommendation No. 7 on National Legislation to Combat Racism and Racial Discrimination, both cited in Hanek 2020 (see Footnote 53) 477.

be sentenced for this crime for which there will be a sentencing maximum prescribed in law. In addition, there is sometimes a "guideline" that is associated with this offence from which judges can get further guidance on the levels of aggravation that should be applied.[56] During the sentencing hearing a judge may (or in some cases must) enhance a sentence where evidence proves that there was a hate-element attached to the offence.[57] In some jurisdictions proof of bias motive at the sentencing stage can rely on a lower standard of proof than that of trial.[58] Under such regimes the offence is also typically recorded as the basic offence only (i.e. assault), with the hate-element making up just one of various aggravating factors that affect the final sentence handed down.

An example of this type of law is found in England and Wales, where under s. 66 of the Sentencing Act 2020 for *any* offence where the offender demonstrates hostility or is motivated (partly) by hostility towards the victim's race, religious beliefs, sexual orientation, transgender identity or disability, the court:

(a) must treat the fact that the offence was committed in any of those circumstances as an aggravating factor, and
(b) must state in open court that the offence was committed in such circumstances.[59]

A study led by this author in England and Wales examined the application of sentence aggravation legislation compared with laws that created substantive hate crime offences.[60] The study reviewed over 100 case

---

[56] See for example assault sentencing guidelines for England & Wales <https://www.sentencingcouncil.org.uk/wp-content/uploads/Assault_definitive_guideline_-_Crown_Court.pdf> accessed 4 December 2021.

[57] Sentencing Act 2020 (UK), s 66.

[58] See for example United States Sentencing Commission, *Guidelines Manual 2018* 324 for reference to use of "preponderance of evidence" as a standard of proof for certain sentencing matters.

[59] See similarly, Canada's Criminal Code, where at s. 718(2)(a) it states:

[...] a sentence should be increased or reduced to account for any relevant aggravating or mitigating circumstances relating to the offence or the offender

[...] evidence that the offence was motivated by bias, prejudice or hate based on [...] sexual orientation, or gender identity or expression [...] shall be deemed to be aggravating circumstances.

[60] Walters, Wiedlitzka and Owusu-Bempah 2017 (see Footnote 32).

5 Legislating for Hate Crime Globally: Putting "Social Justice"... 147

reports, and the authors conducted 71 in-depth qualitative semi-structured interviews with legal practitioners including prosecutors, defence counsel and judges. As this jurisdiction applies both sentence uplifts and substantive offences, the researchers were able to compare and contrast the application of both types of hate crime law. A major theme that emerged from this evaluation was that sentencing aggravation provisions were less likely to be applied consistently in court. During interviews with judges it emerged that the amount of aggravation applied for the hate-element depended on the approach that the judge *generally* took to sentencing such cases. Three general approaches emerged, categorised as:

1. The intuitive approach—no exact percentage or calculation is applied. Judges gauge the level of sentence, intuitively, based on the facts as presented as a whole, as well as their sentencing experience.
2. The sentencing category climber—sentencers do not apply a percentage uplift but instead simply climb to the next sentencing range using the category levels as set out in Sentencing Guidelines.
3. The percentage uplift—the judge follows the guidelines for the general seriousness of the offence and then applies a percentage uplift to the final penalty.

For those judges that increased a sentence by a percentage, these ranged from 30 to 100 per cent, suggesting that there is no single approach to enhancing punishments for hate crime cases in England and Wales.[61]

The amount of sentencing discretion given to judges in most common law jurisdictions means that the amount of enhancement can come down to a "presiding judge lottery".[62] One senior legal practitioner in the study reflected, "it can be just down to judicial discretion ... And that varies so much from judge to judge how seriously they take these things ... it's crazy".[63]

---

[61] It was suggested that crimes motivated by identity-based hostility would attract a greater level of enhancement compared with cases where hostility was demonstrated during the commission of the offence (often in the heat of the moment). However, even here some judges noted that they would apply the same level of enhancement regardless of motivation or demonstration: Walters, Wiedlitzka and Owusu-Bempah 2017 (see Footnote 32).

[62] Walters, Wiedlitzka and Owusu-Bempah 2017 (see Footnote 32) 148.

[63] Walters, Wiedlitzka and Owusu-Bempah 2017 (see Footnote 32) 148.

One way to avoid this potentially inconsistent approach to sentencing hate crime is for legislatures to be more prescriptive in the amount of enhancement that is applied in such cases. In the African jurisdiction of Cabo Verde Article 123 of the Penal Code sets a range of 15–30 years for the crime of murder where the offence is committed "(e) For racial, religious or political hatred or caused by the sexual orientation and gender identity of the victim".[64] This provision still confers a wide degree of discretion on judges when considering the seriousness of the hate-element of such an offence, that is, a range of 15 years. Other jurisdictions have been more prescriptive with the ranges by using a scale system. For instance, under ss. 222A(2), 251D and 325A of the Maltese Criminal Code, it states that:

> The punishments established in the foregoing provisions of this sub-title shall also be increased by one to two degrees when the offence is aggravated or motivated on the grounds of gender, gender identity, sexual orientation […]

Unlike the more flexible approach taken in jurisdictions such as England and Wales, the Maltese courts must choose between a specified amount. While this gives some room to enhance penalties depending on how severe the hate-element is determined to be (as per its role in elevating culpability-harm), it restricts them to a more limited range.

Regardless of the sub-type of sentence enhancement used, a clear advantage in taking this approach to legislate against hate crime is its flexibility. In particular, sentence uplifts that provide for general aggravation across all offence types provide for extensive reach allowing the courts to address the myriad forms of hate-based criminality that occur in society. This approach also avoids legislatures having to enact a whole host of new substantive offences with new sentencing maxima.[65] Legislating against hate crime in this way therefore provides for wider judicial discretion to weigh up the different factors that aggravate and mitigate any given offence, with the hate-element often being just one of many.

Nonetheless, there are significant limitations to the sentence aggravation approach. Perhaps most significant is the fact that sentence uplifts do

---

[64] Compared to 10 to 16 years without the hate-element, art 122.
[65] See next section below.

not change the underlying offence that is prosecuted or convicted. In Chap. 3 I outline why it is important to acknowledge the unique and distinct harms caused by hate crime within a liberal framework of law that aims to tackle social injustice by specifically (re)criminalising such offences. Fair labelling compels a liberal framework of criminal law to recognise hate crime as a distinct classification of offence in *criminal law*. To do otherwise, underplays the moral character of hate crime and neglects to fulfil the expressive function of the law. That is to say, without specific criminalisation the "hate-element" of hate crimes just becomes another factor in a very long list of aggravating factors that a judge may or may not consider at sentencing.[66]

Numerous practical concerns also arise under such an approach. Walters et al. found in their study that evidence of hostility for offences where it does not make up part of the substantive offence is frequently filtered out of the system.[67] Two reasons emerged for this filtering process. The first is that if the hate-element does not make up a substantive element of the offence there is less impetus for the police and prosecutors to carefully investigate and collate evidence of the hate-element to present in court.[68] As one of their interviewees put it:

> [I]t may get forgotten… So we [prosecution managers] do speak to individuals [prosecution lawyers] personally and we will say, 'Well why have you forgotten to mention the uplift?' That's why it's difficult because it's not part of the original offence.[69]

Because the hate-element need not be proved as part of the substantive offence, fewer legal professionals are aware that the legislation exists. This was certainly the case in England and Wales where the substantive hate crime offences were more readily recognised than the sentencing enhancement provisions.

---

[66] And which will often be considered at a lower standard of proof.
[67] Walters, Wiedlitzka and Owusu-Bempah 2017 (see Footnote 32). A similar issue has arisen in Northern Ireland, see Desmond Marrinan, Hate Crime Legislation in Northern Ireland: Independent Review (NI Dept of Justice 2020) 59.
[68] Or a demonstration of hostility as is also permitted in this jurisdiction.
[69] Walters, Wiedlitzka and Owusu-Bempah 2017 (see Footnote 32), 159.

It is not just common law jurisdictions where this filtering out effect occurs. A comparative study by Schweppe et al. on the implementation of hate crime laws in five jurisdictions in the EU indicated that the hate-element of crimes were frequently filtered out of the criminal process in jurisdictions that employ sentence uplift approaches, including in the Czech Republic, Latvia and Sweden.[70] Hanek has similarly concluded in his assessment of sentence aggravation across the OSCE region that "[i]n countries transitioning to a hate crime model … this [type of] provision is rarely or never used".[71]

Other practical concerns linked to sentencing aggravation laws relate to the management of offenders post-conviction. One issue is that if the hate-element does not appear on the offender's criminal record, whether due to it being filtered out of the system or because it does not form a substantive element of the basic offence, it is less likely to come to the attention of justice practitioners who must work with offenders to address their criminal behaviour. I explore in greater detail in Chap. 7 what types of "justice" a social justice liberal approach to combatting hate crime should focus on. It is suffice to say that prison or offender management services cannot adequately address offender behaviour via rehabilitation programmes or community work if a central causal mechanism of the offence remains unknown.

5.5.2 Penalty Enhancements

The second sub-type of sentence uplift includes provisions that create a new range of sentencing enhancements that go beyond that prescribed for the basic offence. These can be referred to as penalty enhancements.[72]

---

[70] Jennifer Schweppe, Amanda Haynes and Mark A Walters, *Lifecycle of a Hate Crime: Comparative Report* (ICCL 2018) 74–75.

[71] See Aleš Gião Hanek, 'International Legal Framework for Hate Crime: Which Law for the "New" Countries?' in Amanda Haynes, Jennifer Schweppe and Seamus Taylor, *Critical Perspectives on Hate Crime: Contributions from the Island of Ireland* (Palgrave 2020) 467–292, 480.

[72] What Gail Mason refers to as the 'Penalty Enhancement Model', which she distinguishes from the "Sentence Aggravation Model": Mason 2009 (see Footnote 11). While I do separate these models into sub-categories I do not categorise each as a separate "type" of legislation; this is because ultimately both provide similar powers to judges that relate only to sentencing.

5 Legislating for Hate Crime Globally: Putting "Social Justice"... 151

Some provide for specific minimum and maximum enhancements, stated in both terms of sentence length and as a percentage addition, as well as additional penalties running concurrently and consecutively. Other statutes prescribe a new enhanced penalty for a specific offence. For instance, under the Penal Code of Uruguay the crime of homicide is punishable by 2 to 12 years in prison. This penalty range is enhanced under Article 312 of the Code:

> (Very special aggravating circumstances) The penalty of imprisonment of fifteen to thirty years shall be applied when the homicide was committed:
> ...
> 7. As an act of discrimination on the grounds of sexual orientation, gender identity, race or ethnic origin, religion or disability.
> 8. (Femicide) Against a woman for reasons of hatred, contempt or belittlement, because of her status as a woman.

This means that homicide committed with a hate-element carries more than double the maximum penalty for the basic offence.

Other jurisdictions enhance penalties based on categories of offence. In France the Criminal Code states that "where a crime or offence is preceded, accompanied or followed by words, writings, images, objects or acts of any kind which are prejudicing the honour or consideration of the victim or of a group of persons to which the victim is a member… by reason of his or her true or perceived sex, sexual orientation or gender identity", the maximum penalties for the basic offence are increased, for example, to life imprisonment when the basic offence is punishable by 30 years; to 30 years of criminal imprisonment when the basic offence is punishable by 20 years; to 20 years of criminal imprisonment when the basic offence is punishable by 15 years, and so on.[73]

Legislating for penalty enhancements is similar to that of other jurisdictions that have created "aggravated" versions of basic offences, but there is a distinction. While penalty enhancement statutes give new powers to extend a sentence beyond that prescribed for the basic offence,

---

[73] Criminal Code (France), art 132-76.

these laws do not establish the hate-element as a constitutive element of a specified criminal offence. In other words, the hate-element is not specifically proscribed in the *criminal law*.

5.6 Hybrid Laws

The number of types, sub-types and variations of sub-types that have emerged through the globalisation of hate crime law makes for a highly complex picture of criminalisation. Complicating this legal landscape further is that some legislatures have utilised elements of both sentencing uplifts and substantive offences, resulting in what I label as hybrid laws. For instance while many US states have enacted so-called penalty enhancements, common law there has determined that the hate-element must be proved beyond reasonable doubt before the trier or fact.[74] This means that in most states where a crime is committed with a hate-element it must *additionally* be charged as "hate crime" (as against the hate-element simply being a factor determined at sentence). As this approach combines features of sentence uplifts (i.e. enhanced penalties) and substantive offences (i.e. the labelling of offences as aggravated at the charging stage) they do not fit neatly within one or other type. To illustrate let us turn to the relevant provisions in California's Criminal Code, which though technically enacting a penalty enhancement provision includes features that also align it with a substantive offence approach. Section 422.55 of the Code states:

For purposes of this title, and for purposes of all other state law unless an explicit provision of law or the context clearly requires a different meaning, the following shall apply:

(a) "Hate crime" means a criminal act committed, in whole or in part, because of one or more of the following actual or perceived characteristics of the victim [disability, gender, nationality, race or ethnicity, religion, sexual orientation, or association with a person or group with one or more of these actual or perceived characteristics].

---

[74] See for example *Apprendi v New Jersey* (99–478) 530 US 466 (2000).

This provision is to be read with a number of other subsections, such as s.422.75 which states that "a person who commits a felony that is a hate crime or attempts to commit a felony that is a hate crime, shall receive an additional term of one, two, or three years in the state prison, at the court's discretion". A defendant is therefore charged with a "felony" and a "hate crime" which acts as a parasitic offence that is layered onto the charge. Where the hate crime is proved at trial it will appear on an offender's conviction record along with the basic offence.

Hybrid laws therefore establish a method of labelling *any* offence on indictment as aggravated by a hate-element without the need to create new substantive offences. Scots law provides another example of this approach to criminalisation. However, instead of layering the hate crime charge on top of a basic offence, the Hate Crime and Public Order (Scotland) Act 2021 allows prosecutors to lay just one charge which includes the label of "aggravated" on the indictment. Section 2 states:

Consequences of aggravation by prejudice
(1) Subsection (2) applies where it is—
(a) libelled in an indictment, or specified in a complaint, that an offence is aggravated by prejudice, and
(b) proved that the offence is so aggravated.
(2) The court must—
(a) state on conviction—
(i) that the offence is aggravated by prejudice, and
(ii) the type of prejudice by which the offence is aggravated (by reference to one or more of the characteristics mentioned in section 1(2)),
(b) record the conviction in a way that shows—
(i) that the offence is aggravated by prejudice, and
(ii) the type of prejudice by which the offence is aggravated (by reference to one or more of the characteristics mentioned in section 1(2)),
(c) take the aggravation into account in determining the appropriate sentence, and
(d) state—
(i) where the sentence in respect of the offence is different from that which the court would have imposed if the offence were not so aggravated, the extent of and the reasons for that difference, or
(ii) otherwise, the reasons for there being no such difference.

The main benefit of this type of legislation is that the legal concept of "hate crime" is not confined to a list of substantive offences that have been (re)criminalised. Drawing on the English and Welsh example again there are 11 such offences on the statute books. Yet there is an estimated 10,000+ criminal offences on the statute books; the vast majority (potentially all) could involve a hate-element.[75] If we are to conceptualise hate crimes as a distinct type of crime which is deserving of fair labelling, we must ask whether it is sufficient to recodify just a tiny fraction of the types of criminal conduct that can be hate-based? While data suggests that the main substantive offences cover a significant proportion of the most common types of hate crime (e.g. assaults, criminal damage, public order offences and harassment), it is clear that different types of hate crime (especially disability hate) can cover other types of offence that are not covered by the range of substantive offences included in the English and Welsh legislation.[76] By only including a sub-set of offences that can be reclassified as "hate crimes" in law, the state unintentionally creates a hierarchy of offences, leaving many thousands of potential offences outside of substantive hate crime laws.

The answer to this quandary has been to capture the remaining types offences through sentence uplifts that cover all offences. However, as we have seen above, these can be insufficient in firstly reflecting the distinct nature and impacts of hate-based offending and secondly because they often result in the filtering out of the hate-element due to the fact it does not make up a substantive element of the offence which must be proved at trial. The hybrid approach therefore creates much-needed simplicity in the law by doing away with dual systems of substantive and sentence enhancements. It will also likely encourage law enforcement agencies to properly investigate and collate evidence of hate for any type of offence that is reported to them, instead of doing so only for the small range of

---

[75] See James Chalmers, 'Frenzied Law Making': Overcriminalization by Numbers' (2014) 67(1) CLP 483.
[76] For example property offences and sexual offences, see Walters, Wiedlitzka and Owusu-Bempah 2017 (see Footnote 32).

offences currently outlined in law.[77] Indeed, a review of Scots hate crime law by Lord Bracadale found that:

> [the] provisions have been extensively used. Having express provisions requires the police (and wider criminal justice system) to be aware of the need to take potential identity hostility into account when investigating crime. Records have been maintained and annual statistics have been published.

The hybrid approach appears to provide an ideal compromise whereby all hate crimes can be labelled and proved in court without the need to enact a range of new substantive offences. Such an approach simultaneously better protects the due process rights of offenders who will only be convicted and labelled as a "hate crime offender" where this has been proved beyond reasonable doubt at trial.

Notwithstanding these potential benefits, a key limitation from a retributive perspective is that the Scots legislation does not extend the sentencing maxima beyond that which is set for the basic offence. From an administrative perspective this can be advantageous, especially in common law jurisdictions, where the lower courts can dispose of most hate crimes (e.g. public order offences) that carry a lower sentencing maximum without the requirement of transferring cases to upper courts, which have greater powers to sentence longer terms of imprisonment. However, there is clearly a mismatch here between the marking of hate crimes out as more serious types of crime while maintaining the same sentencing maxima for the basic version of the offences.[78]

One way around this predicament would be for legislators to set out new sentencing maxima for a range of offences it considers particularly worthy of enhanced punishment (in the English context this could include the 11 offences set out in the CDA). Alternatively, many jurisdictions could simply apply a penalty enhancement such as that used in

---

[77] Though this also depends on a myriad of other structural, political and resource-based factors, see Jennifer Schweppe and Mark Walters, *Establishing a Framework for Implementation of Anti-LGBT Hate Crime Legislation* (Human Dignity Trust 2022).

[78] It is for this reason that the Law Commission in England and Wales rejected this proposed model in their final report on hate crime laws, Law Commission (2021) (see Footnote 35) 317.

California.[79] This latter approach is proposed by Lawrence in his (USA) model bias crime statute in which he states "(1) A person is guilty of a first-degree bias crime if he commits any crime against the person or property in this state's criminal code… (2) A first-degree bias crime is a felony and shall be punished by a term of imprisonment and/or fine that exceeds that of the relevant parallel crime by two levels".[80] Here the statute applies to *any* crime which involves the relabelling of any prosecuted offence as a "bias crime", while prescribing enhanced penalties that go two levels above the basic version of the offence.

A second limitation of the hybrid approach is that although it can capture the full range of basic offences that may have a hate-element, it does not proscribe any new offences that a legislature might consider worthy of criminalisation due to its hateful nature (i.e. conduct-based hate offences); but which fall outside the current framework of criminal laws in any given jurisdiction. As such, any system that incorporates a hybrid approach should remain open to creating new conduct-based substantive offences in order to prevent acts where the expression of hate is in, and of itself, worthy of criminalisation despite there being no parallel basic offence (Fig. 5.1).

5.7 Conclusion

There are multiple ways in which states can attempt to legislate against hate and different legal systems may lend themselves to diverging approaches. As this chapter has expounded there are advantages and drawbacks to each method, meaning that no single type of hate crime law is without limitation. Outlined at the start of this chapter were the criteria for coding of legislation. Consideration was given to the different legal

---

[79] While this approach ensures that higher penalties are maintained for hate crimes, it must be emphasised that the state's focus on enhancing punitive sentences is likely to do little to advance the social justice that hate crime laws could help to achieve. In Chap. 7 I examine in greater detail how a social justice liberal approach to legislation could be framed more centrally around restorative responses to hate crime, while being backed only by threatened punishment that would be used only as a measure of last resort.

[80] Lawrence 1999 (see Footnote 11) 170.

5 Legislating for Hate Crime Globally: Putting "Social Justice"... 157

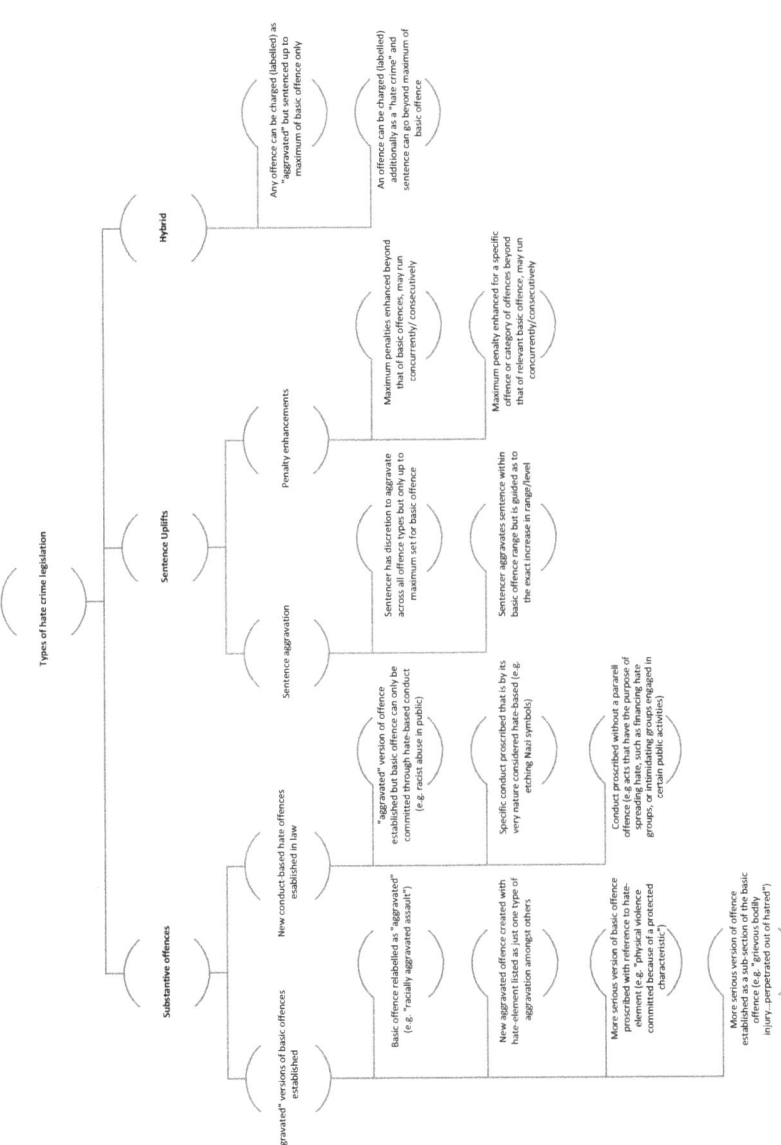

Fig. 5.1 Types of hate crime legislation used globally

systems when doing this, but ultimately nuances in the way some systems work may mean that certain provisions, while appearing on paper to fit a category, in practice might not fit squarely into the types outlined in this chapter.[81] I hope other experts globally who see this work can assist in refining the categories further in the future.

The message that this chapter aims to convey is that legislation ought to recognise hate crime as a distinct type of criminal conduct in the criminal law (code) of any given legal system. Social justice liberalism necessitates the uncovering of hate in its myriad forms and criminal proscription is the strongest means of condemnation. One way this can be achieved is through the enactment of substantive offences which re-label offences and set out appropriate sentences that reflect the harms they cause. Substantive offences are also more likely than sentence uplifts to trigger law enforcement investigations that collate evidence of the hate-element to be proved in court. This reduces the potential for filtering out of the hate-element, while also protecting due process rights by ensuring that defendants can defend against claims before a trier of fact. Substantive offences are also more likely to result in convicted offenders having the hate-element of a crime recorded upon conviction, which in turn increases awareness amongst post-sentence agencies tasked with monitoring offending rates and managing offender rehabilitation. If substantive offences are enforced robustly this should in turn improve confidence amongst communities to report incidents.

Yet while substantive offences are a cogent means of reflecting the distinct harms of hate, practical problems involved in legislating for the many thousands of crimes that can include a hate-element may mean that a hybrid approach is preferred by legislatures. This approach, used in Scotland and in US states such as California, creates a system whereby the hate-element of an offence is labelled on the particulars of a charge and is therefore prosecuted in court as an "aggravated" or "hate crime" offence. Where the hate-element is proved in court, the court must state on conviction that the offence was aggravated by prejudice and this must be reflected in the sentence handed down. Such an approach attempts to

---

[81] Hanek 2020 (see Footnote 71); Joanna Perry, 'The migration and integration of the hate crime approach in India' (2020) 11(1) Jindal Global Law Rev 7.

5 Legislating for Hate Crime Globally: Putting "Social Justice"...

effectuate fair labelling while ensuring that any type of offence with a hate-element can be subjected to the rigour and due process rights afforded within the criminal trial. Notwithstanding the symbolic and practical benefits of hybrid laws, there remains the key limitation that such an approach does not identify or proscribe conduct that is hate-based which is yet to appear on the statute books. Legislatures must therefore remain open to identifying conduct that is considered worthy of criminalisation because of its distinct hate-based harms. As such, legislatures ought to consider utilising both a hybrid and substantive offence approach to criminalising hate.

The "type" of hate crime law that legislatures ultimately choose becomes central to how much conduct is criminalised as hate-based, as well as the extent to which the law becomes a useable tool in challenging hate crime. However, choosing the type of law is only part of what is required when legislating against hate. The next step is to construct a legal model that will enable legal practitioners to put the law on the books into action. In the next chapter I outline the different models that have been used to legislate against hate globally, and set out arguments for the use of those that are considered suitably equipped to actualise the criminalisation of hate as social justice liberalism.

6

Legislating for Hate Crime Globally: Putting "Social Justice" Into Practice, Part 2

6.1 Introduction

In the previous chapter we began to move our exploration from *why* we should criminalise hate to *how* we ought to legislate against it. The chapter examined the different types of hate crime law that are being used globally. It was argued that for hate crime to be treated as a distinct and serious form of offending it must be proscribed within the criminal law, whereby the hate-element makes up a constituent element of an offence. However, determining what types of hate crime law to enact is only part of what can be a highly complex legislative puzzle. Determining *where* hate crime laws should sit within a legal framework does not necessarily tell us how we ought to construct the law. In fact, as we will see, the models of legislation that are incorporated into any given legislative framework can significantly affect the workability and practical application of these laws.

This chapter outlines the diverging ways in which hate crime laws have been codified. The chapter draws on both case law analysis as well as comparative empirical research previously conducted on the application of hate crime legislation in Europe.[1] Using case law analysis, official data, and comparative empirical research on the application of hate crime law, the chapter highlights how the words used to proscribe hate offences impact significantly upon the number of crimes that are successfully prosecuted and convicted in court. In turn, the chapter sets out recommendations on what models of law ought to be employed by legislatures that will likely assist in challenging and preventing hate crime most effectively.

6.2 Models of Hate Crime Legislation

Since the inception of hate crime statutes, two distinct models of hate law have emerged globally, known as the animus model and the discriminatory (group) selection model. Both models are used widely; however, the discriminatory model is more commonly employed across all continents except for Asia.[2]

In order to determine the guilt of hate crime offenders within either model legislation must set out both a conduct-element (actus reus) and a mental state (mens rea) for each offence. Attached to one or both elements of an offence will be a legal test required to prove the hate-element (additional mens rea, e.g. motivation, or by reason of; or additional actus reus, e.g. demonstration).[3] As part of the legal test employed there will be a threshold for which the hate-element must meet (e.g. "hate", "prejudice", "hostility" or "selection due to a protected characteristic") (Fig. 6.1).

6.2.1 The Animus Model

Just over one-third of the legal provisions assessed in this study were identified as employing an "animus model"—also sometimes labelled the

---

[1] With a specific focus on England and Wales.
[2] It should be noted that many jurisdictions use a combination of the models, though as I will outline below where this occurs the legislation is more suitably labelled as an animus model of legislation.
[3] Although as we will see for some offences the hate-element may in fact become the underlying offence. See further discussion on the difference between motivation and demonstration below at 1.1.3.

	Model of law
Animus	Discriminatory selection

	Hate-element
E.g. Hate/prejudice/hostility/intolerance	Selection due to protected characteristic

	Legal test
Mens rea (e.g. "motivation" or "because of")	Actus reus (e.g. "demonstration")

Fig. 6.1 Constructing hate crime provisions

"hatred model".[4] Under this model, a legislative provision refers directly to words such as hatred or prejudice (or other synonyms) which form a substantive element of the legal test to be applied. For example, section 55 of the Criminal Code Act 1907 of Bermuda states:

(2) In sentencing an offender the court shall have regard to—
...
(f) ... **evidence that the offence was motivated by bias, prejudice or hate** based on race, national or ethnic origin, language, colour, religion, sex, age, mental or physical disability, sexual orientation, or any other similar factors

In some jurisdictions, legislation refers directly to a type of prejudice such as racism, xenophobia etc. For instance, section 46(2) of the Criminal Code of Germany states:

When sentencing the court shall weigh the circumstances in favour of and against the offender. Consideration shall in particular be given to the

---
[4] Over 350 legal provisions were coded.

motives and aims of the offender, particularly where they are of a racist or xenophobic nature or where they show contempt for human dignity.[5]

Defining the Hate-Element

It has been asserted that the animus model of legislation best encapsulates the hate-element in "hate crime" by ensuring that an offender's bias is encompassed squarely within the definition of the offence.[6] After all, it is the expression of hate as manifested through criminality that gives hate crime its distinct impacts. It follows therefore that it ought to be a substantive element of a hate crime offence.

There have been numerous ways in which the hate-element in animus models have been prescribed in different jurisdictions. In line with the term "hate crime" itself a number of jurisdictions have used words such as "hate",[7] "hatred"[8] and "hatred or enmity"[9] when defining hate-based crimes in law. In opting for proof of "hate" or "hatred" these jurisdictions will have set a very high evidentiary threshold in law. Not only is it likely that defendants will hold multiple motives in the commission of hate crime,[10] but the emotion of hate/hatred underpinning the defendant's motivation is also likely to be difficult to prove to a criminal standard.

As with most of the terms used under hate crime statutes, the courts will apply the ordinary meaning of the words used. The word hate is defined by the Oxford English Dictionary as "[a] feeling of intense dislike or aversion towards a person or thing". Card notes that hatred is "a much stronger thing than simply bringing into ridicule or contempt, or causing ill-will or bringing into distaste".[11] Indeed in defining "group hate",

---

[5] See similarly Criminal Code (Austria), s 33.
[6] Frederick M Lawrence, *Punishing Hate: Bias Crimes under American Law* (Harvard UP 1999) 11.
[7] Sentencing Act 1995 (Australia's Northern Territory), s 6A.
[8] Criminal Code (Cabo Verde), art 123; Criminal Code (Czechia), § 42; Criminal Code (Slovakia), s 140; Criminal Code (Malta), art 83B.
[9] Penal Code (Kenya), Art.77(3)(e).
[10] Neil Chakraborti and Jon Garland, 'Reconceptualizing hate crime victimization through the lens of vulnerability and "difference"' (2012) 16 Theo Crim 499.
[11] R Card, *Public Order Law* (Jordan 2000) 186, cited in Law Commission, *Hate Crime Laws: A Consultation Paper* (Law Com CP No 250, 2020) 95.

Brogaard states that "[i]t combines resentment for people who belong to a certain group with condemnation of them for their assumed malevolent character".[12] Yet, as research has shown, very few "hate crimes" are the result of such intense dislike or resentment for groups of people's assumed to hold an evil disposition.[13] Much more common is for hate crimes to occur during people's everyday routines where more superficial feelings of animus are demonstrated as people from diverging backgrounds come into contact and conflict.[14] It is perhaps unsurprising, then, that jurisdictions that have used hate or hatred to define hate crime have little case law reporting successful convictions for such offences.[15]

In an attempt to more succinctly reflect the multifarious ways in which hate manifests through criminal offending, most jurisdictions have used words that require a lower threshold including, "bias" used in Indiana (USA),[16] reasons of "discrimination" in Angola,[17] "prejudice" in Cyprus,[18] and Puerto Rico,[19] and "malice" or "ill-will" used in Scotland.[20] Other countries have opted to incorporate a combination of different terms, such as "hatred, contempt or hostility" in Belgium,[21] "hatred, enmity or hostility" in Russia,[22] and "bias, prejudice or hate" in Bermuda (cited above), Canada,[23] the Cayman Islands[24] and Saint Kitts and Nevis.[25]

---

[12] Berit Brogaard, *Hatred: Understanding Our Most Dangerous Emotion* (OUP 2020) 158. See also Brudholm who defines hatred as involving "active desires or wishes for wholesale destruction or elimination of the odious object", Thomas Brudholm 'Hatred Beyond Bigotry' in Thomas Brudholm and Birgitte S Johansen (eds), *Hate, Politics, Law: Critical Perspectives on Combating Hate. Studies in Penal Theory and Philosophy* (OUP 2018) 74–75.

[13] See for example Jack McDevitt, Jack Levin and Susan Bennett, 'Hate crime offenders: An expanded typology' (2002) 58(2) J Soc Issues 303.

[14] See for example Paul Iganski, *Hate Crime and the City* (Policy Press 2008).

[15] For a philosophical exploration of the mean of hatred, which counters the assertion that it is formed of individual pathology, see Brudholm 2018 (see Footnote 12).

[16] Ind. Code Ann. § 35-38-1-7.1.

[17] Criminal Code (Angola), s 68(2)(c).

[18] Criminal Code (Cyprus), art 35A.

[19] Criminal Code (Puerto Rico), s 66.

[20] Hate Crime and Public Order (Scotland) Act 2021, s 1(1)(a).

[21] See for example Criminal Code (1999) (Belgium), art 377.

[22] Criminal Code (Russia), art 63.

[23] Criminal Code (Canada), s 718.2.

[24] Alternative Sentencing Law (Cayman Islands), s 8.

[25] Criminal Code (Saint Kitts and Nevis), s 62.

For example, s. 718 of the Canadian Criminal Code states that:

> evidence that the offence was motivated by bias, prejudice or hate based on race, national or ethnic origin, language, colour, religion, sex, age, mental or physical disability, sexual orientation, or gender identity or expression, or on any other similar factor...
> ... shall be deemed to be aggravating circumstances ...

Of all the words used to describe the hate-element of hate crime, prejudice is most commonly used to conceptualise the meaning of this type of offending.[26] Prejudice is a noun that refers to a feeling, belief or attitude. It is therefore something felt rather than done. Typically prejudice motivates the action of discrimination, or in our case criminal conduct. However, some scholars have extended this basic meaning of prejudice to include action. For instance, Lawrence notes that in the context of hate crime, prejudice is not strictly a personal predilection but rather it refers to antipathies exhibited towards individuals based on faulty stereotypical views of the victim's group.[27] He asserts that this antipathy must exist within a social context and be shared by others in society.

Yet the use of prejudice to define hate-based criminal conduct may in fact cloud the concept.[28] Jacobs and Potter assert that this is because there is no single agreed definition of prejudice, while there are multiple grey areas where biases or prejudices may be considered by most people as socially positive (e.g. anti-fascist), socially negative (e.g. racism) or socially positive or negative, or perhaps both, depending on the group (e.g. anti-Zionism). There might also be crimes where someone is harmed because of their identity characteristics but where this is not a result of a faulty stereotype.[29]

---

[26] Nathan Hall, *Hate Crime* (Routledge 2013) 9.
[27] Lawrence 1999 (see Footnote 6) 11.
[28] James B Jacobs and Kimberly Potter, *Hate Crimes: Criminal Law and Identity Politics* (OUP 1998) 11–16. See generally Nathan Hall, *Hate Crime* (Routledge 2013) ch 5.
[29] For instance, Green et al. point out hate crime can be influenced by economic competition and resentment between ingroups and outgroups. Donald P Green and Rachel L Seher, 'What role does prejudice play in ethnic conflict?' (2003) 6 Annu Rev Polit Sci 509.

6 Legislating for Hate Crime Globally: Putting "Social Justice"... 167

One way to avoid the problems of defining ambiguous concepts such as prejudice is for legislators to use more neutral terminology and to then link this to certain crimes that are targeted against specific groups. Such an approach is taken in New Hampshire (USA),[30] Hawaii (USA),[31] Samoa,[32] New Zealand,[33] England and Wales,[34] Northern Ireland,[35] and numerous Overseas Territories and Crown dependences of the UK, all of which employ the word "hostility". Hostility is an action noun denoting the doing of something; in this case the doing of "aggressive behaviour towards people or ideas".[36] Iganski has asserted that this word arguably signifies the process by which an offender "conveys deleterious notions of difference" in situations where they try to exercise power over the victim.[37] This is a process not necessarily conveyed by the more subjective words of "bias" and "prejudice".

To a large extent it remains unclear what legislators intended the word hostility to encompass as it is not typically defined in law. The Crown Prosecution Service in England and Wales in its guidance to prosecutors states that the word hostility should be given its literal meaning which includes, "ill-will, ill-feeling, spite, prejudice, unfriendliness, antagonism, resentment, and dislike".[38] This very inclusive definition has been open to criticism, with some arguing that the inclusion of "unfriendliness" is too broad and beyond the scope of what hate crime laws should criminalise.[39] In practice, though, the word has typically been interpreted narrowly by the courts; which have often sought to find evidence that an offender is either a bigoted person or that their conduct towards the victim's identity

---

[30] NH Rev Stat Ann § 651:6.1. (f).
[31] Haw Rev Stat Ann § 706-662(6)(b).
[32] Sentencing Act 2016 (Samoa), s 7.
[33] Sentencing Act 2002 (New Zealand), s 9.
[34] Crime and Disorder Act 1998 (England and Wales), s 28.
[35] The Criminal Justice (No. 2) (Northern Ireland) Order 2004, art 2.
[36] As defined by Collins Online Dictionary.
[37] Iganski 2008 (see Footnote 14) 17.
[38] See Crown Prosecution Service, 'Racist and Religious Hate Crime—Prosecution Guidance' (CPS 2020).
[39] Alison Platts, Dawn Griesbach and Fiona Mackay, *One Scotland: Hate Has No Home Here Consultation on amending Scottish hate crime legislation: Analysis of Responses* (Scottish Government 2019) 38.

was aggressive or violent in nature; as against having simply been "unfriendly" to the victim.[40] As we will see further below, the term is also frequently narrowly interpreted in cases where an offender's biased actions are combined with their taking advantage of the victim's *perceived* vulnerability. In such cases the word "hostility", given its ordinary and literal meaning, does not appear to cover crimes where the offender has, for example, befriended their victim in order to draw them into a faux friendship where they go on to exploit, use, and often violently abuse them.[41]

If "hostility" does not encapsulate these more subtle forms of identity-based abuse, incidents that involve the targeting of a victim's perceived vulnerability because of their "difference" may more fittingly fit within words such as "contempt". Fewer legislatures have included the word contempt, with examples including Belgium: "hatred, contempt or hostility"[42] and Malta: "hostility, aversion or contempt".[43] There is little within the caselaw that interprets the meaning of this word. Brogaard refers to "group contempt" as a form of group condemnation on account of group members' "alleged flawed character".[44] She goes on to explain that "[i]n contempt, the attributed character flaw is not malevolence, but vices such as lack of integrity and restraint, an impaired sense of hygiene, low intelligence and animal instincts".[45] Such a definition may more accurately encompasses the pervasive forms of disablist abuse that are so frequently ignored by authorities tasked with combating hate crime.[46] This concern has led one independent review of hate crime legislation in Northern Ireland to recommend that "contempt" be included as a

---

[40] Mark A Walters, 'Conceptualizing "hostility" for hate crime law: Minding "the minutiae" when interpreting section 28(1)(a) of the Crime and Disorder Act 1998' (2014b) 34(1) OJLS 47; Mark A Walters, Susann Wiedlitzka and Abenaa Owusu-Bempah, *Hate Crime and the Legal Process: Options for Law Reform* (University of Sussex 2017) ch 8.

[41] Most common with disability hate crimes, see Jemma Tyson, 'Disablist Hate Crime: A Scar on the Conscience of the Criminal Justice System?' in Jacki Tapley and Pamela Davies (eds), *Victimology: Research, Policy and Activism* (Palgrave Macmillan 2020) 185–212; Walters, Wiedlitzka and Owusu-Bempah 2017 (see Footnote 40) ch 10.

[42] For example Criminal Code (Belgium), art 377.

[43] Criminal Code (Malta), art 222A.

[44] Berit Brogaard, *Hatred: Understanding Our Most Dangerous Emotion* (OUP 2020) 159.

[45] Ibid.

[46] See Tyson 2020 (see Footnote 41); see also Walters, Wiedlitzka and Owusu-Bempah 2017 (see Footnote 40) ch 10.

motivating factor, or type of demonstration, in legislation.[47] The Law Commission for England and Wales has also noted that the law should be interpreted as encompassing "contempt, derision or disregard for the rights of people with the protected characteristics".[48]

While each of the words that have been used to describe the hate-element in hate crime have conceptual limitations, collectively they encompass the wide scope of feelings and action that are applicable to the term "hate crime". The inclusion of words such as bias, prejudice, hostility and contempt reflects the fact that hate crimes are rarely expressions of pure hatred, but more commonly manifest from negative feelings, or antipathies, that are felt and expressed in myriad ways towards certain groups of people. Given the slightly diverging meanings given to each type of words, and that different types of hate crime may manifest more commonly through one or more of these negative feelings and emotions, it is perhaps most fitting for legislatures to list several of these words within legislative provisions.

Legal Tests for Proving Animus: The Use of "Motivation"

Having determined how the hate-element is worded in a statute/code, legislatures must then determine how it is attached to an offence. Most common is to require that the offence is "motivated" by the requisite hate-element. The inclusion of motivation within the definition of an offence has been deemed by many critics to be a radical departure from conventional criminal law principles.[49] Most criminal offences require a mens rea element which must coincide with an *actus reus*. These mental states vary and often include intention or recklessness. The former

---

[47] Desmond Marrinan, *Hate Crime Legislation in Northern Ireland: Independent Review* (NI Dept of Justice 2020) para, 6.114.
[48] Law Commission, *Hate Crime Laws: A Consultation Paper* (Law Com CP No 250, 2020) 365. Though they do not go as far as to recommend including the word "contempt" in the legal test in England and Wales, Law Commission, *Hate Crime Laws: Final Report* (Law Com No 402, 2021).
[49] See Craig Uhrich, 'Hate Crime Legislation: A Policy Analysis' (1999) 36(4) Houston L Rev 1467, 1512–1519; James Morsch, 'The Problem of Motive in Hate Crimes: The Argument Against Presumptions of Racial Motivation' 82(3) J Crim L & Criminol 659; and Alan Norrie, *Crime, Reason and History* (Weidenfeld and Nicolson 1993) ch 3.

typically requires proof that the offender had as their direct purpose the act which took place, or at least that they foresee as a virtual certainty that their conduct would bring about a particular consequence.[50] Recklessness, on the other hand, can be both objective or subjective, but typically involves proof that the offender foresaw from their actions the risk of an outcome and acted regardless.[51] Rarely is either intention or recklessness proved through a thorough assessment of an offender's state of mind (unless an issue of capacity arises). Instead, the mens rea element is something usually assumed based on the offender's actions and the context of the incident.[52]

A person's motive goes beyond explaining whether they meant to do what they did and concerns their *reasons* for doing it. Examining why someone has behaved in a certain way is complex as individual behaviour is often influenced by numerous external and internal factors. These determinants can alter during the course of conduct, and change depending on context, emotion, as well as the behaviour and reactions of others. So complex is human behaviour and our reasons for doing the things we do that, conventionally, motive has fallen beyond the ambit of the criminal law. As one English judge has explained, "[t]he search for a specific motive can be elusive and complex. That is why the establishment of criminal liability does not generally require it".[53]

This is not to say that motive plays no role in criminal law at all. In fact, it is not always clear whether motives and intentions can be disentangled.[54] For some crimes, intention can only really be understood by examining the offender's reason for acting. For example, under s. 9 of the Theft Act 1968 (England and Wales) the offence of burglary is proved,

---

[50] See for example English case of *Woollin* [1999] 1 AC 82.

[51] See for example English case of *R v G* [2004] 1 AC 1034.

[52] For example, as I have noted previously "the person who holds a gun to someone's head and pulls the trigger will be assumed to have had the prerequisite intention to cause the death of her or his victim. There is not normally an investigation into the offender's actual mental state. The jury are left to assume that the defendant intended to kill her or his victim, as it is a natural consequence of the defendant's actions". Mark A Walters, 'Hate crimes in Australia: introducing punishment enhancers' (2005) 29(4) Crim Law J 201, 211.

[53] *DPP v Green* [2004] EWHC 1225 (Admin) [24].

[54] Stephen Mathis, 'Motive, Action, and Confusions in the Debate over Hate Crime Legislation' (2018) 37(1) Crim Just Ethics 1.

not only when someone enters a building as a trespasser and commits theft, but also if they enter with the ulterior intention of committing a further offence, such as inflicting grievous bodily harm or theft. In practice, determining whether someone has ulterior intent requires an investigation into their reason for trespassing, that is what was their motive for entering the property?[55] An offender's motivation can also frequently be considered during the post-conviction stage during sentencing. Bad motives will often serve to aggravate a sentence, especially where a crime is premeditated.

Nevertheless, as we will see, evidencing motivation can be highly inhibitive in proving whether a hate crime has been committed. When emotions or attitudes are tethered to a motivation test, proving even the lowest threshold of a hate-element (such as bias) beyond reasonable doubt can be highly challenging.

The limitations of legal tests that require hate as sole causation have been a common feature of Australian (NSW) case law. In *Ross*[56] the defendant shouted angry racist slurs[57] at a two-year-old infant as he murdered her. Yet despite his angry violent racism the court determined that his acts were not motivated by racial prejudice, the judge holding that "notwithstanding the statements… as to the colour of the deceased, I do not consider that the injuries were inflicted because of hatred or prejudice against a group of people".[58]

It is often those cases where individuals have participated in clearly racist (group) activity, or where there is evidence of premeditation that hate motivation can be proved beyond reasonable doubt.[59] The Australian case of *Katsakis*[60] illustrates the second type of case is captured by motivation tests. In this case four young men arranged by plan to locate and

---

[55] Douglas Husak also provides two examples in *Philosophy of Criminal Law* (Rowman & Littlefield 1987) 146–147.
[56] *Ross v R* [2016] NSWCCA 176 [49].
[57] Which included saying to her "you're a black dog; you're a black c*nt!", *Ross v R* [2016] NSWCCA 176 [32].
[58] *Ross v R* [2016] NSWCCA 176 [49].
[59] See Crown Prosecution Service, 'Racist and Religious Hate Crime—Prosecution Guidance' (CPS 2020).
[60] *DPP v Katsakis* [2013] VCC 1321.

attack gay people. Upon finding two men on the street they engaged in a prolonged attack, repeatedly punching and kicking the victims before robbing them. During police interview, Katsakis stated that he wanted to "fuck up their day because they were gay". Katsakis' confession was sufficient evidence to prove that he had been motivated by "hatred or prejudice".[61]

Yet even cogent evidence that a defendant has been motivated by hatred or prejudice has not always been enough to convince courts that an offence should be aggravated. For instance, in the Australian case of *El Masri*[62] a man was violently attacked in a public toilet after he made a gesture towards El Masri who had interpreted this as a sexual advance. The prosecution submitted during trial that El Masri's violence had been motivated by hatred and prejudice towards the victim based on his sexual orientation. Reminiscent of many of the "gay panic" defence cases of the past,[63] the courts (both at trial and on appeal) ignored the claim making no further mention of sexual orientation hatred or prejudice.[64]

Given that most hate crime offenders have multiple motives, such as where someone is assaulted due to homophobia and thrill-seeking behaviour,[65] or because of racism and a trigger incident which is causal to the incident,[66] or even where there are multiple and intersecting

---

[61] Though note that Gail Mason and Andrew Dyer ("'A negation of Australia's fundamental values": Sentencing prejudice-motivated crime' 36 Melbourne UL Rev (2013) 871, 887) have noted that several NSW cases have shown that a prejudiced motivation can be inferred from racist (and in one case, misogynist) slurs. The case law suggests that there is variation in judicial attitudes towards whether verbal expressions of prejudice prove motive.

[62] *R v Said El Masri* [2005] NSWCCA 167 (29 April 2005).

[63] The use of a partial defence (provocation) where gay men are murdered after making (perceived) sexual advances towards other men who then claim they were "provoked" to kill them. See Stephen A Tomsen, 'Hatred, murder and male honour: gay homicides and the homosexual panic defence' (1994) 6(2) Crim Aust 2. The defence is still used in various parts of the world, see for example Se-shauna Wheatle, 'The Constitutionality of the "Homosexual Advance Defence" in the Commonwealth Caribbean' (2016) 16 Equal Rights Rev 38.

[64] See further evaluation in Mason and Dyer 2013 (see Footnote 61).

[65] See for example Karen Franklin, 'Antigay behaviors among young adults: Prevalence, patterns, and motivators in a noncriminal population' (2000) 15(4) J Interpers Violence 339.

[66] Such as an altercation between neighbours about noise pollution which escalates into racial abuse, see for example Mark A Walters, *Hate Crime and Restorative Justice: Exploring Causes, Repairing Harms* (OUP 2014a).

prejudices,[67] it is prudent to reflect this in legislation. This issue has been problematic in Canada where it remains unclear the extent to which the offender's hate motivation must be causal to the underlying offence charged. In Lawrence and Verdun-Jones' analysis of case law they concluded that the degree of motivation needed for section 718.2(a) has been far from consistent.[68] There have been three levels to which s. 718.2(a) have been applied by the courts, including the offence being motivated "solely" by bias, prejudice or hate; it being "a significant motivating factor" and lower still it being motivated "in part".[69]

Some legislatures have responded to the fact that hate crimes frequently have multiple motivations by including wording to this effect in statute. For instance, s83B of the Maltese Criminal Code states that:

> The punishment established for any offence shall be increased by one to two degrees when the offence is aggravated or motivated, **wholly or in part** by hatred against a person or a group, on the grounds of gender, gender identity, sexual orientation, race, colour, language, national or ethnic origin, citizenship, religion or belief or political or other opinion…

To ensure that other causal factors do not inhibit the successful prosecution of aggravated offences in England and Wales, section 28(3) of the Crime and Disorder Act 1998 states that it is, "immaterial … whether or not the offender's hostility is also based, to any extent, on any other factor".

The use of part motivation tests is certainly likely to increase the rates of successful prosecution. This is illustrated in the English case of *R v Cooke*[70] which involved an organised protest and ensuing riot in the city

---

[67] See for example Hannah Mason-Bish and Irene Zempi, 'Misogyny, Racism, and Islamophobia: Street Harassment at the Intersections' (2019) 14(5) Feminist Criminol 540.
[68] Michelle S Lawrence and Simon N Verdun-Jones, 'Sentencing hate: an examination of the application of s.718.2(a)(i) of the Criminal Code on the sentencing of hate motivated offences' (2011) 57(1) Crim LQ 28.
[69] Similar provisions apply in New South Wales (Australia) where the relevant statute states that the offence must have been "motivated by hatred for or prejudice" (Crimes (Sentencing Procedure) Act 1999, s 21A). In the case of *R v El Mostafa* [2007] NSWDC the court held that despite the fact that the defendant's conduct had been motivated by both political and intra-religious animosities the offence was still "motivated" by religious hatred for the purposes of the statute.
[70] [2015] EWCA Crim 1414.

of Birmingham in the aftermath of the murder of a young British solider Lee Rigby who was killed in a street attack by two men who had claimed they were acting to avenge the killing of Muslims by British soldiers. The defendant was an ex-soldier who had been outraged by Rigby's murder and participated in acts of rioting, joining a group of others who had clearly demonstrated racist motives (including the burning of the Pakistani flag) during the event. The defendant had not been heard making any racist remarks but there was evidence that he was chanting "scum" and that he had taken part in kicking and pushing down fencing around a building site, and that he had hurled missiles at counter protesters made up of young Asian men from the group United Against Fascism (UAF). The defendant was convicted of violent disorder and his sentence was aggravated based on s. 145 of the Criminal Justice Act 2003.[71] On appeal the appellant claimed that his actions were directed towards the UAF which was a political and multi-cultural, multi-ethnic group, albeit one with many Asian and Muslim members. While others had clearly expressed racist and anti-religious hostilities he claimed that had not done so. The court referring to section 28(3) of the Crime and Disorder Act held that the appellant's admission that he wanted to fight the UAF, whose membership was substantially Asian, provided sufficient material from which the judge could infer that the appellant's involvement was, *in part at least*, religiously motivated.

Yet even with the lower part motivation test used in many jurisdictions, the courts can remain reluctant to take prejudice aggravation into account at sentencing. In the Australian (Victorian) case of *O'Brien and Hudson*,[72] two men engaged in a prolonged and extremely violent attack and robbery against a young Vietnamese student, during which the offenders repeatedly used racist slurs. The defendants had been members of a gang called the "Crazy Whiteboys", which O'Brien stated had "morphed into a Neo-Nazi group".[73] During police interview, O'Brien went on to use racist slurs to describe the victim and admitted they were

---

[71] Section 145(b) "the offence is motivated (wholly or partly) by hostility towards members of a racial or religious group based on their membership of that group". This subsection is now consolidated in section 66 of the Sentencing Act 2020.

[72] *R v O'Brien & Hudson* [2012] VSC 592.

[73] *R v O'Brien & Hudson* [2012] VSC 592 [13].

6 Legislating for Hate Crime Globally: Putting "Social Justice"...

"skinheads". Quite astonishingly, the court found while the defendant's concession meant that the test for motivation was met,[74] it was held that racial hatred was "a very small part of the motivation" as the two men had carried out numerous robberies in the past.[75] This in turn meant that the expression of hatred played only a minor role in determining the appropriate sentence.

The decision in *Rintoull and Sabatino*[76] also raises concerns about the use of "motivation" tests, even where there is the inclusion of "partly motivated" in the legislation. Rintoull was convicted of the murder of a 19-year-old man of Sudanese decent. Several days earlier, he had been chased on a group of days by Sudanese men who had been carrying knives. Just before the murder, the offender was heard yelling, "[t]hese blacks are turning the town into the Bronx. I am going to take my town back, I'm looking to kill the blacks" and "I guess I'll go and take my anger out on some n*****".[77] The offender left his house and soon afterwards repeatedly struck the victim killing him. Shortly after the murder, the offender was heard saying, "I bashed a n***** and I think he's dead".[78] The defendant had also been found to have spray painted racist slurs in his home. On appeal the judge concluded that Rintoull's actions were not (partly) motivated by racial prejudice. The judge stated that "[t]o say that this killing was racially motivated is to deny a complex set of factors". These included that he was frustrated by the actions of the Sudanese men who had chased him previously, that he had been in an "aggressive mood", and that he recently taken food to a homeless Sudanese boy. These factors, it was determined, meant that the despite spraying racist slurs on a building, telling people he wanted to kill individuals using the most inflammatory and racist term in existence, and later using the same term to describe his dead victim, the court decided he was not even *partly*

---

[74] In this jurisdiction the test is found under of the Sentencing Act 1991, s 5(2AC)(2) "In sentencing an offender a court must have regard to—(d)(aaa) Whether the offence was motivated (wholly or partly) by hatred for or prejudice against a group of people with common characteristics with which the victim was associated or with which the offender believed the victim was associated".

[75] R v O'Brien & Hudson [2012] VSC 592 [44].

[76] R v Rintoull & Sabatino [2009] VSC 617 [104, 106–108].

[77] R v Rintoull & Sabatino [2009] VSC 617 [76].

[78] R v Rintoull & Sabatino [2009] VSC 617 [77].

motivated by racial prejudice. The extent to which this is a result of limitations to motivation test or a manifestation of institutional racism within the Victorian judiciary is difficult to discern. What is clear is that for some courts, the most objectively extreme forms of racism, when coupled with other causal factors, will mean that an offence will not be considered as hate motivated.

A similar limitation appears to arise in jurisdictions that use "mixed models", where wording draws on both animus and discriminatory selection models.[79] For example, in New Zealand the Sentencing Act 2002, s. 9 states that the court must take into account the following aggravating factors:

> (h) that the offender committed the offence partly or wholly because of hostility towards a group of persons who have an enduring common characteristic such as race, colour, nationality, religion, gender identity, sexual orientation, age, or disability.

Case law there suggests that the "because of" test even when linked "partly" to animus is to be interpreted as meaning "motivated by" that animus. In *C v Police*,[80] the offender, who was very drunk, forced his way into the home of two gay men where he assaulted them. During the commission of his offence he made comments about "gays". The court held that he was not motivated by hostility against the victim's sexual orientation, but instead he had merely made allusions to their sexual orientation.[81]

The conflation of the words "because of" with motivation appears in numerous other cases, such as the more recent case of *Arps v Police*[82] involving a defendant who had distributed video footage of a mass murder carried out in two mosques in Christchurch in 2019. The court interpreting the Sentencing Act 2002 held that section 9 required "a sentencing

---

[79] The latter is discussed more fully below.
[80] *C v Police HC Auckland* CRI 2008-404-307 [2009] NZHC 627 [35].
[81] The demonstration of hostility was still nonetheless deemed an aggravating factor during sentence. *C v Police HC Auckland* CRI 2008-404-307 [2009] NZHC 627.
[82] *Arps v Police* [2019] NZCA 592.

Judge to take into account the defendant's *motivation* for offending based upon hostility towards the victim or victims because of their common characteristic".[83]

It is for these reasons that I do not classify this type of legislation as "mixed" or "combined" in Appendix A. It is clear that where a statute or code requires a hate-element, focus will typically be given to evidencing this when proving the offence. The model used in New Zealand is therefore one of animus, while the use of "because of" or "due to" refers not to the model of legislation but to the standard of proof required to show animus. Hence, whether a hate-element must be proved by "motivation" or "because of" it, ultimately feelings of hate, prejudice or bias must be shown as the main causal element of the offence.

Beyond the case law interpreting the narrow application of motivation tests is empirical research that suggests its use in legislation can be highly inhibitive in prosecuting hate crimes. In the US context, Maldonado a former prosecutor in New York highlighted the difficulty of obtaining reliable evidence to prove bias motivation noting that, "the proof of a nexus between the unlawful physical contact and the bias motivation of the perpetrator is what makes the prosecution of bias crimes extremely difficult".[84] In a more recent study on prosecutorial decision making across 30 US states, Eisenberg found that many prosecutors avoid bringing hate crime charges. Chief amongst the reasons for not doing so was the belief "that proving an actor's motive—what was really driving their actions—is immensely difficult".[85] Part of the issue is obtaining credible evidence of a defendant's reasons for committing the crime, with many cases turning into a exploration of whether they are a genuinely bigoted person.[86] Eisenberg notes that jurors faced with evidence that a

---

[83] *Arps v Police* [2019] NZCA 592, para 48 (emphasis added). See similarly *R v Angelich* [2018] NZHC 2429.

[84] Migdalia Maldonado, 'Practical problems with enforcing hate crimes legislation in New York' (1992–1993) Ann Surv Am L 555. See also, Karen Franklin, 'Good Intentions: The Enforcement of Hate Crime Penalty-Enhancement Statutes' (2002) 46(1) Am Behav Sci 154.

[85] Avlana Eisenberg, 'Hate-Crime Laws Don't Work as Their Supporters Intended' *The Atlantic* (22 June 2021).

[86] Franklin 2002 (see Footnote 84).

perpetrator acted for multiple reasons can acquit on an added hate-crime charge because bias is not the sole or predominant motive.[87]

Research in the European context has produced similar findings. A common theme across Schweppe et al.'s comparative analysis of five European jurisdictions was that the use of motivation within hate crime provisions significantly restricted the application of such laws.[88] In Sweden, interviews with prosecutors showed that "it is difficult to provide evidence of the motivation as a motive is seldom visible… if no oral comments were made in relation to the offence it could be difficult to prove motive".[89] The Czech report similarly notes that the "exceptional difficulty of proving motivation is… the likely reason why the number of hate crimes heard in Czech courts is so low".[90] While the England and Wales study similarly found that the motivation test in England and Wales was rarely used, with some judges and Crown Prosecution hate crime managers stating they had never come across successful prosecutions using the motivation test. Walters et al. assert that this is a significant finding given the fact that the CPS in England and Wales successfully prosecutes approximately 10,000 hate crime cases every year.[91]

Part of the difficulty in proving motive is that it requires the gathering of evidence by officers with specialist investigative skills backed by additional resources that enable enforcement agencies to collate sufficient information that shows the reasons underpinning an offender's behaviour.[92] Even where sufficient evidence of motivation does exist, a further issue has arisen which additionally inhibits the application of the animus model. Research in England and Wales suggests that a focus on motive

---

[87] Eisenberg 2021 (see Footnote 85).
[88] See Jennifer Schweppe, Amanda Haynes and Mark A Walters, *Lifecycle of a Hate Crime: Comparative Report* (ICCL 2018).
[89] Görel Granström and Karin Åström, *Life Cycle of a Hate Crime: Country Report for Sweden* (ICCL 2017) 47.
[90] Václav Walach and others (2017) *Lifecycle of a Hate Crime: Country Report for the Czech Republic* (ICCL 2018) 30.
[91] The reason for the very high rates of prosecution and convictions is explained in the next section.
[92] Walters, Wiedlitzka and Owusu-Bempah 2017 (see Footnote 40); Granström and Åström 2017 (see Footnote 89).

has given rise to a perception that "hate crime" offenders must be "racists" or "homophobes" (for example); to be distinguished from those who have behaved in a racist or homophobic manner, but who do not see it as part of their character to be prejudiced against entire groups of people. Robertson writing in the Canadian context concurs with this finding noting that:

> a focus on motive misconceives the scope of evil the legislature actually seeks to deter. By only looking to motive, the court conceptualizes hate as the product of a deeply held belief and hate crime as necessarily premeditated in nature, ignoring how in the majority of cases hostility manifests social prejudice only in the commission of an offense.[93]

The focus on whether someone is a bad person has provided opportunities for defence counsel to put forward counter evidence that the defendant is not a "real" bigot, rather they have simply behaved badly during a tense situation.[94] Walters et al. reference one seasoned defence counsel who explained that trials can become consumed by testimony from character witnesses, who are called to show that the defendant has friends from the same identity group as the victim. The interviewee explained that by the end of the trial jurors are often convinced that defendant is the "the least racist person in the country and they acquit you of everything—including the crime you were charged with. So actually, it's God's gift to defence I would say".[95]

The risk then is that not only does reliance on motivation give rise to practical difficulties that are so inhibitive that few cases ever meet the required threshold, but the doubt cast by failing to prove that an individual is an out-and-out bigot beyond reasonable doubt may in some cases result in offenders being acquitted for the basic offence as well.

---

[93] Sean Robertson, 'Exception to Excess: Tactical Use of the Law by Outgroups in Bias Crime Legislation' (2012) 37(2) Law Soc Inquiry 456, 462.
[94] A similar finding is highlighted by Franklin 2002 (see Footnote 84).
[95] Cited in Walters, Wiedlitzka and Owusu-Bempah 2017 (see Footnote 40) 125.

Demonstrating Versus Motivation of Hate

An alternative approach to incorporating motive in hate crime legislation is to attach the hate-element to the actus reus of an offence. This method involves constructing the hate-element as a type of action or conduct that accompanies a basic offence, such as where an offender "demonstrates" or "expresses" hate or prejudice during its commission.[96] In England and Wales, section 28(1) of the Crime and Disorder Act 1998 states that an offence is racially or religiously aggravated if:

(a) at the time of committing the offence, or immediately before or after doing so, the offender demonstrates towards the victim of the offence hostility based on the victim's membership (or presumed membership) of a racial or religious group; or
(b) the offence is motivated (wholly or partly) by hostility towards members of a racial or religious group based on their membership of that group.

A constellation of other legal jurisdictions linked to the UK have followed this dual approach,[97] while other jurisdictions following this model include Singapore,[98] and Western Australia.[99] Baroness Hale in the leading case of *Rogers* has interpreted the English and Welsh test as involving an "outward manifestation" of hostility.[100] The breadth of this test has at times been resisted by lower courts which have attempted to conflate demonstration with that of motivation. For instance, in English case of *Woods*[101] an offender had become angry when queuing to enter a nightclub because his friend had been refused entry. This resulted in an altercation with the nightclub's doorman whereby Woods assaulted him, during

---

[96] DC Code § 22–3701.
[97] Kay Goodall and Mark A Walters, *Legislating to Address Hate Crimes Against the LGBT Community in the Commonwealth* (Human Dignity Trust 2019).
[98] Criminal Code (Singapore), s 74.
[99] The Criminal Code (Western Australia), s 80I.
[100] *R v Rogers* [2007] UKHL 8 [6].
[101] *R v Woods* [2002] EWHC 85 (Admin).

which he called the victim a "black bastard". At trial the judge held that the respondent's hostility was:

> borne out of his frustration and annoyance as a result of his companion being denied entry to the premises, and whilst he may have intended to cause offence by the words, this was not 'hostility based on the victim's membership (or presumed membership) of a racial group'.[102]

A similar interpretation of "demonstration" was taken by the District of Columbia (USA) Court of Appeals in *Lucas v United States*[103] where "bias-related crime" is defined as "a designated act that demonstrates an accused's prejudice based on the actual or perceived [characteristics of the victim]".[104] The Court interpreted this provision as requiring proof of motive that is based on a but for test, that is the court must ask: "but for" the defendant's prejudice against the victim's characteristic would the offence have occurred?[105]

However, unlike the upper courts in the District of Columbia, when the English case of *Woods* was appealed the objective application of the demonstration test was reiterated by Maurice Kay J, who stated in the High Court:

> Section 28(1)(a) ... is designed to extend to cases which may have a racially neutral gravamen but in the course of which there is demonstrated towards the victim hostility based on the victim's membership of a racial group. Any contrary construction would emasculate section 28(1)(a).[106]

---

[102] Judgment of lower court quoted in the appealed decision of *R v Woods* [2002] EWHC 85 (Admin) [6].

[103] 240 A.3d 328 (2020), 340–341.

[104] *Lucas v United States* DC Code § 22–3701.

[105] 240 A.3d 328 (2020), 340–341. The court notes that but for can be exchanged for "because of" or "based on". The court also dismissed the state's argument that "demonstrates prejudice" should include incidents where the accused's prejudice is a "contributing cause" of the crime or a motivating factor.

[106] *R v Woods* [2002] EWHC 85 (Admin) [12].

This means that an offender need not be motivated by hostility nor must they be a "racist" in order to fall within the ambit of the legislation.[107] Most cases of this type involve violence or threats of violence where the victim is denigrated for their group characteristic. While it has been shown that slurs and epithets can be used as proof of hate motivation,[108] what is important under the demonstration test is that the offender has actively expressed identity-based hostility which has occurred as part of a basic offence. Why the offence was committed does not matter in law under such a test.

The vast majority of prosecutions and convictions in England and Wales are completed under the demonstration of hostility test.[109] And it is one of the reasons why England and Wales prosecutes more offences as "aggravated" hate offences than any other country in the world.[110] It is clear from the case law considered above that many of the types of "hate crimes" prosecuted in England and Wales, Scotland, and Northern Ireland would almost certainly not succeed in jurisdictions, such as the USA, and especially those that rely on a sole motivation test.

The breadth of the law in both English and Scots law is such that even where there is no discernible victim that the hostility is demonstrated towards, an offender's hostile behaviour may still fall foul of the legislation. For instance, in *Taylor v DPP* two police officers were called to a house by medics, upon entering a heavily intoxicated woman began shouting racist abuse and was asked to leave the premises during which she continued to use racist language, including the N-word.[111] The trial judge found "that anybody hearing that sort of language, black or white,

---

[107] Though defence counsel will still often emphasise that the offender is not a racist in order to encourage a not guilty verdict for the hate-element, as outlined above, see Walters, Wiedlitzka and Owusu-Bempah 2017 (see Footnote 40) 117–131.

[108] See Oxford Pro Bono Publico, *Comparative Hate Crime Research Report: A report prepared for the Hungarian Civil Liberties Union* (University of Oxford 2014).

[109] Walters, Wiedlitzka and Owusu-Bempah 2017 (see Footnote 40).

[110] The country also has one of the most extensive policy and guidance domains, strong political focus on combatting hate crime and an array of training programmes for criminal justice practitioners tasked with responding to hate crime, see Paul Giannasi and Nathan Hall, 'Policing hate crime: Transferable strategies for Improving Service Provision to Victims and Communities Internationally' in Jennifer Schweppe and Mark A Walters (eds), *The Globalization of Hate: Internationalizing Hate Crime* (OUP 2016).

[111] *Taylor v DPP* [2006] EWHC 1202 (Admin).

would be likely to be caused distress thereby".[112] The relevant legislation made it clear that such abuse expressed within the "hearing or sight of a person likely to be caused harassment, alarm or distress thereby" could give rise to liability, and despite none of those present being Black, the appeal court held that the racial hostility was sufficient to aggravate the offence.[113]

One of the main criticisms of this type of animus model is that it is likely to capture expressions of hostility that are directed towards victims, but which are only tangentially causal to the offence. Some hostilities can be expressed in the "heat of the moment" during the commission of an offence, often expressed out of frustration or anger.[114] For some commentators, and judges, these angry expressions of hostility should not be labelled as "hate crimes" at all.[115] This is based on the viewpoint that crimes should only be labelled as "aggravated offences" where the hate-element is directly *causal* to the underlying offence.[116] At its most starkest, we can question whether, in law, we should distinguish between the offender who is driven by hatred and who plans and executes violent acts of prejudice in an attempt to eradicate "difference", from those who, often fuelled by alcohol or drug intoxication, express hate through acts of violence but who are primarily motivated by other extraneous factors.

In answering this question we need to revisit the principles of both culpability and harm.[117] We can start by asking: should an expression of hostility demonstrated in the heat of the moment during a criminal act carry a greater degree of culpability for the crime committed? If we accept that crimes with a hate-element (regardless of motive) cause distinct

---

[112] Ibid. [8].
[113] See also, *DPP v Dykes* [2008] EWHC 2775; in the Scottish context see, *Martin v Bott* 2005 HCJAC 73.
[114] As was the case in *R v Woods* [2002] EWHC 85 (Admin).
[115] See examples in Walters, Wiedlitzka and Owusu-Bempah 2017 (see Footnote 40) s 8.5.
[116] See Jacobs and Potter 1998 (see Footnote 28) 11–16. See generally Nathan Hall, *Hate Crime* (Routledge 2013) 23, Table 1.
[117] See for example James Chalmers and Fiona Leverick, *A Comparative Analysis of Hate Crime Legislation: A Report to the Hate Crime Legislation Review* (University of Glasgow 2017); Kay Goodall, 'Conceptualising 'racism' in criminal law' (2013) 33 LS 215; Mark A Walters, 'Conceptualizing "hostility" for hate crime law: Minding "the minutiae" when interpreting section 28(1)(a) of the Crime and Disorder Act 1998' (2014b) 34(1) OJLS 47.

harms, which are likely to have more serious consequences for victims and social groups, we might impute that the greater seriousness of such acts will equate to a higher degree of culpability for those who commit them. However, before holding someone more culpable for the hate-element of a crime, we ought also to ask what their mental state was in relation to this. In other words, did the offender intend to express hate, were they reckless as to its effects or were they at least aware of them? I have contended elsewhere that it would be a stretch of criminal law doctrine to hold someone liable for an act or consequence which they have no awareness of.[118] I have outlined that demonstrations of hostility should at least be accompanied by an *awareness* that it would be perceived by rightminded people as an expression of identity-based hostility.[119] In reality, it is highly likely that individuals who use racist or other prejudiced language when committing an offence will have done so consciously and purposively. Why else would someone express hatred when committing an act of violence if not aimed at additionally hurting the victim? Indeed, it would take an extraordinary situation for them to have no awareness at all that to do so would be to denigrate the victim's identity.[120] However, where there are legitimate questions over one's awareness of hostility, this should be put to the court as potentially negating a defendant's enhanced culpability.

Nonetheless, if the aim of hate crime legislation is to prevent the proliferation of hate and prejudice in society, then it should matter not, *at least in law*, whether their public display of identity animus is one that is pre-planned or made in a split second. Rarely are offences codified based on how much the offender "wanted" a result to be brought about.[121] As Walters et al. conclude, "[c]ulpability must rest on whether the defendant is a disseminator of hatred (or hostility) within society, and not on whether we believe him or her to be ideologically committed to racism,

---

[118] Walters 2014b (ibid.).

[119] Where an offender is completely unconscious of the fact that certain words have a hostile or prejudiced meaning there should be flexibility within the interpretation of demonstration tests to restrict liability to the parallel offence only. See Walters 2014b (see Footnote 117).

[120] Though there have been some cases where such a situation arises, see Walters, Wiedlitzka and Owusu-Bempah 2017 (see Footnote 40), section 8.

[121] Except for inchoate offences.

islamophobia, homophobia or whatever the prejudice might be".¹²² Hence, it is no excuse within liberal criminal law for an offender who, so often, claims, "well I didn't really mean it, it was the drink talking not me!". Indeed, as one judge remarked in Walters et al., "not everyone when they've had too much to drink refers to people in racially abusive terms, so is it really an excuse?"¹²³ Of course the extent to which planned, intentional or reckless forms of hostility aggravate a sentence should, and often are, taken into account during the sentencing stage of the criminal process.¹²⁴ But this does not detract from the normative position of the criminal law.

Beyond culpability is the important question of harm. The criminal law is tasked not only with recognising how blameworthy someone is for a criminal act, but it must construct offences and their penalties based on how harmful they are. Chapter 3 examined in detail how acts of hate, whether pre-planned or committed in the heat of the moment, will likely have greater (distinct) impacts than those where no hate-element exists. This gives rise to the claim that an enhanced punishment is justified as it recognises the elevated levels of harm caused by the offender. However, some critics have argued that even this approach is unjustified. Dan Kahan has claimed that the penalty enhancements amount to an implicit "bad-value added tax" on violence, based on the assertion that an offender is punished once for the basic offence and then again for hate-element.¹²⁵ Such an argument, it is asserted, is a misconception of how hate crime harms individuals, communities and society. Attempts to compartmentalise basic offences and the hate-element fails to comprehend how the fusion of the two alters the *quality* of the offender's underlying conduct. This is because when joined together, the totality of harms caused by hate-based conduct is greater than the sum of its parts. An expression of hate cannot be simply understood as an individual having "bad values", as contended by Kahan. This is because when the hate-element is "added" to any form of criminality it directly poses an enhanced threat to the

---

[122] See similarly, Goodall 2013 (see Footnote 117).
[123] Walters, Wiedlitzka and Owusu-Bempah 2017 (see Footnote 40) 127.
[124] See Walters, Wiedlitzka and Owusu-Bempah 2017 (see Footnote 40) s 10.
[125] Dan M Kahan, 'Two liberal fallacies in the hate crimes debate' (2001) 20 Law & Phil 175.

victim, and others who share their characteristic (a threat that is absent from non-hate offences). A threat which frequently results in emotional traumas and negative behavioural reactions. These are unique consequences, which have in turn been linked to social marginalisation, feelings of powerlessness, as well as cultural harm (as fully outlined in Chap. 2).

A final comparison between Canada's hate crime statistics and those within England and Wales helps to illuminate the workability of the different tests in reality.[126] In 2017–2018 there were an estimated 184,000 hate crimes that occurred across the two nations of England and Wales.[127] During this same period 94,098 hate crimes were recorded by the police,[128] while 14,151 were prosecuted by the CPS resulting in 11,987 convictions and 7784 declared sentencing uplifts by the courts.[129] In the same year the General Social Survey on Canadians' Safety (Victimization) found that there were an estimated 330,000 criminal incidents that victim's perceived as being motivated by hate.[130] The Canadian police recorded 2073 hate crimes in 2017.[131] The data has to be treated with caution, due to the fact that different definitions are used across the jurisdictions and the population of Canada is two-thirds that of England and Wales.[132] But these differences may also illustrate something important. There will be numerous variables that lead to such a significant divergence in the "justice gap" between these jurisdictions.[133] Nonetheless, it is highly likely that England and Wales' use of a broader legislative definition of hate crime, that includes "demonstrations" of hate, means that

---

[126] For a full analysis of these statistics and the legal process for hate crime in England and Wales see Walters, Wiedlitzka and Owusu-Bempah 2017 (see Footnote 40).

[127] Home Office, *Hate Crime, England and Wales, 2017/18 Statistical Bulletin 20/18* (Home Office 2018).

[128] Home Office 2018 (ibid.).

[129] Crown Prosecution Service, *Hate Crime Annual Report 2017–18* (CPS 2018).

[130] Statistics Canada, 'Police-reported hate crime, 2017' (Statistics Canada 2018).

[131] Statistics Canada 2018 (ibid.). There are no prosecution data publicly available.

[132] As well as the usual limitations to data gathering of this sort, see Mike Maguire and Susan McVie, 'Crime data and criminal statistics: a critical reflection' in Alison Liebling, Shadd Maruna and Lesley McAra (eds), *Oxford Handbook of Criminology* (6th edn, OUP 2017) 163–188.

[133] Including how important hate crime is on the political agenda, the extent to which it is included in policy documentation, public understandings of what hate crime is, and police training on identifying it.

England and Wales records significantly more hate crimes (51 per cent of the total estimated number)[134] than Canada, which relies on a "motivation" test (at 0.6 per cent of the total estimated). If a mere 0.6 per cent of the estimated hate crime in Canada is recorded it is likely that a tiny fraction of incidents is ever successfully prosecuted and that s. 718(2)(a) of the Canadian Criminal Code is applied at sentencing.[135]

If such provisions remain unused to this extent, both the practical and symbolic purpose of hate crime legislation is undermined. This matters greatly. Not only does failure to successfully implement hate crime provisions bring the law into disrepute, but it may also exacerbate identity-based hostilities. As Lawrence notes, if the state fails to punish hate crime more harshly the "implicit message expressed… is that racial harmony and equality are not among the highest values in our society".[136] This can in turn fuel the fire of hate rather than suppress it. In fact research in Australia suggests that where race hate crimes are punished leniently this may result in increased levels of racism amongst the public.[137] As such, given that "demonstration of hostility" models can be "entirely justified",[138] and given that both case law and empirical studies have found motivation tests to be rarely appliable, it is recommended that where animus models are retained by legislatures they include wording that incorporate "outward manifestations" of hate.

6.2.2 The Discriminatory Selection Model

The other main approach to criminalising hate is to construct the legal test around the selection of victims based on their characteristics, removing entirely any direct reference to group-based animus. This approach is

---

[134] It also includes a perception based definition for recording purposes including crimes that are perceived by the victim or any other person as being motivated by hostility or prejudice, see College of Policing, 'Responding to hate' (College of Policing 2020).

[135] For the total number of hate crimes reported through to the number which are convicted and hate crime provisions applied see Walters, Wiedlitzka and Owusu-Bempah 2017 (see Footnote 40) s 5.

[136] Lawrence 1999 (see Footnote 6) 169.

[137] Alison C Sullivan and others, 'The Impact of Unpunished Hate Crimes: When Derogating the Victim Extends into Derogating the Group'(2016) 29 Social Justice Research 310.

[138] As Chalmers and Leverick have also concluded, Chalmers and Leverick 2017 (see Footnote 117) 50–51.

referred to as the discriminatory (or group selection) model and it was the most common form of hate crime legislation found to be used globally during the comparative analysis conducted for this book. Discriminatory model laws typically require prosecutors to prove that an offence was committed "by reason",[139] "because of",[140] "due to",[141] "based on",[142] "on the basis of"[143] or "on the ground of" a protected characteristic. For example, Article 53 of the Criminal Code of Georgia, states that any crime committed:

> on the grounds of race, colour, language, sex, sexual orientation, gender identity, age, religion, political or other beliefs, disability, citizenship, national, ethnic or social origin, material status or rank, place of residence or other discriminatory grounds shall constitute an aggravating circumstance for all the relevant crimes provided for by this Code.

The wording of discriminatory selection models such as Georgia's suggests that an offender need not feel any hatred or animosity towards their victim at all. Rather, all that it required is that they have targeted a victim based on their identity characteristic. Reported case law interpreting the discriminatory model is focused mostly in the USA where the model has been used for the longest period of time. There has been some confusion as to the mens rea element of such offences, primarily whether they require an offender to have *intentionally* selected a victim because of their characteristic or whether it involves evidence of the offender's *motivation* that is linked to a "discriminatory point of view".[144] In *State v Talley*, the Washington Supreme Court interpreted their discriminatory selection statute as "punish[ing] the selection of the victim, not the reason for the selection … The statute is triggered by the victim selection regardless of the actor's motives or beliefs".[145] Case law in New York has also stated

---

[139] For example Ohio Rev Stat Ann § 2927.12.
[140] For example Criminal Code (Angola), art 71(1)(c).
[141] For example Criminal Code (Latvia), art 48(14).
[142] For example Criminal Code (Russia), art 136(2).
[143] For example Criminal Code (Guinea), art 209, 303 & 306(8).
[144] *Wisconsin v Mitchell* 508 US 476, 485. See discussion in Lawrence 1999 (see Footnote 6) 33–34 and Goodall 2013 (see Footnote 117) 224–226.
[145] *State v Talley*, 858 P.2d 217, 222 (Wash. 1993), referenced in Jordan Blair Woods, 'Taking the "Hate" out of Hate Crimes: Applying Unfair Advantage Theory to Justify the Enhanced Punishment of Opportunistic Bias Crime' (2008) 56 UCLA L Rev 489, 500.

that prosecutors need only to show evidence of intent to select a victim based on their characteristic.[146] In the case of *Fox*,[147] the offenders had lured the victim to meet with them via an online chat room under the pretence that they would have sexual relations, but instead they intended to rob him. Evidence, including testimony and past conduct, showed that the defendants believed gay men were easy targets to rob. Upon meeting the victim, the offenders punched him twice before chasing him onto a freeway whereby he was knocked down by a car and killed. In their decision, the court emphasised that the offenders' motivation to gain money was only part of the reason for committing the offence, with their targeting specifically of gay men being central to understanding the nature of the criminality being prosecuted. The Supreme Court of the State of New York interpreting § 485.05(1)(a) of N.Y. Penal Law stated the actions of the defendants were "*tantamount* to a crime motivated by bias, prejudice or hatred".[148]

Nevertheless, it remains to some extent unclear (within the US context at least) whether intentional selection of a victim by reason of their identity involves a subjective analysis of the offender's motives (reasons, including animus) for committing the offence, or whether it simply involves an assessment of intent.[149] As I will outline below, further explanatory notes on how it should be interpreted may help with its practical application.

Does the Discriminatory Model Include Non-hate Conduct?

The omission within this model of legislation to include words such as hate, prejudice or bias has left some commentators to question whether

---

[146] See *People v Fox*, 17 Misc 3d 281, 2007 NY Slip Op 27317, 844 NYS 2d 627 (NY Sup Ct 2007); see also *State v Stalder* 630 So 2d 1072 (Fla 1994).
[147] *People v Fox*, 17 Misc 3d 281, 2007 NY Slip Op 27317, 844 NYS 2d 627 (NY Sup Ct 2007), in reference to New York Penal Law § 485.05(1)(a), which applies to intentionally selecting a victim because of a belief or perception about their protected characteristic.
[148] Emphasis added. Referenced also in both Goodall 2013 (see Footnote 92) and OSCE/ODIHR, *Hate Crime Laws: A Practical Guide* (OSCE/ODIHR 2009).
[149] Goodall 2013 (see Footnote 92) 225.

some of the offences that could fall within its ambit are "hate crimes" at all.[150] Goodall asserts that:

> the offender need not feel any particular animus toward the victim: his or her reason can be expedience... the offender has selected the victim simply because of a stereotype which sees the victim as part of a 'racial' group which has an exploitable characteristic.[151]

The Australian case of *R v Aslett*[152] illustrates such a scenario.[153] In this case the defendants had burgled the home of an Asian family out of the belief that "Asians tended to keep money and jewellery in their homes".[154] The court found that the belief, although based on racial stereotypes, was not motivation of racial hatred or prejudice towards Asians. Mason reflects that by implication the robbery of a Jewish person based on the belief that all Jews are wealthy would not fulfil evidence of prejudice motivation, and nor would the attack of a gay man based on the belief that gay men are all effeminate and unlikely to be able to fight back.[155]

These analyses reveal a position taken by many courts and commentators that victim's targeted because of a stereotype or perception about their identity is not really about hate or prejudice at all but is instead about opportunism, which the offender is exploiting for their own gain. Lord Bracadale in his review of hate crime models comes to this very conclusion in his final report on the Scottish legal framework:

> For example, a bogus workman might target a number of people on a street and be successful in defrauding some of the neighbours but not others. This may be because the particular individuals are more easily deceived, and this could be considered to be related to their age or disability. However,

---

[150] See Goodall 2013 (see Footnote 117).

[151] Goodall 2013 (see Footnote 117) 223.

[152] *R v Aslett* [2006] NSWCCA 49, [124] in reference to Crimes (Sentencing Procedure) Act 1999, s 21A(2).

[153] Discussed in both Goodall 2013 (see Footnote 92) and Gail Mason, 'Hate crime laws in Australia: are they achieving their goals?' (2009) 33(6) Crim LJ 326.

[154] *R v Aslett* [2006] NSWCCA 49 at [124], also cited in Mason 2009 (ibid.) 335. The defendants had also committed sexual assault of a young girl who was in the premises.

[155] Mason 2009 (see Footnote 153).

it is not clear to me that this type of crime is what society would wish to mark out specifically as a hate crime.

Such conclusions reflect an understanding of hate crime and its legal proscription as needing something that goes beyond an offender's bias views about a group's abilities or capacities. Hence, the burglar of only Asian homes or the thief who targets only mentally disabled victims is not prejudiced *enough* to be considered a hate crime offender, but rather they are individuals who have calculated that they will likely get a bigger return from their endeavours by selecting a certain type of victim based on a stereotype that often positions the victim as an easy target. This, it is argued, may well be a matter to be taken into consideration at sentencing, such as where a victim is deemed "vulnerable", but it is not one for hate crime provisions.[156]

Interestingly the examples above make a distinction between offenders' direct feelings of "prejudice" and "hatred" on the one hand (which should fall within the definition of hate crime) and those who stereotype victims and proactively apply these in victimising others (which should not fall within the definition). Yet as Mason points out, stereotyping is at the very heart of defining what prejudice is. Allport defined ethnic prejudice as "an antipathy based upon a faulty and inflexible generalisation. It may be felt or expressed. It may be directed towards a group as a whole, or towards an individual because he is a member of that group".[157] Other common definitions of prejudice do not necessarily refer directly to stereotyping but they still very much bring the actions of offenders who target victims for criminal victimisation because of their identity within its boundaries. For example, Abrams' review of social psychological understandings of prejudice defines it as "bias which devalues people because of their perceived membership of a social group".[158]

---

[156] See for example the English case of *R v Bickley* [2014] 8 WLUK 338, which involved the singling out of a Muslim person's home to burgle during the religious festival of Eid based on the fact that it was more likely to be empty. The court found that this did not amount to religious hostility but was nonetheless an aggravating factor going to culpability.

[157] Gordon W Allport, *The Nature of Prejudice* (Addison-Wesley 1954) 10.

[158] Dominic Abrams, *Processes of Prejudice: Theory, Evidence and Intervention* (EHRC 2010) 3.

In each of these definitions behaviour that is in some way negative towards an individual due to their group identity falls within the definition of prejudice. In transposing definitions of prejudice into law, then, we need to ask the key question of whether the intentional selection of a victim based on their identity is something that is either directly or indirectly negative, or something that devalues them as a group of people? If we return to each of the examples, we might ask the following more specific questions: is attacking a gay person because they are perceived to be effeminate, behaviour that implies some negativity or which devalues gay people as a group? Does the targeting of mentally disabled people because they are an easy target devalue mentally disabled people's position in society? Does the robbery of Jewish people because of a belief that all Jews are rich devalue Jews as a group?

It is asserted that the answer to each of the above questions is yes. I am in agreement with Woods who notes that discriminatory selection in such situations is "distinctly deplorable because unlike typical robberies, they contain a rationally calculative element to exploit unjust economic and social conditions that cause group ostracism and discrimination for personal gain".[159] Similarly, the violence that directed towards someone based on a belief that their sexual orientation makes them effeminate and weak serves to perpetuate a stereotype that frames these individuals in a pejorative way. This is not to say that male effeminacy is something that is essentially negative, far from it, but rather that there is a general attitude which implies negativity towards it. This has the likely effect of increasing perceptions of threat amongst all gay men who are aware that stereotypes attached to their identity increases their risk of violent victimisation. In turn, this can result in gay people changing how they act or even dress, thereby reducing their full and equal participation in society.[160] Likewise, the targeting of mentally disabled people *because* of their disability will likely have a similar marginalising affect. The belief that someone is an easy target because of their identity devalues them, which

---

[159] Jordan Blair Woods, 'Taking the "Hate" out of Hate Crimes: Applying Unfair Advantage Theory to Justify the Enhanced Punishment of Opportunistic Bias Crime' (2008) 56 UCLA L Rev 489, 511.

[160] As outlined in Chap. 3.

when applied to targeted victimisation results in the group experiencing greater levels of social injustice.

Similar conclusions apply to crimes based on the belief that all Jews are rich. Such a belief feeds into a historical narrative that Jews control capital and have unfairly gained wealth over that of other racial groups. Even our primary example of burglars targeting only Asian people due to a perception that they have more money in their homes serves to reduce an entire ethnic group to something which is largely untrue, and which exposes them to targeted victimisation based on this false stereotype. Such crimes therefore involve taking unfair advantage of certain social groups by reason of their identity.[161] In each case, the devaluation of the group through targeted criminal victimisation feeds directly into those groups' experiences of social injustice. I therefore concur with Danner who concludes that a:

> decision to select a member of a protected group as his victim makes the perpetrator more blameworthy: he knowingly or recklessly joins other wrongdoers in a demonstration of bias and discrimination that ultimately harms our society.[162]

It is worth reiterating that hate crime legislation specifies group characteristics *worthy* of special protection under the law because of their marginalised position in society.[163] This is in response to their disproportionate experience of targeted victimisation which results in distinct individual and social harms.[164] The group selection model of legislation reflects and recognises appositely the deeper structural levels of harm experienced by communities of people who are targeted because of the negative stereotypes linked to their group identity; that is conduct that serves to further oppress them because of who they are.[165] If the

---

[161] Woods 2008 (see Footnote 159) 511.

[162] Alison M Danner, 'Bias crimes and crimes against humanity: culpability in context' (2002) 6 Buffalo Crim L Rev 389, 406.

[163] As outlined in Chap. 4.

[164] Chap. 3.

[165] See also Woods 2008 (see Footnote 159) 511; Lu-in Wang, 'Recognizing opportunistic bias crimes' (2000) 80 Boston UL Rev 1399; Danner 2002 (see Footnote 162) 406.

criminalisation of hate is a reflection of the distinct harms attached to the targeted victimisation of certain social groups, and if we accept that intentionally targeting someone because of their group identity is a form of bias, then the group selection model fairly encapsulates the social justice liberal approach to legislating for hate crime.[166]

Nonetheless, even if we accept that group selection is a form of prejudice, there remains a question of whether offenders who select victims by reason of their identity lack the requisite moral culpability that should be required before the label of "hate crime offender" is applied.[167] As I have already discussed above, individuals should only be criminally liable for prejudices that are held sufficiently within their mind during the commission of the offence. In this regard we explored arguments that demonstrations of prejudice, where no intention or motivation of dislike is required at all, can be controversial and that at least some "awareness" on the part of the offender as to the bias nature of their demonstration should be proved before the offender ought to be held culpable for the harms they might have caused.[168] Taking a similar line of enquiry, one might also question whether an offender's conduct that is based on general stereotyping or a biased belief about the victim's identity (which does not amount to them being actively hostile towards the identity) ought to result in a level of culpability that brings them within the scope of hate crime legislation?[169]

Goodall argues that the group selection model is more appropriate for civil law than criminal law, as it recognises the flaws of the society which placed the victim group at a disadvantage but not the culpable mind of a

---

[166] The Organisation for Security and Co-operation in Europe has reflected that the group selection model "may do a better job of addressing the kind of harm that hate crime laws are intended to prevent" ODIHR 2009 (see Footnote 148) 48–49.

[167] Lawrence 1999 (see Footnote 6) 73ff; Goodall 2013 (see Footnote 117) 228.

[168] See Mark A Walters, 'Conceptualizing "hostility" for hate crime law: minding "the minutiae" when interpreting section 28(1)(a) of the Crime and Disorder Act 1998' (2014b) 34(1) OJLS 47; Goodall 2013 (see Footnote 117); in relation to awareness and group selection see also Lawrence 1999 (see Footnote 6) 75–77.

[169] In a similar vein to Hurd's critique that hate crime laws should not punish character, which she argues is outside of the conscious control of the individual. Heidi M Hurd, 'Why liberals should hate "hate crime legislation"' (2001) 20 Law & Phil 215.

"hate crime" offender.[170] She concludes that instead "[w]e may regard it as aggravated on another ground—the pre-planned selection of a vulnerable group victim. There can be enhanced punishment without treating this as a hate crime".[171] The positioning of victims of targeted abuse based on stereotyping as being due to "vulnerability" has been a common approach taken by the courts in England and Wales.[172] While it is true victims are frequently *perceived* by their offenders to be vulnerable, the constant labelling of disabled people, for example, as "vulnerable" may actually serve to perpetuate a false representation of this social group as innately weak and unable to care for themselves. Where this is happening, the criminal process becomes implicated in replicating the same biases that have given rise to the offending behaviour itself.[173]

Given the potential for replicating rather than reducing systemic bias, we must look again at why a perpetrator's decision to offend based on a stereotype—which by definition is a pejorative and negative generalisation about a social group—is felt by so many not to fall within the ambit of a hate crime offence. Goodall asserts that selecting a victim because of a stereotype is "separable" to being motivated by animus towards the victim's identity because the former is a shared societal issue, whereas the latter provides for individual responsibility. However, is it not the case that the "doing" of bias and prejudice as crime, whether based on general stereotypes and negative beliefs or more individually felt forms of hatred,[174] is a matter of both individual and social responsibility?[175] Individuals do not become racists without social context, and systems that sustain negative beliefs about entire groups of people cannot be sustained without individuals perpetuating such attitudes. The fact that culpability is shared between individuals and society as a whole should not

---

[170] Goodall 2013 (see Footnote 117) 221.

[171] Goodall 2013 (see Footnote 117) 228.

[172] See Mark A Walters, Abenaa Owusu-Bempah and Susann Wiedlitzka, 'Hate Crime and the "Justice Gap": The Case for Law Reform' [2018] 12 Crim LR 961.

[173] Walters and others 2018 (ibid.).

[174] Based on what Goodall refers to as "lay" conceptions of racism which are defined in individualistic terms that involve conduct or expressions that people would deem as morally wrong (Goodall 2013 (see Footnote 117) 216).

[175] I explore how individual and social harms and responsibilities can be addressed in Chap. 6.

deter a social justice liberal system of criminal law from seeking out all consciously determined criminal conduct aimed at specific social groups that results in their oppression.

Deciphering whether discriminatory selection of a protected group member is a "hate crime" or not is therefore as much about locating individual blameworthiness as it is about determining the law's normative position in challenging social injustice. Comprehending the legitimacy of the discriminatory selection model within this complex philosophical landscape can be assisted further by reference to general criminal law principles on mens rea. Noteworthy is that critics who have rejected the discriminatory model based on its failure to reflect an offender's conscious intention or knowledge of the hatefulness of their act have drawn little comparison with the huge swathes of criminal offences that do not require an intention to cause an act or bring about certain harmful results. In fact, there is wide range of varying degrees of mens rea for determining guilt for criminal offences, diverging from "direct intention" and "oblique intention",[176] to recklessness (both objective and subjective),[177] knowledge or awareness (both objective and subjective),[178] gross negligence[179] and even negligence.[180] For example, the English offence of manslaughter can be committed where someone causes death, even where the offender foresaw no harm at all and engaged in otherwise lawful conduct before the death of the victim.[181] Other crimes establish liability where a reasonable person in the position of the offender "ought to have known" that their actions would result in certain types of harm.[182] For example, the offence of "stalking... involving serious alarm or distress" is committed where the defendant knows or "ought to know that [their] course of conduct will cause [the victim] serious alarm or distress which has a substantial

---

[176] For example murder, see discussion in *Woollin* [1999] 1 AC 82.

[177] For example arson, see discussion in *R v G* [2004] 1 AC 1034.

[178] For example stalking, see Protection from Harassment Act 1998, s 2A; handling stolen goods, see Theft Act 1968, s 22.

[179] For example manslaughter, see *Adomako* [1995] 1 AC 171.

[180] For example driving without due care and attention, see Road Traffic Act 1988, s 3.

[181] But where they are deemed to have acted in a grossly negligent way, see *R v Adomako* [1995] 1 AC 171.

[182] See for example Protection from Harassment Act 1997, ss 1, 2A, 4 & 4A.

adverse effect on [the victim's] usual day-to-day activities".[183] Under this offence, an offender would be liable to up to 10 years of imprisonment for his actions of stalking even if they honestly did not realise that their behaviour would cause such substantial effects on the victim. It matters only that a reasonable person in possession of the same information would have come to this realisation.

Clearly, then, the mens rea element of numerous very serious criminal offences can be constructed where an offender neither intends nor foresees serious types of harm. In England and Wales, even in the most serious offence of murder, culpability can be constructed where an offender intends to cause serious bodily harm which results in death but did not intend or foresaw death.[184] The reason for these disparate forms of mens rea is that the criminal law imposes different normative standards of culpability depending on the types of activity it aims to prevent. Those individuals whose standards fall below that which we expect of our fellow citizens gives rise to different standards of liability depending on the types of conduct we aim to prevent. This means that for some types of offence, even where the offender does not intend harm, the law must step in to prevent this type of conduct in society.

It is in this same vein that the intentional targeting of marginalised groups because of their identity, whether this is connected to their perceived vulnerability or a pernicious stereotype, should be connected to a normative position on preventing the social injustices caused by bias crimes.[185] The "by reason test" in hate crime law asks whether the offender selected their victim because of the victim's group characteristic. We need not ask whether in doing so they fully intended to subjugate the victim because of enmity for their identity. The moral wrongfulness of their conduct is constructed through the commission of a criminal offence that is combined with a conscious decision to discriminate against the victim's protected identity characteristic. Whether or not in doing so they intend to heighten the social injustice experienced by a group of people

---

[183] Protection from Harassment Act 1997, s 4A.
[184] *R v Vickers* [1957] 2 QB 664.
[185] See also Sean Robertson, 'Exception to Excess: Tactical Use of the Law by Outgroups in Bias Crime Legislation' (2012) 37(2) Law Soc Inquiry 456.

should not impact upon the culpability element of a hate crime offence. It may of course be a factor that weighs heavily on the mind of a sentencer who must discern the most appropriate means of addressing the crime. However, it must not detract from fair labelling of the offence as one which is rooted to bias. Hence, the offender who targets a victim in order to make a material gain by reason of the fact the victim is mentally disabled or gay will have negatively impacted the victim's right to equal participation in society. If the offender claims, "I did not fully comprehend this type of harm", our answer should be: you ought to have.

Further Guidance on Implementing Discriminatory Models

Our exploration of the different ways in which discriminatory selection of a protected group is based largely on harmful stereotypes provides us with a normative framework justifying why this model of legislation should be used for hate crime. However, the various legal tests used for this model do not require proof that an offender consciously stereotyped their victim, only that they intentionally selected their victim by reason of the victim's protected characteristic. While evidence that a victim is selected based on bias perceptions about identity groups may well provide proof of an offender's discriminatory selection, it will not be a requirement in law.

Given that there remains much confusion as to how this test should apply in practice further guidance may be necessary to assist both legal practitioners and finders of fact in identifying what crimes come within the scope of this model. It is here that the rules on causation may come into play. Judges should start by asking: "but for" the victim's protected characteristic would this offence have occurred?[186] A but for test is a matter of "factual causation" and helps the courts to ascertain whether the victim's identity is central to the commission of the offence. However, factual causation should not be the final stop for juries or judges. This is because the but for test may fail to pick up some cases where the offence may or may not have occurred because of the victim's identity but is still

---

[186] Also used by Lawrence 1999 (see Footnote 6) 10, but in relation to proving "bias motivation".

6 Legislating for Hate Crime Globally: Putting "Social Justice"... 199

nonetheless a significant cause of it (see examples below). As such, the courts can gain assistance from rules on "legal causation". Legal causation would require the court to ask whether the protected characteristic was a "substantial" or "significant" factor underpinning the offender's decision to act.[187] This might include: evidence that shows the offender has only targeted victims from a particular identity group; where they have selected the victim due to a perceived weakness in their characteristic; where there is particularly degrading and abusive conduct aimed at dehumanizing or belittling the victim; or testimony from the victim of persistent use of prejudiced language used towards them before, during or after the commission of offence.

Let us take three separate examples involving one type of crime to further explicate the manner in which legal interpretation of the model using factual and legal causation might play out:

1. Burglar A *only* targets Asian or Jewish homes based on the belief these ethnic groups own more valuable jewellery. She has committed two burglaries one from each type of victim. She has a past history of burglaries from victims with the same identity backgrounds. The court can start by asking: but for the victim's identities, would the homes have been targeted by the defendant? If the answer is no it may be satisfied that the offences are hate crimes. However, to be sure the court can also ask whether the identities of the victim were a substantial or significant reason for the commission of the burglary. Although material gain is surely a main reason for committing the offences, given that the offender only targets Asian and Jewish families it might be considered that their characteristics are also significant reasons underpinning the crimes. The offence likely falls within the scope of the legislation.

2. Burglar B *prefers* to target Asian and Jewish homes and has committed two burglaries, one from each type of victim based on the belief these ethnic groups own more valuable jewellery. He has a past history of burglaries from victims with the same identity backgrounds and oth-

---

[187] Lu-in Wang, 'Recognizing opportunistic bias crimes' (2000) 80 Boston UL Rev 1399, 1407.

ers without these identities. The court starts again by asking: but for the victim's identities, would the homes have been targeted by the defendant? The answer is less unequivocal as previous history evidence suggests the offender may have turned to another home were the Asian or Jewish families to have been at home. They must therefore again ask a follow up question: were the victims' identities a significant factor in determining the offender's decision to target the victims' homes? The answer is likely to be yes. The offender clearly shows a bias towards targeting Asian and Jewish people in targeting homes which is significant to his decision to commit the crimes against the victims. The offence likely falls within the scope of the legislation.

3. Burglar C is out walking to the shops to buy some groceries. They have a past history of burglaries from victims of different identity backgrounds. They notice that a home on a side street they have just passed has left a window ajar. There are no cars parked on the front porch. C knows that the area is mostly populated by Muslim families who will likely be out due to a religious festival. They take their chance and break into the property. The court starts by asking: but for the victim's identity, would the home have been targeted by the defendant? The answer is likely to be yes. That is, the offence would likely to have occurred despite the victim's presumed identity. This is because the offender is an opportunist who wants to acquire goods and sees an opportunity that is only partly linked to the victim's identity. We might still ask whether the victim's identity is a substantial reason for the offence? It is likely that it is not, as the offender does not know for sure who the home belongs to. The victim's identity plays a small non-determinative role in the offender's decision to burgle the home and is therefore tangential to the commission of the offence.[188]

The aim of hate crime legislation within social justice liberalism is to prevent crimes that are targeted at groups of individuals which will likely

---

[188] The same would apply to the example provided by Lord Bracadale above. His example of the burglar who has a greater success rate with certain victims simply reveals that more is gained from certain victims, not that his offending was committed by reason of their identity or that they went to systemically target such individuals.

have a disproportionate and marginalising impact on them. While wide in scope, legislation must not be over inclusive so as to criminalise individuals as "hate crime offenders" where they lack intention or awareness that they have targeted a victim because of their marginalised identity. For instance, where victims are targeted in an opportunistic way, which is only tangentially connected to their identity due to context or circumstance, this should not be sufficient to bring them within the scope of hate crime legislation. Ultimately, the case scenarios described above will likely be quite rare. But sceptics are right to be concerned about the overreach of the criminal law given its implications for individual rights. The aim of hate crime law is not to cast the net out widely to include those whose conduct is not directly implicated in the social injustice of marginalised groups. It is there to recognise and prevent crimes where victims are systematically targeted, debased and violently abused because of who they are.

6.3 Conclusion

The way in which hate crime is criminalised has a huge impact on the types and numbers of offenders who are brought before the courts. A great deal depends on our understanding of "hate crime" legislation and what its key purpose is. Within this book, I have argued that hate crime laws should aim to prevent *all* bias and prejudice-based conduct that causes qualitatively distinct individual, community and social harms—impacts which serve to marginalise and disempower entire groups of people thereby inhibiting their equal participation in society. If the criminal law is to play a significant role in furnishing the boundaries of conduct that protects against group oppression it cannot only capture those who directly feel and express the most deeply felt hatred. To do so leaves the criminal law nipping at the very edges of racism, homophobia, transphobia, disablism, amongst other prejudices. If the aim of the criminal law is to prevent harmful conduct, it will fail spectacularly if it is so narrowly defined.

The models and legal tests used by jurisdictions to tackle hate crime matter greatly. While the animus model of legislation most saliently captures the minds of those wanting to tackle hate and prejudice, legislatures must be mindful of both the words used to describe animus and the legal tests that are used within these statutes. Incorporating words such as prejudice, bias, hostility or even contempt will ensure that a broad array of discriminatory conduct underpin the types of hate-based actions that are proscribed. There are a number of legal tests that are used in animus models of legislation including: sole motivation, part motivation, by reason of prejudice, and demonstrations of hostility. Those jurisdictions that employ a sole motivation test combined with proof of hatred (or other similar descriptors) will likely see few offences ever prosecuted as "hate crimes". Such an approach inevitably leaves hate crime provisions lingering on the statute books and brings the aims of hate crime legislation into disrepute. Jurisdictions that utilise a broader objective (actus reus) test to proving animus, such as England and Wales—that require no motivation at all— will ultimately see many more successful prosecutions of hate crime.[189]

Yet even this broader approach to proscribing hate crime can have significant limitations. Most prominent is the fact that many offenders who target marginalised group members based on pernicious stereotypes, but during which they express no outward hostility, and where their motivation cannot be said to directly epitomise the actions of "racist" or "homophobes", are unlikely to be culpable under such models. This is despite the fact that much targeted victimisation serves to subjugate and disempower individuals resulting in further social injustice amongst entire groups of people. Conscious acts that marginalise people because of who they should find space within the hate crime legal framework. This can be most effectively done through the discriminatory selection model where hate crimes can be committed "by reason of" or "because of" a victim's identity characteristic/s.[190]

The aim of this chapter has been to identify the most effective types and models of law that cover the full range of hate and prejudice-based conduct that continues to pervade societies globally. A final substantive point then is to note that legislators need not view models as mutually

---

[189] Though as I have argued this broad test might be supported by a mens rea element of at least awareness that their demonstration is one based on identity-based prejudice so as to ensure culpability rests on both actus reus and mens rea of the hate-element.

[190] Or bias crimes or aggravated crimes as per formal definitions.

exclusive, indeed both an objective animus model and a discriminatory selection model can easily work as an either/or legal test to proscribe hate crime. Only where hate crimes are systematically being tried and convicted in the courts can legislation begin to successfully challenge all criminal manifestations of hate and prejudice.

In concluding this chapter it is important to recognise that disparate cultural factors and political systems of governance may well mean that no matter what "type" or "model" of hate crime law is enacted, "the system" can ensure that it is applied in one way or other, or in some cases not at all.[191] Vital work continues internationally on breaking down cultural barriers that are resistant to addressing discrimination against certain groups and "change agents" remain fundamental to popularising the concept of hate crime within legal systems.[192] Though outside the scope of this chapter, it is also worth highlighting that hate crime legislation is most successfully implemented where there is a framework of education measures, national and regional policies, guidance documents and training programmes that are aimed at promoting awareness of hate crime, where to report it and how law enforcement agencies ought to investigate and collate evidence of the hate-element for presentation before the court.[193]

---

[191] See for example See Aleš Giáo Hanek, 'International Legal Framework for Hate Crime: Which Law for the "New" Countries?' in Amanda Haynes, Jennifer Schweppe and Seamus Taylor, *Critical Perspectives on Hate Crime: Contributions from the Island of Ireland* (Palgrave 2020) 467–292.

[192] See for example Joanna Perry, 'The migration and integration of the hate crime approach in India' (2020) 11(1) Jindal Global Law Rev 7.

[193] See Jennifer Schweppe and Mark A Walters, *Establishing an effective framework for implementation of anti-LGBT hate crime legislation* (Human Dignity Trust 2022). In ensuring that the law on the books is implemented in practice, prosecution services should also resist the use of plea (charge) bargaining, which risks systemic filtering out of the hate-element of offences. For example, in England and Wales the Crown Prosecution Service has an explicit policy "not to accept pleas to lesser offences, or a lesser basis of plea, or omit or minimise admissible evidence of racial or religious aggravation for the sake of expediency". Crown Prosecution Service, Racist and Religious Hate Crime—Prosecution Guidance' (CPS 2020). Research indicates that this policy is mostly strictly adhered to and is just one of the reasons that England and Wales prosecute more hate crime as "aggravated" offences than anywhere else in the world, Mark Walters, Susann Wiedlitzka and Abenaa Owusu-Bempah, *Hate Crime and the Legal Process: Options for Law Reform* (University of Sussex 2017); Jennifer Schweppe, Amanda Haynes and Mark A Walters, *Lifecycle of a Hate crime: Comparative Report* (ICCL 2018).

7

Punish or Repair? Where Is the "Social Justice" in Hate Crime Laws?

7.1 Introduction

Thus far this book has outlined a theory of criminalising hate that has centred on the aims of social justice while maintaining protections to individual liberty. It has said little in relation to the types of sanctions that ought to be imposed where there is a breach of the types of laws outlined in Chap. 5. Almost all hate crime laws that have been enacted globally have as their main purpose the enhancement of penalties. In fact, as outlined in Chap. 5, the internationalisation of hate crime laws has seen the emergence of supranational instruments that *require* its signatories to punish hate crime offenders more severely.[1]

For some critics, the growth in international justice mechanisms that are focused on retributive punishments is a product of the grip that neoliberal policy making has had on Anglo-American states in the twentieth

---

[1] For example, Article 4 of the European Union Framework Decision on Racist and Xenophobic Crime stipulates that member states "shall take the necessary measures to ensure that racist and xenophobic motivation is considered an aggravating circumstance, or, alternatively that such motivation may be taken into consideration by the courts in the determination of the penalties".

and twenty-first centuries.[2] This, they argue, is a result of the decline in social welfarism of the mid-twentieth century and the rise of right wing law and order politics based on the notion that more law, stricter penalties, and a zero tolerance approach to policing would keep crime levels low.[3] As some politicians got "tough on crime" others became even tougher—at least rhetorically.[4] Any previous consideration for the needs and care of individuals gave way to that of focusing on individuals' responsibilities and obligations.[5] For this reason, a number of scholars have been critical of hate crime laws, depicting them as yet another addition to the punitive turn of the latter part of the twentieth century.[6] Meyer asserts that hate crime laws "do more to reinforce existing power imbalances than challenge them" and that the symbolic value of such statutes "pales in comparison to the cost of imprisoning more people, for longer periods of time".[7] I do not disagree that laws that focus on imprisoning more people for longer periods of time do not fit within a socially progressive system of criminal justice. But this does not mean that legislating to criminalise hate should be dismissed as a neoliberal tool of oppression, nor that it need be an endeavour of penal punitivism. The process of identifying when a "hate crime" has been committed and who is impacted by such incidents is significantly restricted where there is no legislative framework specifically proscribing such offences. How would it be officially reported? Who would respond and offer support to those affected?

More importantly, the criminalisation of hate need not automatically result in the imposition of penalty enhancements—at least not as a first response to criminal infractions. Neither does it follow that criminal laws

---

[2] Nils Christie, *Crime Control as Industry* (3rd edn, Routledge 2000); Mark J Findlay, *Governing through Globalised Crime: Futures for international criminal justice* (Willan 2008); David Garland, *The Culture of Control: Crime and Social Order in Contemporary Society* (OUP 2001).
[3] Ralph Henham, *Sentencing Policy and Social Justice* (OUP 2018).
[4] Garland 2001 (see Footnote 2).
[5] Often referred to as 'responsibilization': David Garland, 'The Limits of the Sovereign State: Strategies of Crime Control in Contemporary Society' (1996) 36(4) Brit J Criminol 44; John Muncie, 'The globalization of crime control—the case of youth and juvenile justice: Neo-liberalism, policy convergence and international conventions' 9(1) (2005) Theo Crim 35.
[6] Garland 2001 (see Footnote 2).
[7] Doug Meyer, 'Resisting Hate Crime Discourse: Queer and Intersectional Challenges to Neoliberal Hate Crime Laws' (2014) 22(1) Crit Criminol 113, 120.

are, in and of themself, mechanisms of oppression.[8] Rather, it is the disproportionate enforcement of the law and the ensuing implementation of punitive sanctions that have given rise to the racialized and gendered aspects of criminalisation.

While the application of hate crime laws are clearly open to abuse, as is the enforcement of all laws, I am in agreement with Mason who reflects:

> hate crime laws are an important symbol of state support for those who are victimised… it is time we pushed harder to imagine a path to legislating against hate, and promoting social justice, that is not paved with penal punitiveness.[9]

In this final substantive chapter, I outline how hate crime laws and penalty enhancements need not be mutually inclusive. It is argued that criminalisation, though of fundamental importance to challenging hatred in society, is best served when it is supported by justice mechanisms that aim to repair the intersecting individual and social harms of hate, while simultaneously challenging its underlying causes. In this regard, I draw on research that has examined the use of restorative justice mechanisms in addressing the micro, meso and macro level harms of hate.[10] The aim of the chapter is to present social justice liberalism as a synthesis of law, punishment and restorative justice.[11] I elaborate further on what "justice" might look like within a system of social justice liberalism that has enacted a framework of hate crime legislation. The infusion of communitarian principles, as fostered through processes such as restorative justice, is proffered as yielding the greatest potential in addressing the distinct

---

[8] Chris Cunneen, 'Restorative justice, globalization and the logic of empire' in Sharon Pickering and Jude McCulloch (eds), *Borders and Crime: Pre-Crime, Mobility and Serious Harm in an Age of Globalization* (Palgrave Macmillan 2012) 147–162.

[9] Gail Mason, 'Legislating against hate' in Nathan Hall and others (eds), *The Routledge International Handbook on Hate Crime* (Routledge 2015).

[10] Mark A Walters, *Hate Crime and Restorative Justice: Exploring Causes, Repairing Harms* (OUP 2014a).

[11] Tentatively outlined in a previous work, Mark A Walters, 'Readdressing hate crime: Synthesizing law, punishment and restorative justice' in Thomas Brudholm and Birgitte S Johansen (eds), *Hate, Politics, Law* (OUP 2018) 150–171.

harms caused by hatred.[12] Yet it is argued that for this to truly work, ultimately hate crime laws must still operate within a system that *threatens* punishment.

7.2 Do Enhanced Punishments for Hate Crime Promote Social Justice?

Can penalty enhancements facilitate a social justice liberal society that prevents hate from proliferating, and which reduces individual, social and cultural harm? Duff argues that in achieving the aims of a republican theory of criminal law,[13] the law must be supported by a set of penalties that have as their main purpose the infliction of pain on those who break the rules.[14] Duff asserts that sanctions must be burdensome in order to help offenders understand the wrongfulness of their conduct and to bring forth expiation for their bad actions. This public process of sanctioning an offender should prompt feelings of remorse that assist in inducing moral edification.[15]

Indeed, without punishment the difference between public and private law could well become nebulous, with the criminal law potentially losing its potency as a form of social control. Henry Hart has opined, "[w]hat distinguishes a criminal from a civil sanction, and all that distinguishes it... is the judgment of community condemnation which accompanies and justifies its imposition".[16] Penalties are fixed on to offences in a way that attempts to reflect the wrongdoing and culpability of offenders. This enables sentencers to impose sanctions that reflect both the harmfulness of the conduct and the level of culpability attached to the offender's mental state.

---

[12] Mark A Walters, 'Challenging orthodoxy: towards a restorative approach to combating the globalization of hate' in Jennifer Schweppe and Mark A Walters (eds), *The Globalization of Hate: Internationalizing Hate Crime?* (OUP 2016) 294–313.
[13] Based on the principles of nondomination, freedom and equal concern.
[14] RA Duff, *The Realm of Criminal Law* (OUP 2018).
[15] RA Duff, *Punishment, Communication and Community* (OUP 2001).
[16] Henry M Hart Jr, 'The Aims of the Criminal Law' (1958) 23(3) L & Contemp Prob 401, 404.

In Lawrence's influential work on hate crime laws, he argues that society faces a dichotomous choice between either not responding specifically to hate crime or responding through criminal punishment. In referring to the work of Durkheim he reflects that if the former approach is chosen there is a risk that the bonds of society become relaxed and crime will become more prevalent.[17] Such a position infers that (enhanced) punishment is the best way to prevent hate crime. This perspective dictates that the only way it can be controlled in society is via a system of penalty enhancements that both reflect the harmfulness and culpability of offenders' actions, as well as censuring conduct, thereby preventing reoffending by bringing a greater awareness to offenders of the wrongfulness of their conduct.

Though theoretically quite compelling, there remains a disjuncture between the theory of retributivism and empirical evidence supporting its claims.[18] There is in fact little to no research that I am aware of that shows that public censure via the infliction of burdensome punishment brings forth moral edification or a greater likelihood that the offender will repent and be less likely to reoffend. On the contrary, research shows that desistance from offending is likely to occur over the life course (as individuals mature and leave crime behind them),[19] and through certain effective rehabilitation programmes that focus on underlying causes of offending behaviour (e.g. drug rehabilitation).[20] While countries with lower income inequality, and higher employment rates and health provision typically have lower levels of crime.[21]

Conversely, studies and statistical data suggest that retributive punishments, especially in relation to its most potent form (imprisonment), can have a criminogenic effect that may actually perpetuate social

---

[17] Emile Durkheim, *The Division of Labor in Society* (WD Hall tr, Free Press 1984) 63, cited by Frederick M Lawrence, *Punishing Hate: Bias Crimes under American Law* (Harvard UP 1999) 164.

[18] See further Henham 2018 (see Footnote 3).

[19] Robert J Sampson and John H Laub, *Crime in the Making: Pathways and Turning Points Through Life* (Harvard UP 1993).

[20] See for example Andrew Jones and others, *The Drug Treatment Outcomes Research Study (DTORS): Final Outcomes Report 3rd ed* (Home Office 2009).

[21] See for example Muhammad K Anser and others, 'Dynamic linkages between poverty, inequality, crime, and social expenditures in a panel of 16 countries: two-step GMM estimates' (2020) 9 Economic Structures 43.

marginalisation. Research shows that those who are imprisoned are more likely to self-harm and turn to drugs and alcohol; the latter a causal mechanism of crime.[22] Other studies show that short periods of imprisonment can actually increase the likelihood of reoffending.[23] For example, research by the UK Ministry of Justice found the one year reoffending rate following short term custodial sentences of less than 12 months was higher than if a court had imposed a community order or a suspended sentence order.[24]

In relation to enhanced punishments for hate crime there is, therefore, the concern that short term prison sentences for offenders who might otherwise receive a community order or suspended sentence may actually increase the likelihood of reoffending.[25] Rather than reducing identity group hostilities, enhanced punishments may in fact serve to increase the individual, social and cultural harms of hatred. As such, there is little to persuade even the most ardent of retributivists that higher penalties will do much to transform the socio-structural ills of society.

7.3 Communitarian Principles of Justice: Nondomination, Equality, and Restoration

Given there is little to no evidence to show that *increasing* punishment protects and promotes a free and equal society, it is incumbent upon penal theorists and criminologists alike to identify alternative systems of criminal justice that more effectively achieve these aims. Indeed, if

---

[22] Daniel S Nagin, Francis T Cullen and Cheryl Lero Jonson, 'Imprisonment and Reoffending' in Michael Tonry (ed), *Crime and Justice: A Review of Research* (University of Chicago Press 2009) 115–200.

[23] Nagin and others 2009 (ibid.); Francis T Cullen, Cheryl Lero Jonson and Daniel S Nagin, 'Prisons Do Not Reduce Recidivism: The High Cost of Ignoring Science' (2011) 91(3) (September suppl) Prison J 91 48S.

[24] Georgina Eaton and Aidan Mews, *The impact of short custodial sentences, community orders and suspended sentence orders on reoffending* (Ministry of Justice 2019). See similarly, Aidan Mews and others, *The Impact of Short Custodial Sentences, Community Orders and Suspended Sentence Orders on Re-offending* (Ministry of Justice 2015).

[25] Leslie Moran and Beverley Skeggs, *Sexuality and the Politics of Violence and Safety* (Routledge 2004).

burdensome punishment is a direct route to making "bad people worse",[26] how can the state credibly argue that such a system can assist in fostering a society that guarantees greater freedom and equal concern for its citizens?

What alternative system of justice, then, might provide the "community condemnation" of the criminal law but can assist in reducing (rather than increasing) hate in society? I have previously outlined extensively the benefits and limitations of one such alternative, that of restorative justice.[27] I do not intend to repeat my empirical findings in full here. What this chapter aims to achieve instead is a theoretical synthesis of hate crime law, punishment and restorative justice. The reader may be surprised to read that I intend to advocate a framework that maintains an element of retributive sanctioning given my assertions above. As will become evident below, the maintenance of such a system may well be unavoidable within a system that maintains liberalism at its heart. I will explain why punishment must remain a course of last resort. Before then I set out why communitarian principles of justice must figure first within a system of social justice liberalism.

7.4 Restorative Justice as Social Justice

Duff and Marshall have taken issue with my previous assertions that the criminal justice system should seek to repair harms and directly address offender behaviour.[28] They have argued that hate crimes as public wrongs require a public remedy that cannot be adequately fulfilled through community-based dialogue that focuses on repairing individual and community harms. Such a duty must be fulfilled directly to the state as representative of the public. Social justice liberal criminal law, alternatively,

---

[26] Home Office, *Crime, Justice, and Protecting the Public* (Cm 965, HMSO 1990) 2.7.

[27] See for example Mark A Walters, *Hate Crime and Restorative Justice: Exploring Causes, Repairing Harms* (OUP 2014a); Mark A Walters, 'Challenging orthodoxy: towards a restorative approach to combating the globalization of hate' in Jennifer Schweppe and Mark A Walters (eds), *The Globalization of Hate: Internationalizing Hate Crime?* (OUP 2016) 294–313.

[28] RA Duff and SE Marshall 'Criminalizing Hate?,' in Thomas Brudholm and Birgitte S Johansen (eds), *Hate, Politics, Law* (OUP 2018) 115–149.

seeks to build a bridge between crime as a public wrong and state-level censure required for it, while advancing community-based solutions as a primary response to criminal infringement. That is to say, the criminal law remains an important symbolic and operative tool to addressing hate as a public wrong, but if we are to truly advance a society that promotes social justice, the criminal justice system must move to a position where it can offer interventions that actively seek to address the causes and consequences of social inequality.

Duff and Marshall have argued that all a liberal republic criminal law can demand is for individuals to conduct themselves lawfully.[29] But if a system of justice has been shown to exacerbate social harms by further marginalising perpetrators of violence, while doing little to address the inequalities experienced by victims, must we not question this state of affairs? If the aim of a criminal justice system is to prevent crime, the current regime of enhanced punishment alone, including imprisonment, appears to have failed in its endeavour quite spectacularly. This has left neoliberal policy makers to double down in their position to enact harsher punishments to deter criminal offending. The failure to curb certain crimes is met with more punishment and lengthier terms of imprisonment.[30]

In response to this abject failure to adequately treat the causes and consequences of crime, a growing number of criminologists and justice practitioners have called for a different prism through which we should understand crime and our responses to it.[31] Of growing popularity has been the rise of restorative approaches to criminal offending. Christie's seminal paper "Conflicts as Property" argued that the state had appropriated crimes from those that are directly affected by them.[32] This act of theft has led to the professionalisation of crime control and to the disposal of offences through rigid structures. The needs of victims and those

---

[29] Ibid.
[30] Tim Newburn, '"Tough on Crime": Penal Policy in England and Wales' in Michael Tonry (ed), *Crime, Punishment, and Politics in Comparative Perspective* (UCP 2007).
[31] Nils Christie, 'Conflicts as Property' (1977) 17(1) Brit J Criminol 1; Howard Zehr, *Changing Lenses: A New Focus for Crime and Justice* (Herald Press 1990).
[32] Christie 1977 (ibid.).

of offenders are side-lined in favour of a state-controlled system of justice that seeks only to determine guilt and proportionate punishment.

Christie and other "restorativists" have argued that crimes should instead be understood as conflicts between individuals that occur within communities. The resolution of such conflicts must be returned to the communities where stakeholders of criminal incidents can collectively agree upon methods of reparation. Zehr has asserted that the process of returning conflicts to community requires us to use a new lens to conceptualise what crime is.[33] Rather than crimes being defined as offences against the state, they should instead be understood as harms that have differing impacts on individuals and entire communities of people. It is only through exploring these different harms that we as a society can assist those affected by crime to help heal the wounds caused by conflict. This is best achieved where those affected by a crime (or harmful incident) *encounter* one another via a structured dialogical process that focuses on exploring harm and how it can be best *repaired*.

Braithwaite has added to this discourse by outlining a theory of reintegrative shaming whereby those who have harmed are held accountable through restorative meetings that include a perpetrator's "community of care" who assist in shaming the offender, thereby helping them to see that what they have done is bad, but that they are not a bad person (stigmatic shaming).[34] Social condemnation expressed by those closely connected to the offender (i.e. family and friends) will more likely have a constructive impact on the perpetrator's sense of wrongdoing. The aim is to facilitate the repairing of harm in a way that enables victims to move on, while offenders are reintegrated back into the community with a renewed sense of civic duty. Social condemnation is also expressed implicitly through the active participation in a process that asks participants to repair harms.[35] It is argued that collectively this invokes a sense of remorse in those who have harmed, and who then have a responsibility to actively put things right. The ultimate aim is for the stakeholders to *transform*

---

[33] Zehr 1977 (see Footnote 31).
[34] John Braithwaite, *Crime, Shame and Reintegration* (CUP 1989); John Braithwaite and Valerie Braithwaite, 'Part I. Shame, Shame Management and Regulation' in Eliza Ahmed and others (eds) *Shame Management Through Reintegration* (CUP 2001).
[35] Braithwaite and Braithwaite 2001 (797).

their relationship from one of conflict and injury to that of acceptance and reconciliation.

Braithwaite and Pettit have offered a theoretical foundation for restorative justice as being based on a republican theory of justice, which closely aligns with the aims of social justice liberalism as outlined throughout this book.[36] Two key concepts are central to their theory of justice: freedom and nondomination.[37] Braithwaite asserts, "[j]ustice is that set of arrangements that allow people to make claims against other individuals and institutions in order to secure freedom against the possibility of domination".[38] A republican conception of justice understands the needs of individuals as the needs of communities and collectively as being the needs of society. Freedom from domination is to be contrasted with that of freedom from non-interference; the latter stressing that harming or infringing upon the rights of other individuals is seen as the marker of wrongdoing and injustice. Crime is viewed as disregard for the victim's dominion and in some cases may destroy dominion. The republican notion of liberty emphasises support against interference. The diminishing of dominion affects not just the victim but also the community as a whole. To enjoy dominion is to enjoy the unimpeded life with salient resilience.

As outlined in Chaps. 2 and 3, recognition of dominion of hate crime victims is to recognise individuals as deserving of equal participation in society, free from the fear of targeted victimisation because of their social identity. The harms of hate crime include restriction of personal interests as understood through four faces of oppression: violence, marginalisation, powerlessness and cultural imperialism. To understand the dominion for hate crime victims is, therefore, to comprehend certain groups as requiring freedom from oppression, that which occurs not only as physical violence, but as processes by which certain social groups are subjugated in society.

---

[36] John Braithwaite and Philip Pettit, *Not Just Deserts: A Republican Theory of Criminal Justice* (OUP 1990).

[37] John Braithwaite, 'Restorative Justice: Assessing Optimistic and Pessimistic Accounts' (1999) [25] Crim & Just 1.

[38] Braithwaite (ibid.) 74.

In order for non-interference to be enjoyed it must be protected by law and its institutions. This is a form of what Pettit and Braithwaite refer to as "resilient non-interference". The courts should not have unlimited powers to protect dominion but rather they should attempt to rectify or put right the damage that has been caused by any interference. In other words, in order to protect non-interference some minor interference is required by the state. However, Pettit and Braithwaite emphasise an assumption of "parsimony", which assumes that the onus must always rest on the state justifying legal intrusion. The law and its institutions should only step in to protect an individual from others interfering with their freedoms.

Within a framework of social justice liberalism, we can seek to align such thinking with the way in which hate crime laws operate. Hate crime statutes serve both a symbolic role in denouncing hate crimes while protecting the dominion of individuals, *especially* those from the most marginalised of communities.[39] Pettit and Braithwaite contend that:

> As the opposite of… powerlessness, republican freedom—dominion—requires not just the absence of interference, but security against interference: it requires that for any position that a person occupies—or could realistically occupy—he is never at the mercy of another.[40]

To protect against the harms of hate, laws must first and foremost encourage offenders to recognise the dominion of victims by making amends for what the damage they are, at least partly, responsible for. Pettit and Braithwaite assert that offenders who interfere with dominion are required to first manifest a *recognition* of the victim's dominion, second *recompense* for the material harm that is inflicted and third, provide both the victim and the community with *reassurance* to make up for the damage caused by the crime, sufficient to make up for the damage to the victim and community's subjective sense of enjoying dominion.[41]

---

[39] As per Rawls' "difference principle", John Rawls, *Justice as Fairness: A Restatement* (Harvard UP 2001).
[40] Philip Pettit and John Braithwaite, 'The Three Rs of Republican Sentencing' (1994) 5(3) Current Issues in Criminal Justice 318.
[41] Pettit and Braithwaite (ibid.).

The courts may not always be the best place to effectuate restorative measures and as such criminal trial processes may be best avoided altogether. This can be achieved in the first instance by diverting stakeholders away from the conventional criminal justice system altogether, such as where restorative solutions are sought via conditional cautions or via community resolutions.[42] Where prosecution is preferable, perhaps due to the seriousness of the offence, or dangerousness of the offender, then restorative solutions can be applied post-conviction but before formal sentencing.[43] In England and Wales, sentencers also have the power to utilise the sentencing purpose of "making of reparation by offenders to persons affected by their offence".[44] The framework of restorative interventions can either be outlined in sentencing legislation or sentencing guidelines where it can be explicitly stated that such interventions should be used in the first instance and before retributive sanctions are utilised.

Some US states have begun to legislate for restorative justice for hate crime, though not yet as a primary means of sentencing such crimes. For example, the Penal Code of California states:

> 422.86. (a) It is the public policy of this state that the principal goals of sentencing for hate crimes, are the following:
> (1) Punishment for the hate crimes committed.
> (2) Crime and violence prevention, including prevention of recidivism and prevention of crimes and violence in prisons and jails.
> (3) Restorative justice for the immediate victims of the hate crimes and for the classes of persons terrorized by the hate crimes.

The Code also outlines "penalty enhancements" under s. 422.85; however, these are not aimed at increasing punishment but instead focus on education and restitution, including:

---

[42] These are out-of-court disposals that week to focus on reparation, while avoiding criminalising and labelling especially young offenders. See Mark Walters, 'Developments in the use of restorative justice for hate crime' (2020) 3 International Journal of Restorative Justice 446.

[43] Such as under s 7 Sentencing Act 2020.

[44] As per s 57(2)(e) Sentencing Act 2020.

(1) Complete a class or program on racial or ethnic sensitivity, or other similar training in the area of civil rights… (2) Make payments or other compensation to a community-based program or local agency that provides services to victims of hate violence [and] (3) Reimburse the victim for reasonable costs of counseling and other reasonable expenses that the court finds are the direct result of the defendant's acts.

A similar approach can be observed in Illinois where a recent amendment to section 12-7.1 of the Criminal Code reads as follows:

(b-10) Upon imposition of any sentence, the trial court shall also either order restitution paid to the victim or impose a fine up to $1000. In addition, any order of probation or conditional discharge… shall include a condition that the offender perform public or community service of no less than 200 hours.... In addition, any order of probation or conditional discharge… shall include a condition that the offender enrol in an educational program discouraging hate crimes if the offender caused criminal damage to property consisting of religious fixtures, objects, or decorations. The educational program may be administered, as determined by the court, by a university, college, community college, non-profit organization, or the Holocaust and Genocide Commission.[45]

The reorientation of justice processes to directly involve victims and communities represents a way of democratising criminal justice processes. Such an approach to justice does not reject outright the need for individual responsibility in criminal law. Hate crimes are real life expressions of violent prejudice, involving both individual and social responsibility. The creation of a system of justice that balances individual freedom and social justice is one that will be better equipped to resolve, rather than repeat, the social inequalities that give rise to hate crime. Conceived in this way, hate crime laws must be positioned so as to reflect the individual culpability for the commission of a hate-based offence, while simultaneously being supported by interventions that are better equipped to focus on principles of equality, nondomination and individual and community reparation.

---

[45] The new "educational program" is currently being administered as a restorative justice programme.

Unlike some restorativists, I do not go as far as to contend that the maintenance of retributive sanctions is antithetical to a system of social justice liberalism.[46] The use of punishment, though socially corrosive when applied liberally, remains a vital means of compliance with the law. The *threat* of punishment serves the main purpose of assisting offender engagement in initial measures that are aimed at advancing social justice.[47] This is a maximalist approach to restorative justice that gives primacy to restorative principles as forming both out-of-court justice interventions and secondly sentencing practice.

This means that while RJ comes to the forefront of criminal justice, the wrongdoing-culpability approach that is ordinarily applied to determining offence seriousness within retributive frameworks of justice will remain relevant to the criminalisation of hate crime.[48] There must remain an upper limit to sentencing that can be imposed if, and when, other justice mechanisms fail. Because hate crimes are particularly harmful the sentencing maxima may well be set within a higher range compared with similar non-hate based crimes.

Such a system is also necessary because for restorative justice to really work it must remain a process where stakeholders of an offence voluntarily agree to participate. Stories of harm, empathic listening and reintegrative shaming lack any real potency if an offender refuses to acknowledge the legitimacy or validity of the process. And while restorative interventions,[49] and reparative measures,[50] can still be facilitated in cases where victims do not wish to take part (as where proxy victims, other community representatives or volunteers participate), justice cannot be done, especially as meaningful reparation to victims, if an offender refuses to acknowledge their status. For this reason, where an offender refuses to participate in a restorative intervention, or where having repeatedly

---

[46] See for example Paul McCold, 'Toward a holistic vision of restorative juvenile justice: A reply to the maximalist model' (2000) 3(4) Contemp Just Rev 357.

[47] Note that where victims refuse to participate, RJ interventions can still be used with "proxy" victims and/or other affected community members.

[48] Lawrence 1999 (see Footnote 17).

[49] For example restorative conferencing, direct and indirect victim-offender mediation.

[50] For example material restitution, community payback work.

7.5 Can Restorative Interventions *Help* Repair the Harms of Hate Crime?

The aim of this chapter is not to examine in detail how restorative dialogue is facilitated in cases involving hate crime, or how cultural and identity barriers can restrict and be overcome through different parts of the process.[52] Instead, I explore the possibilities of RJ as a mechanism that can assist in delivering differing aspects of social justice. A question as yet unexplored is to what extent individual offenders of hate ought to recompense and provide reassurance for the individual, community and structural harms that they have contributed to? Below I outline the role of RJ within a framework of justice that can seek to address the individual harms caused by offenders, the broader institutional harms caused by statutory authorities and the cultural harms that can be caused by government policies and rhetoric.

7.5.1 Repairing Individual Harms

In Chap. 3 I outlined the evidence on the individual physical and emotional harms that can be caused by hate crime. The evidence shows that victims are more likely to experience heightened forms of emotional trauma that are linked to a perception of threat (physically and symbolically) caused by hate violence. Such threats result in negative emotions including anger, anxiety, fear and even internalised shame, which in turn can result in harmful behaviours, including changing the way individuals

---

[51] It should be noted here that this perspective does not contend that all crimes should be met first with non-punitive justice measures. There will be numerous cases where the offender poses such a threat to the welfare of society that the courts will have no other choice but to incapacitate the offender in order to prevent reoffending.

[52] For a detailed analysis of this see Mark A Walters, *Hate Crime and Restorative Justice: Exploring Causes, Repairing Harms* (OUP 2014a).

act or even appear in order to avoid victimisation. What then can restorative practice do to mitigate against these elevated individual harms?

In an earlier empirical study into the use of RJ for hate crime in England it was found that restorative processes that carefully adhered to the key principles of "encounter", "repair" and "transformation"[53] significantly reduced the emotional distress caused by targeted victimisation. In one study conducted in London, 17 out of the 23 complainant victims who had participated in a community mediation programme entitled the "Southwark Hate Crime Project" stated that their emotional wellbeing was improved directly as a result of participating in the mediation process. In addition, most participants indicated that their levels of anger, anxiety and fear were reduced directly as a result of having participated in the project.

As well as interviewing each of these participants, 15 observations of direct and indirect mediation meetings were carried out. The study showed that there were a number of key variables that directly assisted in reducing the harms caused by ongoing forms of hate victimisation. The primary factor articulated by interviewees was that they were offered an opportunity to participate in the resolution of their case.[54] This offered victims of hate crime a voice through which they were able to tell their "stories" about what had happened to them and how it had affected their lives and the lives of those around them. Important to these individuals was that they felt that someone was finally listening to them and empathising with their experiences of targeted abuse. During this "story-telling" process, many of the victims were encouraged to talk about their other experiences of discrimination and forms of hate incidents that had previously experienced. These discussions often gave rise to individuals speaking about what it was like for them to be "different" in society and how micro-level daily incidents could chop away at their sense of self and in turn their feelings of safety and security in the community.

At the end of the mediation process an agreement was signed outlining what the parties had agreed to. Most of these included a promise by the

---

[53] Walters 2014a (ibid.).
[54] Walters 2014a (see Footnote 52).

accused perpetrator of desisting from any further hate speech or hate-based violence that had preceded the restorative process. The study found that 6 months after the process had ended 17 out of the 19 cases under investigation had ceased. This was of particular significance as all cases involved medium- to long-term targeted victimisation, with one cases lasting ten years. Such a finding revealed that there are genuine opportunities for preventing hate victimisation via restorative processes. Research on the aetiology of hate crime has consistently shown that very few offenders are motivated by an ideology of hate.[55] More common are for offenders, especially young perpetrators, to express different forms of hate and prejudice during their everyday activities.[56] Indeed, my own research has revealed that hate crimes frequently occur during complex interpersonal disputes where expressions of hate can occur in the "heat of the moment" as an attempt to hurt the victim in the most potent way possible. Such crimes can, and should, be defined as "hate crimes" not least because they are conscious attempts to harm individuals because of their identity, but also because they will likely have distinct impacts.[57] In most of these cases offending is linked causally to multiple variables, such as pervasive stereotyping perpetuated via communication networks (including the media),[58] but are also the result of complex social conditions linked to an offender's own experiences of poverty and social marginalisation.[59]

Restorative dialogue often opens up opportunities for attitudinal and behavioural transformation. Within the 2014 study, some accused perpetrators displayed attitudinal changes that hinted at a greater understanding of the harmfulness of hate victimisation.[60] Such transformations are at least partly the result of a dialogue that pivots on the concepts of equality and nondomination, which in turn helps to humanise the victim's "difference". Indeed, offenders who were able to observe the impacts of

---

[55] Paul Iganski, *Hate Crime and the City* (Policy Press 2008).
[56] Iganski 2008 (ibid.).
[57] See Mark A Walters, 'Conceptualizing "hostility" for hate crime law: Minding "the minutiae" when interpreting section 28(1)(a) of the Crime and Disorder Act 1998' (2014b) 34(1) OJLS 47.
[58] Jack Levin and Jack McDevitt, *Hate Crimes Revisited: America's War on Those Who Are Different* (Basic Books 2002).
[59] For case studies see Walters 2014a (see Footnote 52) ch. 8.
[60] Walters 2014a (see Footnote 52).

hate crime and who listened to the stories of those who had explained how their perceived "difference" had affected their lives were better able to form empathic connections with those they had harmed—despite their being diverging cultural and identity characteristics amongst stakeholders.

There are other opportunities within restorative practice to advance social justice by transforming negative attitudes towards marginalised identity groups. Within some of the reparation agreements under research, restoration included some form of moral learning. In one case a young man convicted of racially and religiously aggravated harassment was asked, at the request of the victim and his family, to undertake a two-week supervised research project on the effects that Nazism had on the Jewish people throughout Europe during WWII. The offender presented his report back to the family along with a reflections document where he set out what he had learned which included a renewed understanding of antisemitism as well as a commitment never to repeat this type of abuse again. Though such forms of reparation remain atypical, they represent genuine opportunities to invoke meaningful transformations in communities blighted by hate crime.

In determining what reparation is appropriate in any given case of hate crime, similar principles of proportionality should apply to that of other theories of punishment. Agreements about how hate crimes are best resolved must be carefully facilitated by practitioners who are mindful of the dominion of the victim and how this is most appropriately restored. The purpose of reparation must be to put a victim back in the position that they were before the offence. Some form of official oversight of the process is to be welcomed in order to ensure that community justice does not become vigilante justice.[61] Oversight might involve a court sanctioning of any agreement made between the stakeholders of a hate crime offence,[62] as well as safeguards upheld by restorative facilitators to ensure

---

[61] Andrew Ashworth, 'Responsibilities, Rights and Restorative Justice' (2002) 42(3) Brit J Criminol 578.

[62] As is the case with youth justice conferencing in New Zealand: Gabrielle M Maxwell and Allison Morris, *Family, Victims, and Culture: Youth Justice in New Zealand* (NZ Social Policy Agency & Institute of Criminology, Victoria U, 1993).

that reparation agreements do not extend beyond that which is required to repair the immediate individual harms of hate crime.[63]

What though must the offender repair? Under restorative justice theory the harm to be repaired is the harm caused. This book has premised the criminalisation of hate crime on both individual *and* socio-structural harms that include marginalisation, powerlessness and cultural imperialism. Within a liberal social justice system are we to expect individual offenders to take on such a responsibility? These are multifaceted micro-meso-macro-level social harms which require complex individual, community and societal solutions. We have observed above how the individual harms of violence (emotional trauma, material damage, damage to interpersonal relationships) can be actively repaired through restorative interventions. How, then, can community and societal level harms be addressed by such processes, and to what extent do individual offenders play in seeking broader societal transformations?

7.5.2 Addressing Marginalisation and Powerlessness

In Chaps. 2 and 3, I identified how hate crimes are violent forms of prejudice that (re)produce the social contexts in which individuals experience powerlessness. This in turn suppresses these individuals' capacities to self-realise and participate as equal members of the polity. One of the most potent ways in which hate victimisation generates marginalisation is through the behavioural reactions of victims and other group members. Figure 3.2 in Chap. 3 illustrated how incidents of hate expand outwards, first heightening group members' perceptions of threat, both in relation to their physical safety and group-based security and rights, before translating into emotional reactions (prominently anger, anxiety and shame), which in turn are causal to certain behavioural reactions (including avoiding certain locales and changing appearance or mannerism in order to "fit in"). Anxiety and fear of repeat victimisation can in some cases trap people within their own homes, leaving them with few opportunities to participate fully in society.

---

[63] Ashworth 2002 (see Footnote 61).

Restorative approaches can play an essential role in transforming these oppressive outcomes by creating spaces where victims and offenders can transform a relationship based on hate and hostility to one of understanding and respect. Clearly not all restorative meetings will generate such ideal outcomes; however, the previous research found that for the majority of victims, average levels of anger, anxiety and fear immediately decreased post-restorative dialogue. As one interviewee noted:

> the incidents have stopped, because the incidents have stopped… I'm healthier again I don't have the stress, I'm not frightened to go out of my own home. Overall everything about my health is better.[64]

Such outcomes were often supported by promises of desistance that were included in reparation or a mediation agreement. These contractual obligations set out in writing that individuals would not express hostility or hatred to one another in the future.

Although RJ meetings between victims and offenders are unlikely to fully repair experiences of marginalisation and powerlessness, there is clearly some scope for restorative outcomes to free people from the constant fear of targeted victimisation and its marginalising effects.[65] However, as explored in Chap. 3, marginalisation and powerlessness are formed not only through individual emotions and behaviour, but as a response to the processes and practices of institutions tasked with protecting victims. Previous research shows that victims are frequently ignored by law enforcement who fail to take action against accused perpetrators, or who have in some cases exacerbated the complainants' experiences of hate by using offensive language when communicating with the victim.[66] These secondary harms are in some cases perceived to be

---

[64] Initially quoted in Mark A Walters, 'Repairing the harms of hate crime: towards a restorative justice approach?' Annual report for 2018 and Resource Material Series No 108 (UNAFEI 2019) 56, 67.

[65] Indeed, while the 2014 study found that restorative meetings reduced feelings of fear and anxiety, the process could not eradicate such emotional traumas. This Walters argues is because the fear remains of other community members targeting individuals because of their identity. Walters 2014a (see Footnote 52) ch 4.

[66] Walters 2014a (see Footnote 52) ch 6.

more severe than those committed by the individuals who had demonstrated identity-based hostility in the first place.

If restorative practices fail to address these institutional barriers to justice, they risk paying mere lip service to advancing social justice for victims in hate crime. Braithwaite reflecting on these risks references the words of Blagg who states, "[j]ustice systems have a tendency to generate and reflect mono-culturalist narratives... Orientalist discourses are, primarily, powerful acts of representation that permit Western/European cultures to contain, homogenize and consume 'other' cultures".[67] Although Blagg is critiquing the use of RJ with reference to indigenous communities subsumed within Western cultures, a similar critique can be made of minority group communities whose social needs are currently not being met within a system still dominated by a White male heterosexual hegemony. However, Braithwaite questions the charge that RJ is likely to repeat the oppressive effects of conventional justice mechanisms. He asserts that the principle of non-domination and the inclusion of plural voices within restorative dialogue can protect against the hegemonic ideologies that serve to maintain social injustice. Nontheless, if RJ as a first and primary response to hate crime is to truly address social injustice it must move beyond the immediate harms caused by conflict between victim and offender and address the secondary harms that can be caused by conventional statutory agencies.

The capacity for restorative practices to challenge secondary harms is found within its flexibility as a process and the independence of practitioners. Independence is best achieved where restorative justice practitioners work within a quasi-official capacity with other justice agencies. This may include practitioners being employed solely as restorative facilitators within parts of the justice system, or preferably where an independent provider is commissioned to work alongside criminal justice agencies. Cases under investigation in London were facilitated by a civil society organisation that was commissioned by local authorities to facilitate conferences. An independent mediator involved multiple participants, through what she described as a "holistic approach" to conflict resolution

---

[67] Harry Blagg, 'A just measure of shame? Aboriginal youth conferencing in Australia' (1997) 37(4) Brit J Criminol 481, referenced in John Braithwaite, 'Restorative Justice and Social Justice' in Eugene McLaughlin and others (eds), *Restorative Justice: Critical Issues* (Sage 2003) 157–163.

that included complainant victims, accused perpetrators, their supporters (family or friends), as well as representatives from state agencies such as school teachers, social workers, housing officers and even community police officers.

The restorative process can be challenged where one or more of these service providers is causal to the social injustice that a victim has experienced. A significant proportion of the cases under research in London were negatively impacted by police and housing officers whose careless or indifferent responses to reports of hate crime further marginalised victims. In some of these cases, facilitators of RJ were able to bring participants into discussion with local authorities to resolve the harms that agency representatives had themselves caused. For example, in one case involving persistent racist abuse that had occurred over a ten-year period numerous complaints were made to a housing association that had failed to take any action against the complainant victim's abuser. In a further twist in the case, a police officer called upon the complainant and served her with a harassment warning insisting that no further complaints were to be made by her to local authorities. The victim finally referred into the Hate Crime Project and after several mediation meetings with the Housing Association the mediator was able to facilitate a discussion between each of the parties (excluding the police) whereby the Association's own hate crime policy was brought to their attention and the victim was finally moved to a new home as a safeguarding measure. A further meeting was then facilitated between the victim and the police Community Safety Unit (specialist hate crime units run by London Metropolitan Police), in which it was revealed that the police officer who had served the victim with a harassment notice was in fact in an intimate relationship with the accused perpetrator of racist abuse. As a result of this meeting, the officer was suspended, the victim's harassment notice was withdrawn, and a formal letter of apology was sent to her by the Metropolitan Police. Finally, the mediator referred the victim to a medical practitioner who provided the victim with counselling support. Though protracted, the flexibility of the Hate Crime Project enabled the facilitator to facilitate a process that focused on harm and the need for harm reparation, which held multiple agencies to account and ultimately transformed the life of the victim.

There is a complex relationship that exists between statutory authorities and the communities that they serve, which means their role in protecting, educating or supporting individuals sees them both as important community providers as well as potential community harmers where biases become institutionalised. School teachers, medical professionals, social workers and housing officers provide essential services that, despite sometimes causing harm, are ultimately needed in order to support the recovery of victims of hate. Previous research has suggested that parties often shared some responsibility for the conflict, with both parties engaging in harmful behaviour.[68] These behaviours could often be linked to socio-economic disadvantage (e.g. unemployment, poverty), as well as mental health issues and drug and alcohol abuse. Without addressing these underlying issues neither "victim" nor "offender" could truly move beyond their conflict and the hate and hostility that had so often turned an interpersonal dispute into a "hate crime". Although RJ could not work to redistribute wealth, or undo the impacts of years of poverty or deficiencies in accessing decent education, facilitators were able to bring state representatives into dialogue in order to support the differing needs of participants.

Numerous cases were observed involving housing officers who worked to rehouse or draw up new contracts to prevent further abuse, or where school teachers and social workers engaged with young people in need of reassurance and emotional support, or where referrals were made to medical practitioners to support serious mental health issues. In fact, out of the 19 cases under research, 6 were only fully resolved after mediators engaged multiple agency representatives within restorative dialogue that addressed *both* parties' needs.[69]

It is important to reiterate that the restorative programme being researched was successful in advancing change at least partly because of its independence from the statutory authorities it engaged in restorative dialogue. For RJ to truly support hate crime legislation it must be administered by practitioners, who though potentially employed by the state,

---

[68] For example, neighbours who had both caused noise pollution, or who had been offensive to one another once a dispute involving family members had occurred. Walters 2014a (see Footnote 52).
[69] Walters 2014a (see Footnote 52) ch 6.

are not working simultaneously as police officers or prosecutors.[70] They must be able to facilitate cases in a holistic way that brings into dialogue multiple community and state representatives who collectively agree on ways to repair harms and support the needs of those affected by hate and prejudice. If this is possible, and I have observed empirically first-hand how it can be, then the criminalisation of hate underpinned by a framework of restorative practices has the potential to address (many of) the social injustices of hate crime.

7.5.3 Addressing Structural and Cultural Harms?

Within a broader framework of social justice liberalism, emphasis should be placed on protecting individual liberty while simultaneously unearthing social injustices caused by individual, social psychological and structural biases linked to group identity, in order to ensure that all individuals, regardless of background or wealth, can self-realise. However, ancient structures and culturally embedded institutions make this move to a fairer society challenging to achieve. As was discussed in Chap. 4, the power of social movements to bring about social and political change is a central part of the development of a happier and healthier (social) liberal society. In this regard, these movements must not only call for the criminalisation of hate-based violence directed at marginalised communities, but also seek structural reform to ensure that those in government are not causal to the social environments where expressions of hate continue to flourish.

The "hostile environment" in the UK towards immigrants and refugees is a case in point. In 2018 the Home Office was accused of generating such an environment. Known as the Windrush Scandal, it eventually saw the UK government apologise and set up a compensation fund for deporting and threatening to deport those who had emigrated to the UK from the late 1940s, many of whom had travelled from the Caribbean (with one of the first ships to arrive named the Empire Windrush). As

---

[70] See Walters 2014a (see Footnote 52) ch 5.

7 Punish or Repair? Where Is the "Social Justice" in Hate Crime... 229

well as those who were deported, many others were detained, lost their jobs and/or homes and were denied social benefits or health care.[71]

Although the government apology and compensation scheme were a welcomed step in repairing what had happened, it does little to empower those affected to share their experiences of harm so that lessons can be learned for the future. What is worse is that the compensation scheme proved incapable of processing claims quickly, demonstrating a lack of care towards those affected by the scandal.[72] How might social justice for these individuals be achieved? The problem of institutionalised racism, and other institutional prejudices, that are cultivated by state institutions must be addressed at their very roots. A restorative solution to building better institutions that not only resists prejudice and discrimination, but actively unearths social injustices is one that starts by holding open dialogue about the historical harms that are caused by policies, institutions and laws that disadvantage entire communities of people.

Such a process has been attempted in various contexts across the globe. For instance, the Truth and Reconciliation Commission (TRC) established in South Africa (SA) in 1995 was one of the first macro-level processes guided by restorative principles to help repair the structural harms inflicted during apartheid. The TRC had six main purposes, including: to record the extent and nature of the incidents; to name those responsible; to provide a public forum for victims to express themselves; to make recommendation to prevent future violations; to make reparations to victims and to grant amnesty to those who made full disclosure.[73] Over a period of seven years over 2000 victims and witnesses participated in public hearings, while 21,000 provided testimony via statements to the Commission.[74] Individuals who were responsible for the atrocities of

---

[71] Harriet Agerholm, 'Windrush generation: Home Office "set them up to fail", say MPs' *The Independent* (London, 3 July 2018).

[72] The scheme has since paid out £14.3 million in compensation, National Audit Office, *Investigation into the Windrush Compensation Scheme* (NAO 2021).

[73] Chris Cunneen, 'Exploring the Relationship Between Reparations, the Gross Violation of Human Rights, and Restorative Justice' in Dennis Sullivan and Larry Tifft (eds), *Handbook of Restorative Justice: A Global Perspective* (Routledge 2007) 362.

[74] See Truth and Reconciliation Commission, 'Amnesty hearings and decisions' (n.d.).

apartheid were given an opportunity to testify and in return could request amnesty.[75]

The TRC aimed to promote reconciliation at four different levels; these included: individual—coming to terms with painful truths; interpersonal—between victims and offenders; community—the role of local populations; and national—the role of the state and non-state institutions.[76] This was one of the first national level processes to offer an alternative approach to criminal prosecution that sought to facilitate a process of "truth-telling".[77] The Constitutional Court of South Africa reflected on the symbolic importance of the Commission, stating:

> The families of those unlawfully tortured, maimed or traumatized become more empowered to discover the truth, the perpetrators become exposed to opportunities to obtain relief from the burden of a guilt or an anxiety they might be living with for many long years, the country begins the long and necessary process of healing the wounds of the past, transforming anger and grief into a mature understanding and creating the emotional and structural climate essential for the 'reconciliation and reconstruction' which informs the very difficult and sometimes painful objectives of the amnesty.[78]

The TRC was perceived by many to be transformative in South Africa's transition from a system of institutionalised racial segregation to democratic republic with a constitution that focuses on principles of racial equality and minority rights. However, it was not without its limitations

---

[75] Amnesty was granted in 849 cases and refused in 5,392 cases: Truth and Reconciliation Commission (ibid.).

[76] Cunneen 2008 (see Footnote 73).

[77] Elgar GM Weitekamp and others, 'How to deal with mass victimization and gross human rights violations: A restorative justice approach' in Uwe Ewald and Ksenija Turković (eds), *Large-Scale Victimisation as a Potential Source of Terrorist Activities: Importance of Regaining Security in Post-Conflict Societies* (IOS Press 2006) 217–241.

[78] *Azanian People's Organisation (AZAPO) and Others v President of the Republic of South Africa and Others*, 1996 (8) BCLR 1015 (CC at 17), 1996 SACLR LEXIS 20 at 37–8. The perceived success of the TRC resulted in the establishment by the UN General Assembly of the Basic Principles and Guidelines on the Right to a Remedy and Reparation for Victims of Gross Violations of International Human Rights Law and Serious Violations of International Humanitarian Law in 2005.

or criticism.⁷⁹ For instance, while the TRC provided some reparations it did not extend these to everyone affected directly and indirectly by the system of segregation.⁸⁰ Furthermore, most of the structural harms caused by state and non-state institutions under the fourth level of reconciliation were not fully explicated or resolved.⁸¹

The challenge for RJ at the macro-level is that its practices must resist operating in such a way as to reproduce outcomes that partly sustain an unequal society. Cuneen asserts that the restorative dialogue at this level may simply create an "individualized sense of civic obligation" that reproduces the role of law and conventional processes of criminalisation as maintained by Western neoliberal systems of justice that disproportionately impact upon already marginalised communities.⁸² Such a reality may well be true were RJ's future to operate on the periphery of a criminal justice system that remains anchored to neoliberal commitments to penal punitiveness. However, a system of governance that is framed by principles of restorative justice can serve to uncover and heal the harms of social injustice, so long as that system operates to protect dominion and rectify inequality. This book is a call for a vision of what justice can look like in the future if it is anchored to social justice liberalism. For a social justice liberal criminal law to be truly realised we must work to shed the entrenched ideological commitment to seeking justice only through punishment. Though typically a popular response to crime, it is not one that

---

⁷⁹ For instance, Lin has asserted that the TRC was no more than a reflection of the political interests of achieving less legal pluralism and more centralisation. In addition she argues that the international community has perpetuated a 'restorative justice mythology' that was expressed by influential figures including Bishop Desmond Tutu and Dr Alex Boraine. Olivia Lin, 'Demythologizing restorative justice: South Africa's Truth and Reconciliation Commission and Rwanda's Gacaca courts in context' (2005) 12(1) ILSA J Int'l & Comp L 41, 56–63.

⁸⁰ Lars Waldorf, 'Rwanda's failing experiment in restorative justice' in Dennis Sullivan and Larry Tifft (eds), *Handbook of Restorative Justice: A Global Perspective* (Routledge 2007) 422–432.

⁸¹ Elgar GM Weitekamp and others, 'How to deal with mass victimization and gross human rights violations: A restorative justice approach' in Uwe Ewald and Ksenija Turković (eds), *Large-Scale Victimisation as a Potential Source of Terrorist Activities: Importance of Regaining Security in Post-Conflict Societies* (IOS Press 2006) 217–241.

⁸² Chris Cunneen, 'Restorative justice, globalization and the logic of empire' in Sharon Pickering and Jude McCulloch (eds), *Borders and Crime: Pre-Crime, Mobility and Serious Harm in an Age of Globalization* (Palgrave Macmillan 2012) 147–162, 148. See also, George Pavlich, 'Transforming Powers and Restorative Justice' in Theo Gavrielides, *Routledge International Handbook of Restorative Justice* (Routledge 2019) ch 30.

is always supported by members of the public. Indeed, a recent study on attitudes towards sentencing hate crime offenders showed that members of the LGBT+ community preferred justice as restoration over the use of enhanced punishments.[83]

7.6 Conclusion

The criminal law plays a fundamental role in furnishing the boundaries of acceptable behaviour, both for individuals and state actors. Conventionally what distinguishes criminal law from other forms of law is its focus on punishment. This book offers an alternative paradigm shift which reimagines the criminal law, not as a tool of inflicting pain, but as a means through which to prevent it. However, if this is to be effective the criminal justice system must shift its primary basis from one of punishment delivery to that of harm reparation. This does not mean that there is no role for punishment in society, rather it becomes secondary to the purposes of criminal justice. Within a system of social justice liberalism, it is conceded that the threat of punishment must remain attached to criminal offences if the criminal justice system is to function as a comprehensive mechanism for crime control. The threat of punishment acts as a form of insurance, ensuring that ultimately all members of the polity are answerable to their actions of hate. However, in promoting a more inclusive and cohesive society, the criminal justice system must become attuned to the social harms that are likely to accrue where forms of punishment (especially imprisonment) are used as foci for preventing hate crime. Without the reframing of law and justice in this way, far from preventing hate, the state risks repeating the individual, institutional and structural harms caused by identity-based prejudices.

---

[83] See Mark A Walters, Jenny L Paterson and Rupert Brown, 'Enhancing Punishment or Repairing Harms? Perceptions of Sentencing Hate Crimes Amongst Members of a Commonly Targeted Victim Group' (2020) 61(1) Brit J Criminol 61. Recent research has shown that 61 per cent of LGBTQI surveyed on their preferences for the use of an enhanced punishment versus restorative justice for hate crime, preferred the use of RJ. Furthermore, experiments showed that RJ for even violent hate crime was perceived to be better at reducing reoffending and supporting victims.

7 Punish or Repair? Where Is the "Social Justice" in Hate Crime...

If the criminal law is to serve more than a mere means through which to stigmatise offenders, its institutions must be underpinned by a framework of restorative and community-based interventions that aim to address the multifarious individual and social causes and consequences of hate-based criminality. Restoration as the cornerstone of criminal justice can be achieved where a framework of practices is systemised within and outside of the criminal justice system. Interventions can be used at all stages of the criminal process, from alternatives to formal cautioning or prosecution,[84] through to RJ activities being implemented post-conviction but pre-sentencing,[85] as part of a sentence,[86] or—where punishment becomes necessary—as part of post-sentence activities.[87] Beyond the criminal justice system, broader interventions must then be instituted at the state level to address the historical and structural harms perpetrated by the government and its institutions.

---

[84] For instance, community mediation services commissioned by local authorities, including examples such as the Southwark Hate Crime Project, or the use of police restorative disposals as part of "community resolutions" implemented by restorative justice practitioners who work for police services, but who are not police officers. See for example the Sussex Police scheme Restore DiverCity which uses restorative conferencing for "low-level" hate crimes, outlined in Mark Walters, 'Developments in the use of restorative justice for hate crime' (2020) 3 International Journal of Restorative Justice 446.

[85] See for example s.1ZA(6) of the Powers of the Criminal Courts (Sentencing) Act 2000, which provides for powers to defer sentence for RJ activities but which is largely unused due in part to there not being a systemic framework of practice to refer cases into.

[86] See for example Criminal Code (Illinois), s. 12-7.1.

[87] See for example Mark A Walters, '"I thought 'he's a monster'... [but] he was just... normal": Examining the therapeutic benefits of restorative justice for homicide' (2015) 55(6) Brit J Criminol 1207, which details a case where the offender convicted of murdering a young gay man participated in restorative meetings facilitated by a probation service with the victim's family members.

8

Conclusion: Expanding the Criminal Justice Lens

The twenty-first century has paid witness to the globalisation of hate crime legislation. Research undertaken for this book uncovered many hundreds of legislative provisions that have been enacted across 190 jurisdictions covering all six inhabited continents. There is much to celebrate in this global movement towards preventing hate-based criminal conduct. Yet while these laws are a marker of progress in tackling criminal manifestations of hatred, they are also a reflection of a neoliberal drive to bring in more punitive measures to prevent crime more generally. The international legal landscape is one that situates offences within systems of justice that are failing to adequately address both the structural causal mechanisms of hate-based conduct and its individual, community and societal harms. Part of the reason for this is that "hate" has been understood as a discrete feature of a crime that is attached to an offence as a form of "aggravation". Such frameworks of law have done little to unearth the myriad ways in which hate is expressed through action, while punishment enhancements remain largely impotent in mitigating against hate crime's distinct harms.

This book departs from current thinking on legislating for hate crime by reimagining the role of law in criminalising it. Hate crime is defined as hate-based conduct (as distinguished from speech alone), which includes acts, omissions or states of affair, that is considered by lawmakers to be worthy of criminal proscription, based primarily on an assessment of the harms it is likely to cause. The word "hate" (or "hate-element") is inclusive of both states of mind and actions that demonstrate hatred, bias, prejudice, identity-based hostility and/or contempt towards a victim with a protected characteristic, and which underpins, or partly forms, the proscribed conduct. Central to this definition is harm. The book reconceptualises the harms of hate-based conduct as a form of social injustice. Law as social justice liberalism puts the unearthing of social injustice at the heart of criminal law. Based on social liberal political theory, it is argued that criminal law ought to play an active role in identifying and combating harms that are causal to social inequality. Social injustice occurs where individuals are faced with individual and structural obstacles to equal participation in society. This in turn reduces an individual's capacity to self-realise, or as many philosophers have put it, to enjoy a "good life". Few have recognised hate-based criminal conduct as a salient form of social injustice; instead defining it simply as an offence already proscribed in law that has a hate motivation and which is likely to "hurt more". But hate crime is much more than this. When understood as a form of oppression, hate crime can be more comprehensibly explained as forming an intersectional and mutually reinforcing cycle of harm that occurs as violence, marginalisation, powerlessness and cultural imperialism. Hate as a form of oppression does not just conceptualise hate crimes as simply hurting victims "more", but instead it shows us how acts of hatred sustain social environments within which entire groups of people are rendered without sufficient capacity to participate equally in society.

Understanding hate-based harms in their wider context enables us to build a framework of laws, and justice measures, that extend beyond traditional conceptions of criminal wrongdoing. This is not to suggest that all discriminatory conduct or biased expressions of norms and values ought to be criminalised. Rather, it is a call for a more a holistic understanding of harm that comprehends the intersecting and multi-layered injustices that targeted violence and abuse cause entire groups of people. While criminal law theorists have traditionally rejected the criminalisation of remote harms as being too nebulous to accurately calculate, or because they are open to myriad external causal factors, I hope to have outlined sufficient empirical evidence in this book that shows direct causal linkage between hate crime and the harms of violence, marginalisation, powerlessness and cultural imperialism.

Central to this more holistic conceptualisation of harm has been group identity. Oppression is directly linked to social groups who are disproportionately subjected to targeted victimisation. The oppressive effects of hate are casually linked to group members' perceptions of threats, as they relate to collective identity. Perceptions of threat are experienced in relation to individuals' sense of physical safety as well as to their rights to participate fully in society free from group-based inequality and discrimination.[1] It is these threats that result in emotional responses, most distinctively anger, anxiety and shame. These emotions occur not just amongst direct victims but are experienced vicariously by others who share their characteristics. They also predict certain behaviours, including changing appearance, avoiding certain public locations and avoiding visible markers in public that reveal one's identity. These are distinct harms and are partly what give "hate crime" its unique character as a type of crime.

Given that hate crime is a form of group-based oppression, there is good reason to ensure that the criminal law is structured to protect those groups' identities that are most commonly targeted *and* that experience the distinct harms of social injustice. Chapter 4 outlined criteria that can guide legislatures when making important decisions about which groups should fall behind the protective shield of the criminal law. Such a task is assisted greatly through forms of participatory democracy that include the voices and work of political activists, civil society organisations and NGOs, as well as academics. Collectively, these individuals are fundamental to creating greater awareness of the social injustices experienced by certain groups. They too will play an important role in providing evidence that certain individuals are experiencing the oppressive effects of targeted victimisation. Yet they cannot do this alone. It is important that government agencies work directly with groups across society in an ongoing and mutually reinforcing engagement process that ensures multiple voices representing intersecting identities inform the development of hate crime policy and law.

---

[1] See Chap. 3, Part 2.

Putting these policies and laws into practice involves the construction of a legal framework that recognises hate as a distinct moral wrong and a system of justice interventions that aim to repair its harms. Chapter 5 explored the myriad ways in which hate has been criminalised globally, revealing three main types of hate crime law, each containing subcategories and variations. The different methods of legislating for hate crime each have theoretical and practical advantages and disadvantages. And beyond what is written in the statute books, there will be nuances across and between legal systems that will impact on how each of these "types" are practised. Indeed, in the US where modern hate crime laws originated, there are far fewer recorded "hate crimes" than in other jurisdictions such as the UK.[2] This is despite the fact that the UK has a population one-fifth the size of the US. There are a multitude of factors affecting recording and prosecution practices,[3] but prominent amongst these is the way in which hate crime laws have been constructed on paper. Research explored in this book suggests that provisions that apply only at the sentencing stage (whether in common or civil law jurisdictions) are more likely to result in the hate-element of an offence being filtered out of the criminal process. Where the hate-element does not make up a constitutive element of a criminal offence it is less likely to be taken seriously by the statutory authorities tasked with enforcing and applying the law. Jurisdictions yet to enact hate crime laws, or those currently involved in reform processes, must reflect carefully on whether the maintenance of laws that are proving to be ineffective in practice will ultimately erode trust in the state's commitment to preventing hate crime.

The task of criminalising different forms of hate is by no means a simple one. Hybrid models offer a partial solution to the practical problem of legislatures creating thousands of new hate-based offences, by ensuring that any offence in law can be charged as hate-based and upon conviction labelled as such. Yet even this approach is significantly limited by the fact that it fails to unearth hate-based conduct and activities yet to be legally proscribed. The enactment of new substantive (aggravated) offences may

---

[2] See Chaps. 5 and 6.

[3] Including: group members' willingness to report, effectiveness of recording systems, the training levels amongst statutory authorities and the willingness among statutory authorities to prioritise hate crime.

therefore be an important step in taking hate crimes more seriously. Under such an approach, legislatures ought to label hate crime offences for what they are, whether they be formally enacted in legislation as "hate crimes"[4] or "bias offences",[5] or through other labels that reflect the prejudiced nature of such offences. This task is not just about re-labelling existing offences which may involve a hate-element. A social justice liberal approach to criminalisation also requires legislatures to proactively unearth and identify conduct that results in social injustice. This proactive approach to enacting legislation will likely result in new conduct and activity being proscribed where it infringes personal interests; understood as violence, marginalisation, powerless and cultural imperialism. In some cases, conduct identified as hateful by its very nature should be a worthy candidate for criminal proscription, regardless of whether there exists a parallel offence. Many of these new laws will likely relate to online hate, something I have said little about in this book, but which a next step of evaluation might lead. Online hate is a place where "speech" and "conduct" often meet (from offensive speech to threats of violence) and where new realms of criminal responsibility for hate may extend beyond private citizens to that of commercial platforms. A social justice liberal framework of criminalising online hate is one where the unique nature of hateful online activity, understood in term of the distinct harms it likely causes, will dictate the ways in which new offences are crafted and enforced.[6] Legislatures will need to explore ways of creating individual culpability that more saliently reflects the specific harms of different types and levels of online hate. In fact, research suggests these may well be different from offline hate crime.[7] Given the current practical difficulties involved in policing such offences, it may also involve exploring ways of establishing new forms of liability for online platforms that host hate-based material.[8] Such a multi-method approach to preventing the spread

---

[4] For example California Penal Code § 422.55.
[5] For example Oregon, Or Rev Stat § 166.155.
[6] See for example Chara Bakalis, 'Rethinking cyberhate laws' (2017) 27(1) Information and Communications Technology Law 86.
[7] Harriet Fearn, *The impacts of cyberhate* (Doctoral thesis, University of Sussex 2017).
[8] Including new methods of regulating content, including via communication regulators. See for example the new Online Safety Bill 2021 (UK).

of hate extends beyond individual responsibility by extending the reach of legal regulation to capture corporate entities that operate globally.

Once a legislator has identified the forms of hate-based conduct it wishes to proscribe and the *type* of law that best reflects their wrongfulness, it must then decide the model and legal test that will be used to operationalise the legislation. These too can have a significant impact upon the way hate crime laws are put into practice. Two main models of law were examined in this book: the animus model and discriminatory selection model. As with types of law, these both had advantages and disadvantages in their operationalisation. Animus models incorporate a "hate-element" directly into a legal test that must then be proved in court. While this model seemingly reflects an important element of what makes a crime a "hate crime", there have been significant issues both conceptually and practically in attaching animus to a criminal offence. First, there appears to be no single word that captures all types of emotion, belief, attitude and behaviour that embody the "hate" of hate crime. Some jurisdictions have chosen to narrowly define hate crimes as those involving "hate" or "hatred".[9] While this may on face value appear commonsensical, given we are dealing with the phenomenon of "hate crime", it is clear that the types of conduct that are directed at certain groups, from which social injustice ensues, are linked to much broader concepts including, but not limited to, bias, prejudice, hostility and contempt.[10]

Yet even when these broader concepts are included in law, they each have definitional boundaries that may be inclusive or exclusive of different subjective motives and physical expressions that a social justice liberal approach to criminalising hate might seek to capture. Complicating the legal nomenclature for hate further is that the hate-element can either be attached to the mens rea and/or actus reus of an offence. Most legislatures have chosen to attach the hate-element to mens rea, most commonly through "motivation" or "part motivation". While the inclusion of motive has been contested theoretically, its real issue is with its application in practice. Research in both the US and Europe suggests that proving motive beyond reasonable doubt is so problematic that it has had the

---

[9] See Chap. 6, Sect. 6.2.1.
[10] Ibid.

effect of significantly restricting the applicability of hate crime law. Alternatively, some jurisdictions have chosen to attach the hate-element to the actus reus of an offence. In doing so they have criminalised hate where prejudice or identity-based hostility is "demonstrated" during the commission of an underlying offence. Such an approach, used in UK jurisdictions, has had the effect of capturing many more offences as "hate crimes" when compared with those jurisdictions that have used only the mens rea element. This book has defended the use of such a legal test, but there remains a question mark as to whether a demonstration, such as a verbal expression of hate made during the commission of an offence, would be challenged as breaching free speech rights, particularly in the US context.[11]

A second method of constructing hate crime offences is to use a discriminatory section model. This more commonly used model of law does not require a direct form of animus to prove an offence. Instead, the hate-element is incorporated indirectly by criminalising conduct which is committed *by reason* of a victim's identity. There have been concerns that the model is overly inclusive and will capture conduct that is not intended to express hate to a group, but which instead directs harm at individuals for their perceived vulnerability, invariably linked to either a faulty stereotype or a belief that the victim's identity makes them innately weak.[12] It was argued that these concerns are based on a perception that the law should only criminalise hate-based conduct where the offender *intentionally* expresses prejudice through their action. However, what is less clear from critics of the model is why the selection of a victim based on a faulty stereotype or belief they are weak is not tantamount to selecting a victim because of a bias or prejudice; especially given that stereotyping is central to defining the latter. I argue that the criminal targeting of group members because of a stereotype or because the victim is perceived to be weak, are prime examples of prejudices and biases that serve to oppress certain identity groups. Despite an offender not always literally "hating" their victim, they ought still to be culpable where they have consciously

---

[11] Though it has been held that it can be used as evidence to prove motive, *Wisconsin v Mitchell* 508 US 476, 489.
[12] See Chap. 6, Sect. 6.2.2.

selected a victim because of their *protected* characteristic in order to make a gain at their expense. As with so many types of crime, we need not require mens rea of the consequences of their action (as per result crimes) so long as the offender intentionally commits the act. We are interested here in the normative position of the criminal law, and to a mental state that considers whether a reasonable citizen ought to know an act is harmful or risks harm. Hence, where the offender exclaims "I didn't know my actions resulted in the oppression of a marginalised identity group" we might respond "you ought to have known"—much in the same way that liability can be constructed for crimes such as harassment, stalking and even murder.[13]

While the discriminatory model covers the types of conduct that a social justice liberal approach to criminalisation might be interested in criminalising, it too will have its limitations. Such as where expressions of hatred are demonstrated during a criminal act but where the offence is not committed because of the victim's identity. Given that there are limitations to both models, legislators ought to consider incorporating a mixture of models and legal tests that are capable, both in theory and practice, of capturing the myriad forms of hate-based criminality that pervade societies globally.

Some liberal theorists reading this book may initially balk at the idea of extending the scope of criminal law to cover such a broad range of social harms through such wide-ranging models and legal tests. Such a concern is particularly relevant where the primary response to criminalisation is the infliction of pain through punishment. However, this book does not envisage a criminal justice landscape that expands the carceral estate. The construction of hate crime laws that are aimed at tackling social injustice cannot be sustained where the state focuses its postconviction response on enhancing punitive sanctions. The liberal application of punitive sanctions is likely to exacerbate the problem of hate and may be implicated in perpetuating social injustice where the law fails to address its underlying causes. In fact, a system of law that centres punitive sanctioning may also risk repeating institutional and structural processes

---

[13] Ibid.

8 Conclusion: Expanding the Criminal Justice Lens

of marginalisation that disproportionately target already marginalised groups through law enforcement activities.

The criminal justice system envisaged in this book is one that pivots on communitarian principles of reconciliation and restoration. It is orientated towards a collection of innovative interventions that comprehend hate crimes as individual, community and structural harms. The final chapter of this book outlined how restorative solutions to hate can be delivered at micro, meso and macro levels. This involves a change in the way that justice is delivered, and it requires a state that is open to the possibilities of repairing harms, not simply by facilitating restorative dialogue between affected parties, but by taking on obligations to resolve the harms that public institutions have caused. Such a repositioning is radical in and of itself, but the system I propose is not one of complete abolition. For a primary system of restoration to work it must be layered upon a secondary system of threatened punishment, which would continue to operate upon more traditional notions of harm-culpability and the setting of proportionate punishments. These threatened sanctions must operate only as an option of last resort and this ought to be stated in law.

If we are to truly take hate crime seriously, we can no longer tolerate a system of justice that treats "hate" as a secondary factor that *might* aggravate a selection of a few offences. Unless criminal manifestations of hate are properly understood as being directly causal to social injustice, the law will continue to focus its attention on inflicting pain on individuals for their "aggravated" offending. Social justice liberalism urges us to expand our lens of what hate-based harms are, it calls for new legal frameworks that recognise and challenge the oppression of minority groups, and it seeks to repair harms through dialogical processes of justice.

Appendix A: Examples of Hate Crime Laws from Around the World[1]

---

[1] This Appendix provides a sample of hate crime laws from jurisdictions across six continents. It is not an exhaustive list of legislation but instead aims to provide examples of the different types and models of legislation that have been enacted globally. Note that due to the extensive range of incitement to hatred legislation used globally only some examples of these laws are provided in the tables for those jurisdictions where incitement can be committed through "acts" and where other types of hate crime legislation are not used.

Asia

Jurisdiction	Type of Legislation	Model	Hate-element	Characteristics covered	Legal provision
Armenia	Sentence uplift—aggravation	Discriminatory selection	motives	ethnic, racial or religious … or for religious fanaticism	Criminal Code, Art. 63(1)(6)
	Substantive offences—aggravated	Animus	motives of hate/hatred	nationality, race or religious or for religious fanaticism	Criminal Code, Arts. 104(13), 112(12), 113(7), 119(7), 185(4), 265(2)
	Substantive offence—conduct-based	Discriminatory selection	for reasons of	nationality, race, sex, language, religion, political or other views, social origin, property or other statuses	Criminal Code, Art. 143
China	Substantive offence—conduct-based	Through conduct	illegally deprive or encroach on	citizens' right to religious belief; … minority nationalities' customs or habits	Criminal Law of the People's Republic of China, Art. 251
India	Substantive offence—conduct-based	Animus	promot[es] enmity, or organises for violence	between different religious, racial, language or regional groups or castes or communities …. any religious, racial, language or regional group or caste or community	Penal Code, Art. 153A(1)(b) and (c)
Singapore	Sentence uplift—penalty enhancement	Animus	motivated (wholly or partly) by hostility or demonstrated hostility	racial or religious group	Penal Code, Art. 74
Uzbekistan	Sentence uplift—aggravation	Animus	on the grounds of … hatred or enmity	racial or ethnic	Criminal Code, Art. 56(I)
	Substantive offences—aggravated	Animus	on grounds of hatred or prejudice	interethnic or racial, religious	Criminal Code, Arts. 97(2)(k) and (m), 104(2)(j) and (z), 105(2)(j) and (z), 173(2)(a)

Appendix A: Examples of Hate Crime Laws from Around the World

Africa

Jurisdiction	Type of Legislation	Model	Hate-element	Characteristics covered	Legal provision
Angola	Sentence uplift—aggravation	Discriminatory selection	because of discrimination on account of	race, colour, ethnicity, place of birth, gender, sexual orientation, illness or physical or psychological disability, belief or religion, political or ideological convictions, social condition or origin or any another form of discrimination	Penal Code, Art. 71(1)(c)
	Substantive offence—aggravated	Animus	motive of hatred	racial, religious, political, ethno-linguistic or regional	Penal Code, Art. 149(c)
	Substantive offence—aggravated	Discriminatory selection	directed at a person on account of	race, colour, ethnicity, place of birth, gender, sexual orientation, illness or physical or psychological disability, belief or religion, political or ideological convictions, social condition or origin or any another form of discrimination OR a human group characterised by race, colour, ethnicity, place of birth, gender, sexual orientation, illness or physical or psychological disability, belief or religion, political or ideological convictions, social condition or origin or any other form of discrimination or another relevant reason in respect to the people that constitute it	Penal Code, Art. 170(3) and (4)
	Substantive offence—conduct-based	Discriminatory selection	because of	race, colour, ethnicity, place of birth, gender, sexual orientation, illness or physical or psychological disability, belief or religion, political or ideological convictions, social condition or origin or any other reason in respect to its members or holders of its corporate boards	Penal Code, Art. 212

(continued)

(continued)

Jurisdiction	Type of Legislation	Model	Hate-element	Characteristics covered	Legal provision
	Substantive offences—aggravated	Discriminatory selection	for reasons of	race, colour, ethnicity, place of birth, gender, sexual orientation, illness or physical or psychological disability, belief or religion, political or ideological convictions, social condition or origin, having or not an illness or a physical or psychological disability, or for supposedly being or not being a member of a determined organisation	Penal Code, Arts. 221, 222 with 223
Cabo Verde	Substantive offences—aggravated	Animus	because of hatred	racial, religious, or political, sexual orientation and gender identity	Penal Code, Art. 123(e)
Eritrea	Sentence uplift—aggravation	Animus	motivated by bias, prejudice or hate motive	religion, national or ethnic origin, language, sex, or race, or otherwise acted out of a base or evil	Penal Code, Art. 67(1)(c)
	Substantive offence—aggravated	Animus	for reasons of bias or hatred	ethnicity or religion	Penal Code, Art. 276
Gabon	Sentence uplift—aggravation	Discriminatory selection OR Animus	based on OR offence is preceded, accompanied or followed by words, writings, images, objects or acts of any kind which affect the honour or consideration of victim because of	ethnicity, nation, race or religion	Penal Code, Art. 55-6

Appendix A: Examples of Hate Crime Laws from Around the World

Country	Offence type	Category	Trigger	Protected characteristics	Citation
	Substantive offences—aggravated	Discriminatory selection	based on	ethnic group, nation, race, or religion	Penal Code, Art. 296
Guinea	Substantive offences—aggravated	Discriminatory selection	on the basis of	ethnic group, nation, race or religion	Penal Code, Arts. 209, 303 and 306(8)
	Substantive offences—aggravated	Discriminatory selection	by reason of, or on grounds of	origin, sex, family status, physical appearance, the family name, place of residence, state of health, disability, genetic characteristics, morals, age, political opinions, trade union activities, ethnic group, nation, race or religion	Penal Code, Arts. 313, 314
	Substantive offence—aggravated	Discriminatory selection	on the basis of	ethnic group, nation, a race, religion, political opinion or other form of discrimination	Penal Code, Arts. 233 and 234
Kenya	Substantive offence—conduct-based	Animus	subversive intention intended or calculated to promote feelings of hatred or enmity	races or communities	Penal Code, Art. 77(3)(e)
Mali	Substantive offences—conduct-based	Animus	likely to establish or give rise to discrimination… aimed at provoking or maintaining the spread of regionalism	racial, ethnic or regionalism	Penal Code, Art. 58

(continued)

(continued)

Jurisdiction	Type of Legislation	Model	Hate-element	Characteristics covered	Legal provision
Sao Tomé and Principe	Substantive offences—aggravated	Animus	motivated by hatred	racial, religious or political, colour, ethnic or national origin, sex or sexual orientation	Penal Code, Art. 130
South Africa (draft govt bill)	Hybrid	Animus	motivated by prejudice or intolerance	age, albinism, birth, colour, culture, disability, ethnic or social origin, gender or gender identity, HIV status, language, nationality, migrant or refugee status, occupation or trade, political affiliation or conviction, race, religion, sex, which includes intersex, or sexual orientation.	(Draft) Prevention and Combating of Hate Speech Bill, ss. 3, 6

Central and South America (including the Caribbean)

Jurisdiction	Type of Legislation	Model	Hate-element	Characteristics covered	Legal provision
Bermuda	Sentence uplift—aggravation	Animus	motivated by bias, prejudice or hate based on	race, national or ethnic origin, language, colour, religion, sex, age, mental or physical disability, sexual orientation or any other similar factors	Criminal Code Act 1907, s. 55(2)(f)(i)
	Substantive offences—aggravated	Animus	antipathy … on account of	race, colour or place of origin	Criminal Code Act 1907, ss. 200A and 200B
Brazil	Substantive offences—conduct-based	Animus	discrimination or prejudice based on	race, colour, ethnicity, religion or national origin	LAW No. 7.716, of January 5, 1989, ss. 1, 3 to 18
	Substantive offences—conduct-based	Animus	for the purposes of	promoting Nazism	LAW No. 7.716, of January 5, 1989, s. 20
	Substantive offences—aggravated	Discriminatory selection	due to prejudice of	race, colour, ethnicity, religion or origin	Penal Code, Art. 149
Cayman Islands	Sentence uplift—aggravation	Animus	motivated by bias, prejudice or hate based on	race, national or ethnic origin, language, colour, religion, sex, age, mental or physical disability, sexual orientation or any other similar factor	Alternative Sentencing Law (2008 Rev.) s. 4(c)(i)

(continued)

(continued)

Jurisdiction	Type of Legislation	Model	Hate-element	Characteristics covered	Legal provision
Cuba	Substantive offences—conduct-based	Discriminatory selection and Animus	for reasons of	sex, race, colour or national origin	Penal Code, Art. 349
Mexico	Sentence uplift—penalty enhancement	Discriminatory selection	gender-based	woman	Penal Code, Art. 51
	Substantive offences—conduct-based	Discriminatory selection	on grounds of	ethnic or national origin or belonging, race, skin colour, language, gender, sex, sexual preference, age, marital status national or social origin, social or economic status, health, pregnancy, political or any other opinion that is contrary to human dignity or nullifies the rights and freedoms of individuals; or restricts labour rights, mainly on the basis of gender	Penal Code, Art. 149 B
	Substantive offence—aggravated	Discriminatory selection	on the basis of	gender/a woman	Penal Code, Art. 325
Puerto Rico	Sentence uplift—aggravation	Animus	motivated by prejudice towards and against	race, colour, sex, sexual orientation, gender, gender identity, origin, ethnic origin, marital status, birth, handicap, or physical or mental condition, social condition, religion, age, ideologies, political or religious beliefs or being homeless	Penal Code, Art. 66

Appendix A: Examples of Hate Crime Laws from Around the World

	Substantive offences—conduct-based	Discriminatory selection	on the grounds of	political ideology, religious belief, race, skin colour, sex, gender, social status or national or ethnic origin, or on the grounds of political ideology, religious belief, race, skin colour, sex, gender, social status, national or ethnic origin, or homelessness	Penal Code, Art. 180
Uruguay	Sentence uplift—penalty enhancement	Discriminatory selection	on the grounds of	sexual orientation, gender identity, race or ethnic origin, religion or disability	Penal Code, Art. 312(7)
	Sentence uplift—penalty enhancement	Animus	for reasons of hatred, contempt, or belittlement	status as a woman	Penal Code, Art. 312(8)
Territories and Dependencies					
Saint Kitts and Nevis	Sentence uplift—aggravation	Animus	motivated by bias, prejudice or hate based on	race, national or ethnic origin, language, colour, religion, sex, age, mental or physical disability, sexual orientation, or any other similar factors	Criminal Code, Art. 62 with 3
Sint Maarten	Substantive offences—conduct-based	Discriminatory selection	on the basis of	religion, other beliefs, political persuasions, race, colour, language, national or social origins or physical, psychological or mental handicap or their gender or heterosexual or homosexual orientation, or their membership of a national minority	Criminal Code, Art. 2:63; see 2:60

(continued)

Appendix A: Examples of Hate Crime Laws from Around the World

(continued)

Jurisdiction	Type of Legislation	Model	Hate-element	Characteristics covered	Legal provision
Sint Maarten	Substantive offences—conduct-based	Discriminatory selection	on the grounds of	race	Criminal Code, Art. 2:64
Trinidad and Tobago	Substantive offences—aggravated	Discriminatory selection	because of	race, religion, nationality or country of origin	Offences Against the Person Act, s. 4E(g)
US Virgin Islands	Sentence uplift—penalty enhancement	Animus	maliciously motivated by prejudice	race, colour, religion, national origin, sex, ancestry, age, disability, sexual orientation or gender identity	V.I. Code 14-3047 with § 14-3048

Appendix A: Examples of Hate Crime Laws from Around the World

Europe

Jurisdiction	Type of Legislation	Model	Hate-element	Characteristics covered	Legal provision
Belgium	Sentence uplift—penalty enhancement	Animus	hatred against, contempt for or hostility to a person on the grounds of	presumed race, colour of skin, ancestry, national or ethnic origin, nationality, sex, sexual orientation, marital status, birth, age, wealth, religious or philosophical conviction, current or future state of health, disability, language, political conviction, trade union conviction, a physical or genetic characteristic or social origin	Criminal Code, Arts. 377bis, 405 quarter, 422 quarter, 438bis, 442ter, 453bis, 514bis, 525bis, 532bis, 534quarter, 543.
Cyprus	Sentence uplift—aggravation	Animus	motivation of prejudice against	race, colour, national or ethnic origin, religion or other belief, descent, sexual orientation or gender identity	Criminal Code, Art. 35A
Czech Republic	Sentence uplift—aggravation	Animus	motive of hatred, or another particularly condemnable motive	racial, ethnic, religious, class or other similar	Criminal Code, § 42
	Substantive offences—aggravated	Discriminatory selection	for	race, ethnic affiliation, nationality, political opinion, religion or belief or real or perceived lack thereof	Criminal Code, §§ 140(3)(g), 145(2)(f), 146(2)(e), 149(2)(c), 170(2)(b), 171(2)(b), 172(3)(b), 175(2)(f), 183(3)(b), 228(3)(b), 329(2)(b), 352(2), 378(2), 379(2)(d), 380(2)(c), 381(2)(c), 382(2)(c)
Georgia	Sentence uplift—aggravation	Animus	based on; with motives of intolerance	race, colour, language, sex, sexual orientation, gender identity, age, religion, political or other opinion, disability, citizenship, nationality, ethnic or social belonging, origin, material or social status, place of residence, other signs of discrimination	Criminal Code, Art. 53(3-1)

(continued)

(continued)

Jurisdiction	Type of Legislation	Model	Hate-element	Characteristics covered	Legal provision
	Substantive offences—aggravated	Animus	due to intolerance	racial, religious, national or ethnic	Criminal Code, Arts. 109(2)(d), 117(5), 118(3), 126(2)(g)
	Substantive offences—conduct-based	Discriminatory selection	on the grounds of	language, sex, age, nationality, origin, birthplace, place of residence, material or rank status, religion or belief, social belonging, profession, marital status, health status, sexual orientation, gender identity and expression, political or other views or of any other signs of having substantially breached human rights	Criminal Code, Art. 142
	Substantive offence—conduct-based	Discriminatory selection	based on	race, colour, national or ethnic belonging	Criminal Code, Art. 142-1
	Substantive offence—conduct-based	Discriminatory selection	due to	persons with disabilities	Criminal Code, Art. 142-2
	Substantive offence—conduct-based	Discriminatory selection	because of	political, public, professional, religious or scientific activities	Criminal Code, Art. 156
	Substantive offence—conduct-based	Nature of conduct is hate-based	interfere, using violence etc.	political, public or religious associations	Criminal Code, Art. 166
	Substantive offence—aggravated	Animus	due to intolerance	racial, religious, national or ethnic	Criminal Code, Art. 258
France	Sentence uplift—penalty enhancement	Animus	prejudicial to the honour because of	race, ethnicity, nation or religion	Criminal Code, Art. 132-76

Appendix A: Examples of Hate Crime Laws from Around the World

Country	Type	Model	Connector	Protected characteristics	Citation
	Sentence uplift—penalty enhancement	Discriminatory selection	prejudicial to the honour because of	sex, sexual orientation or gender identity	Criminal Code, Art. 132-77
	Substantive offence—aggravated	Discriminatory selection	because of	ethnic group, a particular nation, alleged race or religion, sex, sexual orientation or gender identity	Criminal Code, Art. 222-13(5)(a) and (b)
	Substantive offence—conduct-based	Discriminatory selection	on the basis of, or on the grounds of	origin, sex, family status, pregnancy, physical appearance, particular vulnerability resulting from their apparent or known economic situation, surname, place of residence, health, loss of autonomy, disability, genetic characteristics, morals, sexual orientation, gender identity, age, political opinions, trade union activities, ability to express themselves in a language other than French, ethnic group, nation, alleged race or religion	Criminal Code, Arts. 225-1, 225-1-1
Germany	Sentence uplift—aggravation	Animus	motives and aims	racist or xenophobic or showing contempt for human dignity	Criminal Code, Art. 46(2)
Hungary	Substantive offence—aggravated	Discriminatory selection	because of	national, ethnic, racial or religious group or a certain group of population; especially due to a disability, sexual identity or sexual orientation	Criminal Code, Art. 216
Latvia	Sentence uplift—aggravation	Discriminatory selection	due to	racist, national, ethnic or religious motives	Criminal Code, Art. 48(14)
	Substantive offence—conduct-based	Discriminatory selection	due to	racial, national, ethnic or religious belonging or for the violation of the prohibition of any other type of discrimination	Criminal Code, Art. 149.1

(continued)

258 Appendix A: Examples of Hate Crime Laws from Around the World

(continued)

Jurisdiction	Type of Legislation	Model	Hate-element	Characteristics covered	Legal provision
Malta	Sentence uplift—penalty enhancement	Animus	aggravated or motivated by hatred against	gender, gender identity, sexual orientation, race, colour, language, national or ethnic origin, citizenship, religion or belief or political or other opinion	Criminal Code, Art. 83B
	Sentence uplift—penalty enhancement	Animus	demonstrates or is wholly or partly motivated by hostility, aversion or contempt based on	a particular gender, gender identity, sexual orientation, race, colour, language, national or ethnic origin, citizenship, religion or belief or political or other opinion	Criminal Code, Arts. 251D and 325A with 222A
Russian Federation	Sentence uplift—aggravation	Animus	motivated by hatred or enmity or hostility	political, ideological, racial, ethnic or religious hatred or hatred or enmity towards a social group	Criminal Code, Art. 63(1)(e)
	Substantive offences—aggravated	Animus	on the grounds of hatred or enmity	political, ideological, racial, ethnic or religious ... or hostility towards any social group	Criminal Code, Arts. 105(2)(l), 111(2)(e), 112(2)(e), 115(2)(b), 116(2)(b), 117(2)(h), 119(2), 213(1)(b)
	Substantive offences—aggravated	Animus	motivated by hatred or enmity or hostility	political, ideological, racial, ethnic or religious hatred or hatred or enmity towards any social group	Criminal Code, Art. 214(2)
	Substantive offence—aggravated conduct-based	Animus	on the grounds of hatred or enmity or hostility	political, ideological, racial, ethnic or religious hatred or enmity or hatred or hostility towards a social group, ... [or] the victims of fascism or the fight against fascism	Criminal Code, Art. 244(2)(b)
	Substantive offence—conduct-based	Discriminatory selection	based on	sex, race, nationality, language, origin, property or official status, place or residence, attitude to religion, convictions, or affiliation with public associations or any social groups	Criminal Code, Art. 136(2)

Appendix A: Examples of Hate Crime Laws from Around the World

Country	Model	Basis	Wording	Protected characteristics	Citation
Slovakia	Sentence uplift—penalty enhancement	Animus	hatred against	race, nation, nationality, ethnic group; or origin, colour of skin, sex, sexual orientation, political beliefs or religion	Criminal Code, Art. 140(e)
Sweden	Sentence uplift—aggravation	Animus	motive for the offence was to insult on grounds of	race, colour, national or ethnic origin, religious belief, sexual orientation or transgender dentity or expression, or another similar circumstance	Criminal Code, Ch .29, s. 2(7)
	Substantive offence—conduct-based	Discriminatory selection	discriminates against a person on grounds of	race, colour, national or ethnic origin, religious belief, sexual orientation or transgender identity or expression	Criminal Code, Ch. 16, s. 9
United Kingdom					
England and Wales	Substantive offences—aggravated	Animus	motivated (wholly or partly) by hostility or demonstrated hostility	racial or religious group	Crime and Disorder Act 1998, ss 28-32
	Sentence uplift—aggravation	Animus	motivated (wholly or partly) by hostility or demonstrated hostility	racial or religious group, sexual orientation, disability, transgender	Sentencing Act 2020, s. 66
Northern Ireland	Sentence uplift—aggravation	Animus	motivated (wholly or partly) by hostility or demonstrated hostility	racial or religious group, sexual orientation or disability	Criminal Justice (No. 2) (Northern Ireland) Order 2004, s. 2
Scotland	Hybrid	Animus	motivated (wholly or partly) by malice or ill will or demonstrated malice or ill will	age, disability, race, colour, nationality (including citizenship) or ethnic or national origins, religion or, in the case of a social or cultural group, perceived religious affiliation, sexual orientation, transgender identity, variations in sex characteristics	Hate Crime and Public Order (Scotland) Act 2021, ss. 1-2
	Substantive offences—aggravated	Animus	motivated (wholly or partly) by malice or ill will or demonstrated malice or ill will	race, colour, nationality (including citizenship) or ethnic or national origins	Hate Crime and Public Order (Scotland) Act 2021, s. 3

North America

Jurisdiction	Type of Legislation	Model	Hate-element	Characteristics covered	Legal provision
Canada	Sentence uplift—aggravation	Animus	motivated by bias, prejudice or hate based on	race, national or ethnic origin, language, colour, religion, sex, age, mental or physical disability, sexual orientation, or gender identity or expression, or on any other similar factor	Criminal Code 718.2(i)
	Substantive offence—aggravated	Animus	motivated by bias, prejudice or hate based on	colour, race, religion, national or ethnic origin, age, sex, sexual orientation, gender identity or expression or mental or physical disability	Criminal Code 430(4.1)
USA Federal	Substantive offence—aggravated	Discriminatory selection	because of	race, colour, religion or national origin, gender, sexual orientation, gender identity or disability	The Matthew Shepard and James Byrd, Jr. Hate Crimes Prevention Act of 2009, 18 U.S.C. § 249
	Substantive offence—conduct-based	Discriminatory selection	because of	race, colour, religion, sex, handicap or national origin	Criminal Interference with Right to Fair Housing, 42 U.S.C. § 3631
	Substantive offence—aggravated/conduct-based	Discriminatory selection	because of	race, colour, or ethnic characteristics of any individual associated with	Damage to Religious Property, Church Arson Prevention Act, 18 U.S.C. § 247
	Substantive offence—conduct-based	Discriminatory selection	because of	race, colour, religion or national origin	Violent Interference with Federally Protected Rights, or Title I of the Civil Rights Act of 1968 § 245

Appendix A: Examples of Hate Crime Laws from Around the World

USA State/Federal District	Type	Model	Connector	Protected characteristics / description	Citation
Alabama	Sentence uplift—penalty enhancement/hybrid	Discriminatory selection	motivated by	race, colour, religion, national origin, ethnicity or physical or mental disability	Code of Alabama § 13A-5-13
California	Substantive offence—conduct-based	Discriminatory selection	interfere with enjoyment of right or privilege	disability, gender, nationality, race or ethnicity, religion, sexual orientation or association with a person or group with one or more of these actual or perceived characteristics	California Penal Code § 422.6
	Sentence uplift—penalty enhancement/hybrid	Discriminatory selection	because of	disability, gender, nationality, race or ethnicity, religion, sexual orientation or association with a person or group with one or more of these actual or perceived characteristics	§§4.22.7, 422.75, 422.85 and 422.865 with §422.55
	Substantive offence—conduct-based	Animus	for the purpose of/in reckless disregard of terrorising	sign, mark, symbol, emblem, or other physical impression, including, but not limited to, a Nazi swastika any/owner or occupant	California Penal Code § 11411
	Substantive offence—conduct-based	Animus	for the purpose of/in reckless disregard of terrorising	religion, or from engaging in a religious service	California Penal Code § 11412
	Substantive offence—conduct-based	Animus	for the purpose of/in reckless disregard of terrorising	church, temple, synagogue, mosque or other place of worship; buildings, offices, and meeting sites of organisations that counsel for or against abortion or among whose major activities are lobbying, publicising or organising with respect to public or private issues relating to abortion	California Penal Code § 11413

(continued)

(continued)

Jurisdiction	Type of Legislation	Model	Hate-element	Characteristics covered	Legal provision
Hawaii	Sentence uplift—penalty enhancement/hybrid	Animus	intentionally selected because of hostility towards	race, religion, disability, ethnicity, national origin, gender identity or expression, or sexual orientation	Haw. Rev. Stat. Ann. § 706-662(6)
Illinois	Substantive offence—aggravated	Discriminatory selection	by reason of	race, colour, creed, religion, ancestry, gender, sexual orientation, physical or mental disability, or national origin	720 Ill. Comp. Laws Ann. 5/12-7.1
	Sentence uplift—penalty enhancement/hybrid	Discriminatory selection	by reason of	race, colour, creed, religion, ancestry, gender, sexual orientation, physical or mental disability, or national origin	720 Ill. Comp. Laws Ann. 5/5-5-3.2(a)(10)
	Substantive offence—aggravated	Discriminatory selection	by reason of	race, colour, creed, religion, ancestry, gender, sexual orientation, physical or mental disability, or national origin of another individual or group of individuals, regardless of the existence of any other motivating factor or factors	720 Ill. Comp. Laws Ann. 5/21-1.2
	Sentence uplift—aggravation	Discriminatory selection	selected because of	characteristic, trait, belief, practice, association or other attribute the court chooses to consider, including but not limited to … colour, creed, disability, national origin, race, religion or sexual orientation	Ind. Code Ann. § 35-38-1-7.1 with 10-13-3-1
New Hampshire	Sentence uplift—penalty enhancement/hybrid	Animus	substantially motivated because of hostility towards	the victim's religion, race, creed, sexual orientation; national origin, sex or gender identity	N.H. Rev. Stat. Ann. § 651:6

Appendix A: Examples of Hate Crime Laws from Around the World

Jurisdiction	Type	Model	Protected characteristics	Citation
New York	Substantive offence—aggravated	Discriminatory selection	intentionally selects because of a belief or perception; or intentionally commits act in whole or in substantial part because of a belief or perception	race, colour, national origin, ancestry, gender, gender identity or expression, religion, religious practice, age, disability or sexual orientation of a person	N.Y. Penal Law § 485.05, § 485.10, with CPL § 200.50.
	Substantive offence—aggravated	Discriminatory selection	because of	race, colour, national origin, ancestry, gender, gender identity or expression, religion, religious practice, age, disability or sexual orientation	N.Y. Penal Law § 240.30(3)
	Substantive offence—aggravated/conduct-based	Discriminatory selection	because of	race, colour, national origin, ancestry, gender, gender identity or expression, religion, religious practice, age, disability or sexual orientation	N.Y. Penal Law § 240.31
Oklahoma	Substantive offence—aggravated	Discriminatory selection	because of	race, colour, religion, ancestry, national origin or disability	Oklahoma Stat. tit. 21 § 850
Rhode Island	Sentence uplift—penalty enhancement/hybrid	Animus	intentionally selected because of hatred or animus toward	disability, religion, colour, race, national origin or ancestry, sexual orientation, or gender of that person or the owner or occupant of that property	R.I. Gen. Laws § 12-19-38

Appendix A: Examples of Hate Crime Laws from Around the World

Oceania

Jurisdiction	Type of Legislation	Model	Hate-element	Characteristics covered	Legal provision
Australia					
New South Wales	Sentence uplift—aggravation	Animus	motivated by hatred for or prejudice against	a group of people ... such as people of a particular religion, racial or ethnic origin, language, sexual orientation or age, or having a particular disability	Crimes (Sentencing Procedure) Act 1999, s. 21A(2)
Northern Territory	Sentence uplift—aggravation	Animus	motivated by hate against	a group of people	Sentencing Act 1995, s. 6A(e)
Tasmania	Sentence uplift—aggravation	Animus	motivated to any degree by hatred for or prejudice against	on racial grounds	Sentencing Act 1997, s. 11B
Victoria	Sentence uplift—aggravation	Animus	motivated (wholly or partly) by hatred for or prejudice against	a group of people with common characteristics	Sentencing Act 1991, s. 5(2)(daaa)
Western Australia	Substantive offences—aggravated	Discriminatory selection	intends to harass	a racial group, or a person as a member of a racial group	Criminal Code Act Compilation Act 1913, ss. 80A, 80B, etc. with ss. 80E-80J
Western Australia	Substantive offences—aggravated	Discriminatory selection	in circumstances of racial aggravation	racial group	Criminal Code Act Compilation Act 1913, ss. 313, 317, 317A, 338B, 444 with 76, 80F and 80I
Marshall Islands	Substantive offence—conduct based	Discriminatory selection	commits an act of discrimination	gender	Gender Equality Act 2019, §§ 729 with 702 and 730
Marshall Islands	Substantive offence—conduct based	Discriminatory selection	on the basis of	disability	Rights of Persons with Disabilities Act, 2015, § 1147

Appendix A: Examples of Hate Crime Laws from Around the World

New Zealand	Sentence uplift—aggravation	Animus	partly or wholly because of hostility towards	a group of persons who have an enduring common characteristic such as race, colour, nationality, religion, gender identity, sexual orientation, age or disability	Sentencing Act 2002, s. 9
Samoa	Sentence uplift—aggravation	Animus	partly or wholly because of hostility towards	a group of persons who have an enduring common characteristic such as race, colour, nationality, religion, gender identity, sexual orientation, age or disability	Sentencing Act 2016, s. 7
Vanuatu	Substantive offence—conduct-based	Discriminatory selection	by reason of	sex, ethnic or racial origin, or religion	Penal Code, Art. 150
Pitcairn etc. Islands	Sentence uplift—aggravation	Animus	partly or wholly because of hostility towards	a group of persons who have an enduring common characteristic such as race, colour, nationality, religion, gender identity, sexual orientation, age or disability	Sentencing Ordinance 2017, s. 8

Author Index[1]

B

Bakalis, Chara, 9n45, 103, 106, 107n52
Bracadale, Lord, 155, 190, 200n188
Braithwaite, John, 213–215, 225, 225n67
Brown, Rupert, 59, 63n51, 232n83
Byrd, James Jr., 96, 98

C

Chakraborti, Neil, 16n64, 78, 100, 101, 107, 108, 116n86, 164n10

D

Duff, RA, 60, 85, 87, 208, 211, 212

F

Feinberg, Joel, 56, 64, 67

G

Garland, Jon, 16n64, 100, 101, 107, 108, 164n10, 206n5
Goodall, Kay, 130, 190, 194, 195, 195n174

H

Al-Hakim, Mohamad, 6n30, 71, 102, 103, 109
Hall, Steve, 20n7, 29, 30, 116n86
Hardy, Stevie-Jade, 78
Harel, Alon, 9, 9n46, 10, 50, 101
Hurd, Heidi M, 7, 65, 194n169

---

[1] Note: Page numbers followed by 'n' refer to notes.

Author Index

I
Iganski, Paul, 4, 5, 7n33, 167

J
Jacobs, James B, 11, 15, 16, 64, 68, 131n11, 166
James, Zoe, 75

L
Lagou, Spiridoula, 5, 5n23, 7n33, 63n51
Lawrence, Frederick M, 57, 86, 100, 131n11, 156, 166, 173, 187, 209
Lawrence, Stephen, 98

M
Marshall, Sandra, 211, 212
Mason, Gail, 7n32, 9, 11, 101–103, 102n35, 107, 116, 116n86, 131n11, 150n72, 172n61, 190, 191, 207
Mill, John Stuart, 55

O
Owusu-Bempah, Abenaa, 138n37, 147n61, 182n107, 186n126, 187n135, 203n193

P
Parchomovsky, Gideon, 9, 10, 50, 101
Paterson, Jenny L, 63n51, 72, 76, 232n83
Pettit, Philip, 214, 215
Potter, Kimberly, 11, 15, 16, 64, 68, 131n11, 166

R
Rawls, John, 29, 38, 39n97, 49, 56, 57

S
Schweppe, Jennifer, 11n52, 103, 122, 139n41, 140, 145n53, 150, 178, 203n193
Shepard, Matthew, 96, 98
Simester, A. P., 56, 57, 73, 79

V
Von Hirsch, Andrew, 56, 57, 73, 79

W
Walters, Mark A, 63n49, 63n51, 71, 75, 113n66, 116, 137, 147n61, 149, 170n52, 178, 179, 182n107, 182n110, 184, 185, 187n135, 203n193, 216n42, 219n52, 224n64, 224n65, 227n68, 232n83, 233n87
Wiedlitzka, Susann, 138n37, 147n61, 182n107, 187n135, 203n193
Winlow, Simon, 20n7, 29, 30

Y
Young, Iris Marion, 14, 15, 28, 39–41, 40n101, 40n102, 46, 80

Place Index[1]

C

Crime Survey for England and Wales, 23, 48, 66, 88

O

Office for Democratic Institutions and Human Rights (ODIHR), 3, 98n20, 130, 194n166
Organization for Security and Co-operation in Europe (OSCE), 130, 150

S

Sussex Hate Crime Project (SHCP), 69–72, 77

T

Truth and Reconciliation Commission (TRC), 229–231, 230n78, 231n79

---

[1] Note: Page numbers followed by 'n' refer to notes.

Subject Index[1]

Aggravated offences, *see* Hate crime laws, types of

Communitarian principles of justice
  equality, 210–211
  nondomination, 210–211
  restoration, 210–211
Criminalisation of hate
  harm principle, 55, 56, 60, 81, 104, 105
  legal moralism, 9, 55, 59
  public wrong, 60, 86

Deterrence, 85–91
Due process, 155, 158, 159

Fair protection paradigm
  fair labelling, 15, 136, 143, 149, 154, 159, 198
  fair punishment, 15
  proportionate sentencing, 15

Group identity, 11, 12, 15, 33, 40–42, 40n99, 40n100, 45, 46, 49, 50, 57, 69–72, 100, 101, 103, 106–113, 120, 126, 143, 179, 192–194, 198, 199, 210, 222, 228, 237, 241, 242
  identity politics, 11

---

[1] Note: Page numbers followed by 'n' refer to notes.

H

Harm
  additive fallacy, 65
  conjunctive harm, 58n29, 73, 74, 79
  cultural harm/ imperialism, 13, 15, 26, 40, 50, 65, 80, 81, 84, 92, 99, 106, 112, 125, 186, 208, 210, 219, 223, 228–232, 236, 237
  direct and indirect, 69, 71, 76, 92, 220
  distinct wrongs, 85
  individual and group identity, 69–71, 106, 109, 111, 113, 126, 193, 228, 237
  institutional harm, 76–79, 219
  remote harm, 58n29, 79, 80, 236
  See also Victimisation
Hate crime laws, types of
  hybrid approach, 154–156, 158
  sentence uplifts
    penalty enhancements, 17, 150–152
    sentence aggravation, 17, 144–152
  substantive offences
    aggravated offences, 17, 132–138, 238
    conduct-based, 17, 131, 138–144, 156
Hate crime law, the practice of
  educative deterrence, 85–91
  evidence gathering, 178
  filtering out, 150, 154, 158, 203n193
  monitoring, 158
  policing, 206, 239
  sentencing discretion, 147
  symbolic messaging, 71, 125
  training, 182n110, 186n133, 203, 217
Hate crime legislative language
  phrasing, 64
  words to conceptualise hate
    bias, 3n10, 17, 128, 136, 163, 202
    hate, hatred, 3n10, 17, 128, 163, 202
    hostility, 3n10, 17, 128, 202
    prejudice, 3n10, 17, 128, 136, 163, 202
Hate crime models
  animus, 162–164, 176–178, 184, 187, 190, 195, 201–203, 240, 241
  discriminatory or group selection, 162, 188
Hate crime victim groups
  disability, 113
  gender identity, 36, 96, 129n4, 141, 148, 151, 166, 173, 176, 188
  LGBT, 69, 74
  racial and ethnic, BAME, 21, 22, 43, 45
  religious, 113
  sexual orientation, 106
Hate element in offences
  bad character or bad conduct, 8, 65
  blameworthiness or moral culpability, 6
  extraneous or inherent, 64

standard of proof
  demonstration, 162, 169, 202n189
  motivation, 17, 162, 169, 171, 177, 180, 240

Identity politics, 11, 11n52, 15, 16, 114–125
Intergroup Emotions Theory (IET), 69

LGBT, *see* Hate crime victim groups
Liberal theories of justice
  classical liberalism
    individual liberty, 53
    non-discrimination, 52
    personal autonomy, 55
  egalitarian liberalism, 50
    redistribution, 27, 29, 49
  neoliberalism
    non-state interference, 55
    populism, 26
  socialism, 27, 37
    collectivism, collective identity, 111
  social justice liberalism (*see* Social justice)
  state control, 36

Protected characteristics
  group identity, 100, 198, 199, 241
  identity politics, 11

victim groups (*see* Hate crime victim groups; Victim group criteria)
Punishment, 3, 4, 7, 9, 10, 12, 13, 15, 17, 18, 25, 54, 54n13, 65, 67, 87, 107, 131, 147, 148, 155, 156n79, 170n52, 173, 185, 195, 205, 207–213, 216, 218, 219, 222, 231–233, 232n83, 235, 242, 243
Punishment theory
  consequentialist, 4, 25
  retributive, 4, 25

Restorative justice
  community-based mechanisms, 212, 233
  indigenous models of justice, 130
  repairing individual harms, 211
Retributive justice
  crime control, 212
  responsibilisation, 25

Social justice
  communitarian (*see* Communitarian principles of justice)
  difference principle, 38, 49, 57
  disadvantage, 21, 28, 32, 38, 39, 45, 58, 92, 137, 143, 194, 227, 229
  fair protection (*see* Fair protection paradigm)

Social justice (*cont.*)
   oppression and domination, 2,
      10, 12, 14, 15
   pluralism, 14, 34, 52
   redistribution, 28, 29, 49, 92
   restorative (*see* Restorative justice)
   socio-structural inequality, 80,
      210, 223
   Young's criteria
      cultural imperialism,
         40, 41, 80
      exploitation, 40
      marginalisation, 15, 40
      powerlessness, 40, 46
      violence, 15, 40, 49, 93

V

Victim group criteria
   disadvantage, 102–104, 107, 109
   distinct harms, 105, 106, 113
   equality, 102–105, 112
   group identity, 100, 101,
      103, 106–113
   hierarchy, 101, 103
   targeted, 101–104, 106–111, 113
   vulnerability and difference, 100,
      101, 107
Victimisation
   emotional trauma, 5, 68, 219
   perceived threat, 2, 32, 40, 81
   physical and psychological
      injury, 56
   shame, 70, 71, 74, 106, 219,
      223, 237
   social marginalisation and
      disempowerment,
      47, 186
   targeted, 4, 8, 12, 64, 71, 73, 74,
      91, 101–104, 106,
      108–111, 114, 117, 125,
      129, 188, 190, 193–195,
      199–202, 214, 220, 221,
      224, 237

GPSR Compliance

The European Union's (EU) General Product Safety Regulation (GPSR) is a set of rules that requires consumer products to be safe and our obligations to ensure this.

If you have any concerns about our products, you can contact us on

ProductSafety@springernature.com

In case Publisher is established outside the EU, the EU authorized representative is:

Springer Nature Customer Service Center GmbH
Europaplatz 3
69115 Heidelberg, Germany

www.ingramcontent.com/pod-product-compliance
Lightning Source LLC
LaVergne TN
LVHW011006250326
834688LV00004B/98